15
Canadian
Poets
plus 5

23 - Valedictn

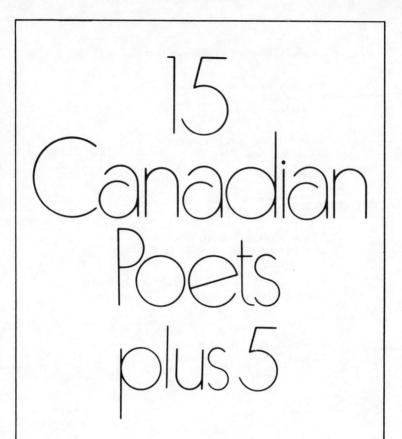

15 Canadian Poets plus 5

Edited by GARY GEDDES
and PHYLLIS BRUCE

Toronto
Oxford University Press
1978

Canadian Cataloguing in Publication Data

Main entry under title:

15 Canadian poets plus 5

Earlier ed. published in 1970 under title:
15 Canadian poets.

Bibliography: p.
Includes index.
ISBN 0-19-540289-8

1. Canadian poetry (English) – 20th century.*
I. Geddes, Gary, 1940-   II. Bruce, Phyllis.

PS8279.F54 1978   C811'.5'408   C78-001355-7
PR9195.7.F54 1978

© Oxford University Press Canada 1978
ISBN 0-19-540289-8
1 2 3 4 5 6 - 3 2 1 0 9 8
Printed in Canada by
Webcom Limited

CONTENTS

Contents | vii

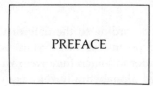

PREFACE

15 Canadian Poets was first conceived in 1970 to meet a very specific need to provide a representative selection of the best post-war Canadian poetry in English, and to offer enough poems by each poet to give a sense of that poet's range and development. In selecting the original fifteen poets, we purposely included mature writers (Birney, Layton, Souster, Avison, and Purdy), writers in the middle of their poetic careers (Nowlan, Cohen, Jones, and Mandel) and young writers (Atwood, Newlove, Bowering, MacEwen, Coleman, and Ondaatje). In this way, we hoped to reflect something of the poetic tradition in Canada and to suggest ways in which the craft was developing and changing.

In our revised and expanded edition, we have continued this pattern by adding three established poets (Dorothy Livesay, P. K. Page, and Phyllis Webb), who have written some of their most important work during the post-war years, and two newer poets (Pat Lowther and Patrick Lane) whose work is receiving increasing attention. We have also updated the selection of poetry from the original fifteen poets. Ultimately, there are no prescriptive criteria to offer for choices that are highly subjective; it can only be hoped that the enjoyment of these poets and poems will stimulate the reader to range more widely and to create his or her own ideal anthology.

It was again necessary to give extra space to several poets in order to include poems, especially longer poems, that seemed indispensable. Readers can explore a wide range of poetic forms, from short lyrics to long narratives. Birney's 'November Walk Near False Creek Mouth', Layton's 'A Tall Man Executes a Jig', Jones's 'Kate, These Flowers ... (The Lampman Poems)', Livesay's 'Call My People Home', Lowther's 'Chacabuco, The Pit', and Webb's 'Naked Poems' should provide some incentive to seek out recent book-length narratives, such as *The Journals of Susanna Moodie* and *The Collected Works of Billy the Kid*, as well as earlier narratives by D. C. Scott and E. J. Pratt.

The poets appear according to the date of their first published collection; and their poems, as far as it is possible to ascertain exactly, are in the order in which they were written. The notes on each poet are printed alphabetically for easy reference. They are followed by an abbreviated list of relevant general and specific criticism and secondary materials.

Once again, our thanks to the poets and to the many friends who have offered criticism and advice and admonition in the matter of selections, especially William Toye of the Oxford University Press. In the interest of being up-to-date, we have reluctantly had to forgo the use of some of Sheldon Grimson's fine photographs from the original book.

G. G.
P. B.

ACKNOWLEDGEMENTS

MARGARET ATWOOD Reprinted by permission of Margaret Atwood and The House of Anansi: 'The Islands' from *The Circle Game* by Margaret Atwood; 'They Eat Out' from *Power Politics* by Margaret Atwood.

Reprinted by permission of the Oxford University Press Canada: 'The Animals in That Country', 'A Night in the Royal Ontario Museum' and 'Progressive Insanities of a Pioneer' from *The Animals in That Country* by Margaret Atwood; 'Further Arrivals', 'Death of a Young Son by Drowning', and 'The Immigrants' from *The Journals of Susanna Moodie* by Margaret Atwood; 'Game After Supper' and 'Girl and Horse, 1928' from *Procedures for Underground* by Margaret Atwood.

Reprinted by permission of Margaret Atwood: 'Newsreel: Man and Firing Squad' from *You Are Happy* by Margaret Atwood; 'You Begin', 'All Bread', and 'Five Poems for Dolls' from *Two-Headed Poems* by Margaret Atwood.

MARGARET AVISON 'Snow', 'The World Still Needs', 'New Year's Poem', 'To Professor X, Year Y', 'The Swimmer's Moment', 'Voluptuaries and Others', and 'Birth Day' reprinted from *Winter Sun* by Margaret Avison by permission of Miss Avison.

'Pace', 'Black-White Under Green: May 18, 1965', 'July Man', 'The Absorbed', 'In a Season of Unemployment', and 'A Nameless One' reprinted from *The Dumbfounding*, poems by Margaret Avison by permission of W. W. Norton & Company, Inc. Copyright 1966 by Margaret Avison.

EARLE BIRNEY All poems reprinted by permission of Dr Birney and The Canadian Publishers, McClelland and Stewart Limited, Toronto: 'November Walk Near False Creek Mouth' from *Selected Poems 1940-1966* by Earle Birney; 'El Greco: *Espolio*' from *The Collected Poems of Earle Birney*; 'There Are Delicacies' from *Ghost in the Wheels: Selected Poems* by Earle Birney; the remaining poems from *The Poems of Earle Birney*.

GEORGE BOWERING Reprinted by permission of The Canadian Publishers, McClelland and Stewart Limited, Toronto: 'The Night Before Morning' and 'Grandfather' from *Points on the Grid* by George Bowering; 'To Cleave', 'The Swing', and 'Esta Muy Caliente' from *The Man in Yellow Boots* by George Bowering; 'Indian Summer' and 'Albertasaurus' from *Rocky Mountain Foot* by George Bowering; 'The Breath, Release' from *In the Flesh* by George Bowering.

'The House,' 'The Egg', 'Dobbin', and 'Our Triple Birth' reprinted from *The Gangs of Kosmos* by George Bowering by permission of Mr Bowering and The House of Anansi.

LEONARD COHEN 'God Is Alive' reprinted from *Beautiful Losers* by Leonard Cohen by permission of The Canadian Publishers, McClelland and Stewart Limited, Toronto.

'Ballad of the Death of a Lady's Man' Written by Leonard Cohen Copyright © 1977 Stranger Music, Inc. Used by permission. All rights reserved.

The remaining poems reprinted from *Selected Poems 1956-1968* by Leonard Cohen by permission of The Canadian Publishers, McClelland and Stewart Limited, Toronto.

VICTOR COLEMAN All poems reprinted by permission of Mr Coleman: 'The Lady Vanishes' and 'Kenkyusha: Day Nine' from *one/eye/love* by Victor Coleman; 'The Devil' and 'Fish : Stone : Song' from *Light Verse* by Victor Coleman; 'Parking Lots for Greg Curnoe' is uncollected.

D. G. JONES 'Portrait of Anne Hébert', 'Odysseus', 'Beautiful Creatures Brief as These', 'For Françoise Adnet', and 'These Trees Are No Forest of Mourners' reprinted from *The Sun is Axeman* by D. G. Jones by permission of University of Toronto Press. Copyright, Canada, 1961 by University of Toronto Press.

'Summer Is a Poem by Ovid', 'I Thought There Were Limits', 'On a Picture of Your House', and 'The Stream Exposed With All Its Stones' reprinted from *Phrases from Orpheus* by D. G. Jones by permission of Oxford University Press Canada.

'Spring Flowers', 'Words From the Aviary', and 'Kate, These Flowers . . . (The Lampman Poems)' reprinted from *Under the Thunder the Flowers Light Up the Earth* by D. G. Jones by permission of Mr Jones.

PATRICK LANE 'The Bird', 'Wild Horses', 'Elephants', 'Mountain Oysters', and 'Passing into Storm' reprinted from *Beware the Months of Fire* by Patrick Lane by permission of Mr Lane and The House of Anansi.

Reprinted by permission of Patrick Lane: 'White Mountain' from *Passing into Storm* by Patrick Lane; 'Unborn Things' and 'Macchu Picchu' from *Unborn Things: South American Poems* by Patrick Lane; 'From the Hot Hills', 'The Carpenter', 'Stigmata', 'Albino Pheasants', and 'Of Letters' from *Albino Pheasants* by Patrick Lane.

IRVING LAYTON All poems reprinted by permission of The Canadian Publishers, McClelland and Stewart Limited, Toronto: 'If I Lie Still' from *Balls for a One-Armed Juggler* by Irving Layton; 'Marché Municipale' from *The Shattered Plinths* by Irving Layton; 'Rhine Boat Trip' and 'Israelis' from *The Poems of Irving Layton*; the remaining poems from *The Collected Poems of Irving Layton*.

DOROTHY LIVESAY All poems reprinted by permission of Dr Livesay: 'Summer Landscape: Jasper' from *Ice Age* by Dorothy Livesay; the remaining poems from *Collected Poems: The Two Seasons* by Dorothy Livesay.

PAT LOWTHER 'Touch Home', 'Wanting', and 'Regard to Neruda' reprinted from *Milk Stone* by Pat Lowther by permission of The Borealis Press Ltd.

'Early Winters', 'Notes From Furry Creek', 'Coast Range', 'Chacabuco, The Pit', and 'The Dig' reprinted from *A Stone Diary* by Pat Lowther by permission of the Oxford University Press Canada.

GWENDOLYN MACEWEN Reprinted by permission of McGraw-Hill Ryerson: 'You Cannot Do This' and 'Arcanum One' from *A Breakfast for Barbarians* by Gwendolyn MacEwen.

The remaining poems reprinted by permission of The Macmillan Company of Canada: 'The Red Bird You Wait For', 'The Discovery', 'Inside the Great Pyramid', 'One Arab Flute', and 'Dark Pines Under Water' from *The Shadow-Maker* by Gwendolyn MacEwen: 'Memoirs of a Mad Cook' from *The Armies of the Moon* by Gwendolyn MacEwen; 'Poems in Braille', 'Green With Sleep', 'Manzini: Escape Artist', 'Poem Improvised Around a First Line', 'The Child Dancing', and 'The Film' from *Magic Animals: Selected Poems Old and New* by Gwendolyn MacEwen.

ELI MANDEL Reprinted by permission of Mr Mandel: 'A Castle and Two Inhabitants', 'Acis', and 'Pillar of Fire' from *Fuseli Poems* by Eli Mandel; 'The Meaning of the I CHING', 'Houdini', 'Pictures in an Institution', 'Woodbine', 'The Speaking Earth', 'From the North Saskatchewan', and 'Marina' from *An Idiot Joy* by Eli Mandel.

'Thief Hanging in Baptist Halls' reprinted from *Black and Secret Man* by Eli Mandel by permission of McGraw-Hill Ryerson Limited.

Reprinted by permission of Press Porcepic Ltd.: 'On the 25th Anniversary of the Liberation of Auschwitz', which first appeared in *The Canadian Forum*; 'Two Dream Songs for John Berryman', 'Agatha Christie', and 'On the Death of Ho Chi Minh' from *Stony Plain* by Eli Mandel.

JOHN NEWLOVE Reprinted by permission of The Canadian Publishers, McClelland and Stewart Limited, Toronto: 'The Arrival', 'Then, If I Cease Desiring', 'The Flowers', and 'Verigin, Moving in Alone' from *The Fat Man* by John Newlove; 'Crazy Riel', 'Everyone', 'Lady, Lady', 'Ride Off Any Horizon', and 'In This Reed' from *Black Night Window* by John Newlove; 'The Engine and the Sea', 'Warm Wind', 'The Flower', and 'Doukhobor' from *The Cave* by John Newlove.

ALDEN NOWLAN Reprinted by permission of Alden Nowlan: 'Beginning' and 'Warren Pryor' from *Under the Ice* by Alden Nowlan; 'God Sour the Milk of the Knacking Wench' and 'For Nicholas of All the Russias' from *Wind in a Rocky Country* by Alden Nowlan.

Reprinted by permission of Clarke, Irwin & Company Limited: 'I Icarus', 'And He Wept Aloud, So That the Egyptians Heard It', 'Britain Street', 'In Those Old Wars', and 'July 15' from *Bread, Wine and Salt* by Alden Nowlan; 'The Mysterious Naked Man', 'Another Parting', 'For Claudine Because I Love Her', 'Ypres: 1915', and 'The First Stirring of the Beasts' from *the mysterious naked man* by Alden Nowlan; 'The Middle-Aged Man in the Supermarket' and 'The Broadcaster's Poem from *I'm a Stranger Here Myself* by Alden Nowlan; 'Land and Sea' from *Smoked Glass* by Alden Nowlan.

MICHAEL ONDAATJE All poems reprinted by permission of Mr Ondaatje: 'We're at the Graveyard', 'The gate in his head', 'Postcard from Piccadilly Street', 'Letters & Other Worlds', and 'White Dwarfs' from *Rat Jelly* by Michael Ondaatje; 'Bearhug' first appeared in *Saturday Night*; the remaining poems are from *The Dainty Monsters* by Michael Ondaatje.

P. K. PAGE All poems reprinted by permission of P. K. Page: 'A Grave Illness' first appeared in *Queen's Quarterly*; 'Sestina for Pat Lane after Reading "Albino Pheasants"' first appeared in *The Malahat Review*; the remaining poems are from *Poems Selected and New* by P. K. Page.

AL PURDY Reprinted by permission of The Canadian Publishers, McClelland and Stewart Limited, Toronto: 'The Cariboo Horses', 'Song of the Impermanent Husband', and 'Transient' from *The Cariboo Horses* by Al Purdy; 'Eskimo Graveyard' and 'Arctic Rhododendrons' from *North of Summer* by Al Purdy; 'Detail', 'Interruption', 'Lament for the Dorsets', and 'The Runners' from *Wild Grape Wine* by Al Purdy; 'The Beavers of Renfrew' from *Sex and Death* by Al Purdy; 'Alive or Not' from *Sundance at Dusk* by Al Purdy.
'A Handful of Earth: To Réne Lévesque' reprinted from *A Handful of Earth* by Al Purdy by permission of Mr Purdy and Black Moss Press.

RAYMOND SOUSTER Reprinted by permission of McGraw-Hill Ryerson Limited: 'Young Girls', 'Lagoons, Hanlan's Point', 'The Lilac Poem', 'Downtown Corner News Stand', 'Study: The Bath', 'Flight of the Roller-Coaster', 'The Six-Quart Basket', and 'The Death of the Grenadiers' from *The Colour of the Times* by Raymond Souster; 'A Morning in Brussels', 'Memory of Bathurst Street', and 'St Catherine Street East' from *The Elephants on Yonge Street* by Raymond Souster.
Reprinted by permission of Oberon Press: 'All This Slow Afternoon', 'The Embarrassment' 'On the Rouge', 'Night Raider', and 'Among the Willows' from *Double-header* by Raymond Souster; 'The First Two Acorns' and 'Get the Poem Outdoors' from *So Far So Good* by Raymond Souster; 'A Letter to Archibald Lampman' and 'Pictures of a Long-Lost World' from *Extra Innings* by Raymond Souster; 'The Nest' from *The Years* by Raymond Souster.

PHYLLIS WEBB All poems reprinted by permission of Phyllis Webb: 'Occasions of Desire' from *The Sea is Also a Garden* by Phyllis Webb; 'For Fyodor' and 'Treblinka Gas Chamber' from *Mountain Day Moving*; the remaining poems are from *Selected Poems 1954-1965* by Phyllis Webb.

PHOTOGRAPH CREDITS

ATWOOD © 1978 Thomas Victor. AVISON, BOWERING, LAYTON, MACEWEN, SOUSTER Sheldon Grimson. BIRNEY, LOWTHER © Vancouver Sun. COHEN CBS. COLEMAN Taki Bluesinger. JONES Michael Ondaatje. LANE Ian Corrance. LIVESAY David Street. MANDEL Ann Mandel. NEWLOVE Peter Milroy/Collodion. NOWLAN Charles Clark. ONDAATJE Stephen Jones. PAGE Graeme Gibson. PURDY Richard Harrington. WEBB Betty Fairbank.

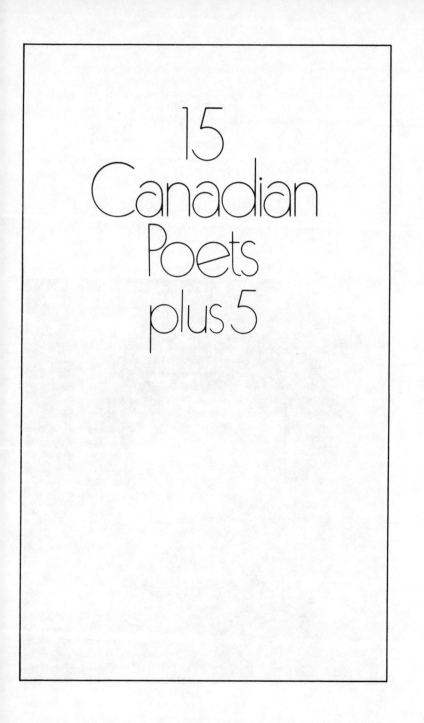

15
Canadian
Poets
plus 5

Dorothy
Livesay

Fire and Reason

I cannot shut out the night—
Nor its sharp clarity.

The many blinds we draw,
You and I,
The many fires we light
Can never quite obliterate
The irony of stars,
The deliberate moon,
The last, unsolved finality of night.

Going to Sleep

I shall lie like this when I am dead—
But with one more secret in my head.

Green Rain

I remember long veils of green rain
Feathered like the shawl of my grandmother—
Green from the half-green of the spring trees
Waving in the valley.

I remember the road
Like the one which leads to my grandmother's house,
A warm house, with green carpets,
Geraniums, a trilling canary
And shining horse-hair chairs;
And the silence, full of the rain's falling

Was like my grandmother's parlour
Alive with herself and her voice, rising and falling—
Rain and wind intermingled.

I remember on that day
I was thinking only of my love
And of my love's house.
But now I remember the day
As I remember my grandmother.
I remember the rain as the feathery fringe of her shawl.

The Lake

Go out: go in canoes
Over the still brown water
Too deep for any knowing.

Go out: you will not find his boat,
Nor his long, quiet body
Twisted among the reeds.

Seek long in the early dawn
Among the islands
And the green, hushed lagoons,

Seek long

You will not find the place
Where death came suddenly and laid its hand
Like sun, upon his face . . .

Go out: go in canoes.
He was not made to answer any voices
Save the too urgent, too insistent calling
Of his dream.

Spain

When the bare branch responds to leaf and light
Remember them: it is for this they fight.
It is for haze-swept hills and the green thrust
Of pine, that they lie choked with battle dust.

You who hold beauty at your finger-tips
Hold it because the splintering gunshot rips
Between your comrades' eyes; hold it across
Their bodies' barricade of blood and loss.

You who live quietly in sunlit space
Reading The Herald after morning grace
Can count peace dear, when it has driven
Your sons to struggle for this grim, new heaven.

Call My People Home

A Documentary Poem for Radio or Choral Presentation

ANNOUNCER:

Now after thirty years come from a far island
Of snow and cherry blossoms, holy mountains,
To make a home near water, near
The blue Pacific; newcomers and strangers
Circled again and shaped by snow-white mountains,
These put down their roots, the Isseis:*
The older generation. This is their story.

CHORUS OF ISSEIS:

Home, they say, is where the heart is:

*Isseis—generation born in Japan.

Transplanted walls, and copper-coloured gardens
Or where the cherry bough can blow
Against your pain, and blow it cool again—
This they call home.

But for ourselves we learned
How home was not
Even the small plot, raspberry laden
Nor shack on stilts, stooping over the water,
Nor the brown Fraser's whirl,
Sucking the salmon upward.

Home was the uprooting:
The shiver of separation,
Despair for our children
Fear for our future.

Home was the finding of a dry land
Bereft of water or rainfall
Where water is cherished
Where our tears made channels
And became irrigation.

Home was in watching:
The fruit growing and pushing
So painfully watered;
The timber hewn down
The mill run completed.

Home was in waiting:
For new roots holding
For young ones branching
For our yearning fading...

ANNOUNCER:

His ancestors had lived near water
Been fishermen under Fujiyama's shadow.

Each season in the new land found him struggling
Against the uncertain harvest of the sea,
The uncertain temper of white fishermen
Who hungered also, who had mouths to feed.
So these men cut his share
From half to one-eighth of the fishing fleet:
But still he fished, finding the sea his friend.

FIRST FISHERMAN:

Home was my boat: T.K. 2930—
Wintering on the Skeena with my nets
Cast up and down the river, to lure and haul
The dogfish. (His oil, they said, was needed overseas
For children torn from home, from a blitzed town.)
We made good money, and the sockeye run
That summer had outdone all the remembered seasons.
Now I could own my boat, *Tee Kay*, the Gillnetter
The snug and round one, warm as a woman
With her stove stoked at night and her lanterns lit
And anchor cast, brooding upon the water
Settled to sleep in the lap of the Skeena.

Now after thirty years, come from an island
To make a home near water: first on a sailing vessel
Towed, each season, to the fishing grounds:
Then the small gasboat, the gillnetter, that belonged
Not to the man who fished, but to the cannery.
Now after thirty years a free man, naturalized,
A man who owned his boat! I smelt the wind
Wetting my face, waves dashing against the *Tee Kay's*
    sides
The grey dawn opening like a book
At the horizon's rim. I was my own master—
Must prove it now, today! Stooping over the engine
Priming the starter, opening the gas valve,
I felt her throbbing in answer; I laughed
And grasped the fly wheel, swung her over.
She churned off up the river—my own boat, my home.

That was before Pearl Harbor: before a December day
Spent on a restless sea; then anchor in the dusk
And down to bunk to have a bowl of rice.
By lantern light I turned the battery set
To hear brief messages from fishermen
From boat to shore, to learn the weather forecast.
Must have been dozing when I woke up sharp—
What was he saying? Some kind of government order?
'All fishing craft on the high seas must head at once
To the nearest port, report to authorities.'
Did they not want our fish, the precious oil?
'No,' said the voice, 'Our boats were to be examined, searched
For hidden guns, for maps, for treachery . . . '
I heard, but could not understand. Obeyed,
But as a blind man. The numb fear about my boat,
Tee Kay, found no release in port, off shore,
Rubbing against a fleet of trollers, frail gillnetters
All heading down for Inverness and Tusk
All in the dark, with rumour flying fast.
No one knew more than his fear whispered,
No one explained.
We thought: perhaps it's all a mistake
Perhaps they'll line us up and do a search
Then leave us free for Skeena, Ucluelet—
The time is ripe, the season's fish are running.

SECOND FISHERMAN:

There was no mistake. It wasn't a joke:
At every fishing port more boats fell in.
Some had no wood, no gasoline; and some
Barely a day's store of food aboard.
So we waited at the Inlet's mouth, till the 16th.

FIRST FISHERMAN:

How speak about the long trip south, the last
We ever made, in the last of our boats?
The time my life turned over, love went under

Into the cold unruly sea. Those waves
Washing the cabin's walls
Lashed hate in me.

SECOND FISHERMAN:

We left Rupert in two long lines of sixty boats
Strung to the seiners, met and tugged
By *Starpoint* and the naval escort, the corvette.
All day we watched the gloomy sea roughed up
By westerlies, but had to tough it out
Glued to the wheel, weary for sleep, till 2 a.m.

Then, at Lowe Inlet, had brief anchorage.
At Milbanke Sound we ran into heavier seas
The buffeted boats like so many bobbing corks
Strung on a thin rope line that over and over
Would break, be mended by the corvette's men
And then again be snapped by snarling sea.

Day merged into night and day again
Found us with six boats broken loose; some torn
And others gashed with bumping in the dark—
If some drugged fisherman fell off to sleep
And left craft pilotless,
Smashing like blind birds through a log-strewn sea.
Some boats that had no gasoline to keep
Heart thumping in their engines, these
Were plucked aloft in fistfuls by the waves
Then brought down with a thud—
Propellers spinning helpless in mid-air.
So we proceeded into colder, rougher seas,
Seasick and sore, nodding at the wheel,
Then stamping up and down to keep the winter out.

FIRST FISHERMAN:

Christmas at sea. The bitterest for me
That any year had given. Even so
Some had a celebration, pooled their funds

And bought the only chicken left in Alert Bay.
Others boiled cabbages in salt sea water,
Pulled out the playing cards and shrugged, and laughed.
As we set sail at midnight, now a thousand boats
Chained to the naval escort, steadily south
Into familiar waters where the forests cooled their feet
At rocks'-end, mountains swam in mist—
As we set sail for home, the young ones, born here, swore
Not softly, into the hissing night. The old men wept.

The rest takes little telling. On the fifteenth night
We passed Point Grey's low hulk, our long line wavered
   shoreward.
Dirty and hungry, sleep lying like a stone
Stuck in our heads, we nosed our broken craft
Into the wharf at Steveston, 'Little Tokyo.'
The crowd on the dock was silent. Women finding their men
Clung to them searchingly, saying never a word,
Leading them home to the *ofuro** and supper.
Others of us, like me, who knew no one,
Who had no place near the city's centre
Stood lonely on the wharf, holding the *Tee Kay*'s line
For the last time, watching the naval men
Make a note of her number, take my name.
That was the end of my thirty years at the fishing
And the end of my boat, my home.

ANNOUNCER:

These their children, the Niseis,† were born
Into the new world, called British Columbia home,
Spoke of her as mother, and beheld
Their future in her pungent evergreen.

GIRL'S VOICE:

We lived unto ourselves
Thinking so to be free

*Ofuro—the bath.
†Niseis—generation born in Canada.*

Locked in the harbour
Of father and mother
The children incoming
The tide inflowing.

BOY'S VOICE:

Sometimes at remote midnight
With a burnt-out moon
An orange eye on the river
Or rising before dawn
From a house heavy with sleepers
The man touching my arm
Guiding my hand through the dark
To the boat softly bumping and sucking
Against the wharf;
We go out toward misty islands
Of fog over the river
Jockeying for position;
Till morning steals over, sleepy,
And over our boat's side, leaning
The word comes, Set the nets!
Hiding the unannounced prayer
Resounding in the heart's corners:
May we have a high boat
And the silver salmon leaping!

GIRL'S VOICE:

We lived unto ourselves
Locked in the harbour

BOY'S VOICE:

I remember the schoolhouse, its battered doorway
The helter-skelter of screaming children
Where the old ones went, my sisters
Soberly with books strapped over their shoulders:
Deliberately bent on learning—
(And learned, soon enough, of
The colour of their skin, and why
Their hair would never turn golden.)

GIRL'S VOICE:

But before the bell rang
For me
My turn at becoming
Before the bell rang
I was out on the hillside
Reaching high over my head for the black ones
The first plump berries of summer;
A scratch on the arm, maybe, a tumble
But filling my pail and singing my song
With the bees humming
And the sun burning.

Then no bell rang for me;
Only the siren.
Only the women crying and the men running.
Only the Mounties writing our names
In the big book; the stifled feeling
Of being caught, corralled.
Only the trucks and a scramble to find
A jacket, a ball, for the bundle.

My blackberries spilled
Smeared purple
Over the doorway.
Never again did I go
Blackberry picking on the hillside.
Never again did I know
That iron schoolbell ringing.

BOY'S AND GIRL'S VOICES:

The children incoming
The tide inflowing.

ANNOUNCER:

From the upper islands of the coast
With only one day's notice to depart

Came these, and hundreds like them: Mariko and her
   mother.
In the re-allocation centre, Hastings Park
Mariko writes a letter.

THE LETTER:

I wonder where in the inner country
On what train shooting between two mountains
You fly tonight, Susumu?
When I explain to you how it is here
You will understand, perhaps,
Why I have not been able to tell my mother
About you and me.

It is this: she is continually frightened—
Never having lived so, in a horse stall before.
My bunk is above hers, and all night I lie rigid
For fear to disturb her; but she is disturbed.
She has hung her pink petticoat from my bunk rail
Down over her head, to be private; but nothing is private.
Hundreds of strangers lie breathing around us
Wakeful, or coughing; or in sleep tossing;
Hundreds of strangers pressing upon us
Like horses tethered, tied to a manger.

My mother lies wakeful with her eyes staring.
I cannot see her, but I know. She is thinking:
This is a nightmare. She is back in her home
Embroidering blossoms on a silk kimono
Talking to me of Yosh (the boy I mentioned,
The one I grew up with). She is making plans
To visit the go-between; to bake for a wedding.

My mother cannot believe her dream is over,
That she lies in a manger with her hands tethered.
So you will understand now, Susumu:
I have not been able to tell my mother.
It is hard for me to believe, myself,

How you said the words, how you spoke of a garden
Where my name, MARIKO, would be written in
    flowers. . . .
I wonder where in the inner country
On what train far from this animal silence
This thick night stifling my heart, my nostrils—
Where like a rocket shooting between two planets
Have you flown, Susumu? Have you gone?

ANNOUNCER:

Between the fury and the fear
The window-breaking rabble and the politician's
    blackout,
(Wartime panic fed
On peacetime provocations)
Between the curfew rung
On Powell Street
And the rows of bunks in a public stable
Between the line-ups and the labels and the presentation
    of a one-way ticket
Between these, and the human heart—
There was in every centre one man, a white man—
A minister, a layman—a mayor.

THE MAYOR:

That year the snow came early, lay lightly on our hills
Cooling their colours, pointing up the evergreen
Scribbled over the ledges; at valley's end
Snow muffled with its mantle the gaunt shape,
The smokeless chimney of the copper smelter.

I stood on the station platform reading the message
Telegraphed from Vancouver: 'The first contingent,
Sixty-eight persons, arriving on the night train.'
Then I looked down our narrow, funnelled valley
My ghost-town village, with hotels closed up
Since gold-rush days; post office perched
Upon a down-hill lurch, leaning towards empty stores.

At seven-fifteen the evening train pulled in.
I stood alone on the platform, waiting.
Slowly the aliens descended, in huddled groups,
Mothers and crying children; boys and girls
Holding a bundle of blankets, cardboard boxes,
A basket of pots and pans, a child's go-cart—
Looking bewildered up and down the platform,
The valley closing in, the hostile village. . . .

I stepped forward, urged into sudden action.
The women cowered, fell back, cried words
In panic to the old men standing surly, helpless.
I collared a young kid, bright, with his eyes snapping:
'You there, you speak English?' 'Why, yah! You bet.'
We eyed each other, and I smiled. 'You see,'
I said, 'I'm mayor here . . . your mayor.
This is your home. Can you tell the people that?
Tell them I'm here to meet them, get acquainted,
Find a place for them to sleep.' The boy
Nodded. 'Okay, I'll tell my mother, sure.
The rest will believe whatever she says to do.'

Their conference began. I waited, tense;
Then plunged into the job of lifting crates
And scanty furnishings, getting local lads
To pile it up on trucks; until I felt
A timid touch upon my arm; I turned
And saw the Issei mother.
                              Putting out my hand
I felt hers move, rest for a moment in mine—
Then we were free. We began to work together. . . .

Then I went out to find some carpenters
To build a village in a single day. . . .
It was cold. Light snow covered the hills.
By spring, I vowed, those people would be mine!
This village would be home.

ANNOUNCER:

These were the fathers, mothers, those
Who had to choose another home, another way.
What would they choose? The questioner
Paused with his pencil lifted; gave them a day
To talk together, choose.

THE WIFE:

Either to be a ghost in mountain towns
Abandoned by the seekers after gold,
There to sit with idle hands,
Embroidering the past upon a window-pane
Fed on foreign food
And crowded together in government huts
The men torn from our arms, the family parted,
Or to face the longer, stranger journey
Over the mountain ranges, barred from the sea—
To labour in uncertain soil, inclement weather
Yet labour as one—all the family together?

THE HUSBAND:

We looked at each other, you and I, after
So many doubtful years binding our struggles:
Our small plot grown to wider green
Pastured within the Fraser's folds, the shack
Upbuilded to a cottage, now a house—
The cherry trees abloom and strawberry fields
White with the snow of blossom, of promise.

THE WIFE:

Had it all to be done again, worked at again
By our gnarled hands, in a harsh new land
Where summer passes like a quick hot breath
And winter holds you chained for half the year?
You took my hands, and said: 'It's the children's country.
Let them choose.' They chafed for independence
Scenting the air of freedom in far fields.

Therefore we had no choice, but one straight way:
The eastward journey into emptiness,
A prairie place called home.

THE HUSBAND:

It was harder than hate. Home was a blueprint only.
We lived in a hen coop perched on a farmer's field
Soaked by the sudden storms, the early rains of April.
Yet there was time for ploughing, time to sow
Beet seed upon the strange black soil in rows
Of half an acre; we saw in neighbouring fields'
Bleak tableland, the stabbing green
Of the young wheat; and heard the sweet
Heart-snaring song of meadow-larks; in grass
Withered and brown saw maps move, empty patches
Purple with crocus underneath our feet.

In summer the sun's beak
Tore at our backs bending over the rows
Endless for thinning; the lumpy soil left callouses
Upon our naked knees; mosquitoes swarmed
In frenzied choruses above our heads
Sapping the neck; until a hot wind seared
The field, drove them away in clouds.

THE WIFE:

I think we had nearly given up, and wept
And gone for government help, another home—
Until, one evening lull, work done
You leaned upon the poplar gate to watch
A lime green sky rim the mauve twilight
While in the pasture fireflies danced
Like lanterns of Japan on prairie air.

Leaning the other way spoke our new friend
The neighbour from the Ukraine;
Touching your arm, using words more broken
Than yours, like scraps of bread left over.

'See how tomorrow is fine. You work
Hard, same as me. We make good harvest time.'
He came from a loved land, too, the mild
Plains of the Dneiper where, in early spring
(He said) the violets hid their sweetness. 'This land
Is strange and new. But clean and big
And gentle with the wheat. For children too,
Good growing.'
He lifted up his hands, his praise; we heard
Over the quickening fields a fresh wind blowing.

ANNOUNCER:

This one was young, a renegade. He wanted the world
In his two hands. He would not make the choice,
But cast it back in their teeth.

NISEI VOICE:

They can't do this to me, Shig said
(Once a Jap, always a Jap)
Why, I went to school with those kids
Vancouver's my home town.

They can't do this to me, Shig said
(Once a Jap, always a Jap)
I'll spend my life in a road camp
In a freight car bunk in the bush.

They'll get tired of me, Shig said
(Once a Jap, always a Jap)
And some dark night I'll buckle my belt
And hitch-hike to the sea.

The Mounties won't get me, Shig said
(Once a Jap, always a Jap)
I'll say I'm a Chinese, see?
It's the underworld for me.

They picked Shig up on a robbery charge

(Once in jail, always in jail)
There were only a few of us such as he
But he blackened our name
Shut the gates to the sea.

ANNOUNCER:

This one was young; but he wanted the world
For others. A philosopher,
He accepted the blow, Pearl Harbor.
He learned the way of waiting.

THE PHILOSOPHER:

To be alone is grace; to see it clear
Without rancour; to let the past be
And the future become. Rarely to remember
The painful needles turning in the flesh.

(I had looked out of the schoolroom window
And could not see the design, held dear
Of the shaken maples; nor the rain, searing and stinging
The burning rain in the eye.

I could not see, nor hear my name called:
Tatsuo, the Pythagoras theorem!
I could not think till the ruler rapped
On the desk, and my mind snapped.

The schoolroom faded, I could not hold
A book again in my hand.
It was the not knowing; the must be gone
Yet the continual fear of going.

Yes, to remember is to go back; to take
The path along the dyke, the lands of my uncle
Stretching away from the river—
The dykeside where we played

Under his fruit trees, canopied with apples,

Falling asleep under a hedgerow of roses
To the gull's shrill chatter and the tide's recurrent
Whisper in the marshland that was home. . . .)

So must I remember. It cannot be hid
Nor hurried from. As long as there abides
No bitterness; only the lesson learned
And the habit of grace chosen, accepted.

CHORUS OF NISEIS:

Home, we discover, is where life is:
Not Manitoba's wheat
Ontario's walled cities
Nor a B.C. fishing fleet.

Home is something more than harbour—
Than father, mother, sons;
Home is the white face leaning over your shoulder
As well as the darker ones.

Home is labour, with the hand and heart,
The hard doing, and the rest when done;
A wider sea than we knew, a deeper earth,
A more enduring sun.

Bartok and the Geranium

She lifts her green umbrellas
Towards the pane
Seeking her fill of sunlight
Or of rain;
Whatever falls
She has no commentary
Accepts, extends,
Blows out her furbelows,
Her bustling boughs;

And all the while he whirls
Explodes in space,
Never content with this small room:
Not even can he be
Confined to sky
But must speed high and higher still
From galaxy to galaxy,
Wrench from the stars their momentary notes
Steal music from the moon.

She's daylight
He is dark
She's heaven-held breath
He storms and crackles
Spits with hell's own spark.

Yet in this room, this moment now
These together breathe and be:
She, essence of serenity,
He in a mad intensity
Soars beyond sight
Then hurls, lost Lucifer,
From heaven's height.

And when he's done, he's out:
She leans a lip against the glass
And preens herself in light.

Without Benefit of Tape

The real poems are being written in outports
on backwoods farms
in passageways where pantries still exist
or where geraniums
nail light to the window
while out of the window boy in the flying field
is pulled to heaven on the keel of a kite.

Stories breed in the north:
men with snow in their mouths
trample and shake at the bit
kneading the woman down under blankets of snow
icing her breath, her eyes.

The living speech is shouted out
by men and women leaving railway lines
to trundle home, pack-sacked
just company for deer or bear—

    Hallooed
across the counter, in a corner store
it booms upon the river's shore:
on midnight roads where hikers flag you down
speech echoes from the canyon's wall
    resonant
    indubitable.

The Unquiet Bed

The woman I am
is not what you see
I'm not just bones
and crockery

the woman I am
knew love and hate
hating the chains
that parents make

longing that love
might set men free
yet hold them fast
in loyalty

the woman I am
is not what you see
move over love
make room for me

The Artefacts: West Coast

I

In the middle of the night
I hear this old house breathing
a steady sigh
when oak trees and rock shadows
assemble silence
under a high
white moon

I hear the old house turn
in its sleep
shifting the weight of long dead footsteps
from one wall to another
echoing the children's voices
shrilly calling
from one room to the next
repeating those whispers in the master bedroom
a cry, a long sigh of breath
from one body to another
when the holy ghost takes over

In the middle of the night
I wake
and hear time speaking

II

History the young say
doesn't make sense
and what can I say
in rejoinder?

The history of this house
if explored
is perhaps only reiterated pattern
being made over and over
by the young, now—
so there's nothing gained or lost
from the not-knowing
from the non-pattern?

> First it was forest; rock;
> hidden ups and downs
> a hill where oaks and pines
> struggled
> and if a stranger climbed
> the topmost pine
> he'd see the ocean flattening the mountains
> the forest, serried—
> below, only the sculpted bays
> native encampments
> ceremonial lodges, totem poles
> and winter dances
> the Raven overall
> giver-of-light, supervising
> and the white whale imminent
> evil lurking
> to be appeased with ritual
> long hair dancing
> feathered masks

And today
> at Wreck Bay, Long Beach
> the long hairs dance
> shaking their necklaces

they do not paint their faces
            nor wear masks
are vulnerable to the whale
unprotected think to find safety
in nakedness

            (in the cities
            the young are wiser
            stave off the whale's power
            with maxi-minis, fringes, tokens, charms
            LONG HAIR)

but history begins
                        the woman said
when you are thirty
that tomtom, time
begins to beat
to beat for you

III

And in this house, look
examine the door lintels
striated cleverly and crowned
by the encircled eye:
egg-and-dart

examine out of doors
those arabesques, supporting eaves
leaves leaves entwined
those shingled sidewalls
scalloped leaf imprinted
over leaf; the forest
pattern brought to shape the house;
and turrets high!   and branching rooms
and eaves where swallows nest.

And in this city on the brink

of forest—sea—
history delights that Queen Victoria
made marriage with the totem wilderness
the cedar silences
the raven's wing

IV

Now ravens build here still
Seagulls spiral
the hippie children in these attics
breathe and cry
unwittingly
the names of history
tumble from their lips:
Nootka   Nanaimo
Masset   Ucluelet
The map leaps up
                here did I live
                    was born and reared
                here died

So: Chief Maquinna   Jewitt   Emily Carr

The map leaps up
from namelessness
to history
each place made ceremonial
when named
and its name
peopled!
events shouted!

                here the waters divided
                here the whale bellowed

V

In the middle of the night
the house heaves, unmoored
launched on a vast sea.

Summer Landscape: Jasper

The mountains are cold husbands
they stare
stony and white-capped
shrouded in mist

Below, by chill brown water
deer and elk graze   mindlessly
the grass is sulky green
the evergreens   undifferentiated
in a drift of rain

Chill gloom, no face
of man
only a speeding car
whose lights devour the highway
brief as brightness is
caught between dark and dark

The mountains are
remote as brotherhoods
bereft of women
in these valleys
no cries of children

Earle
Birney

From the Hazel Bough

I met a lady
  on a lazy street
hazel eyes
  and little plush feet

her legs swam by
  like lovely trout
eyes were trees
  where boys leant out

hands in the dark and
  a river side
round breasts rising
  with the fingers' tide

she was plump as a finch
  and live as a salmon
gay as silk and
  proud as a Brahmin

we winked when we met
  and laughed when we parted
never took time
  to be brokenhearted

but no man sees
  where the trout lie now
or what leans out
  from the hazel bough

Bushed

Bush fever insanity

He invented a rainbow but lightning struck it
shattered it into the lake-lap of a mountain
so big his mind slowed when he looked at it

Yet he built a shack on the shore
learned to roast porcupine belly and
wore the quills on his hatband

At first he was out with the dawn
whether it yellowed bright as wood-columbine
or was only a fuzzed moth in a flannel of storm
But he found the mountain was clearly alive
sent messages whizzing down every hot morning
boomed proclamations at noon and spread out
a white guard of goat
before falling asleep on its feet at sundown

When he tried his eyes on the lake   ospreys
would fall like valkyries
choosing the cut-throat
He took then to waiting
till the night smoke rose from the boil of the sunset

But the moon carved unknown totems
out of the lakeshore
owls in the beardusky woods derided him
moosehorned cedars circled his swamps and tossed
their antlers up to the stars
Then he knew   though the mountain slept   the winds
were shaping its peak to an arrowhead
poised

And now he could only
bar himself in and wait
for the great flint to come singing into his heart

1951

A Walk in Kyoto

All week   the maid tells me   bowing
her doll's body at my mat   is Boys' Day
Also please Man's Day   and gravely
bends deeper   The magnolia sprig in my alcove
is it male?   The ancient discretions of Zen were not shaped
for my phallic western eye   There is so much discretion
in this small bowed body of an empire
the wild hair of waterfalls combed straight
in the ricefields   the inn-maid retreating
with the face of a shut flower   I stand hunched
and clueless like a castaway in the shoals of my room

When I slide my parchment door to stalk awkward
through Lilliput gardens framed and untouchable
as watercolors   the streets look much the same
the Men are being pulled past on the strings of their engines
the legs of the Boys are revolved by a thousand pedals
and all the faces as taut and unfestive as Moscow's
or Chicago's   or mine

Lord Buddha help us all there is vigor enough
in these islands and in all islands reefed and resounding
with cities   But the pitch is high as the ping
of cicadas   those small strained motors concealed
in the propped pines by the dying river   and only
male as the stretched falsetto of actors mincing
the women's roles in *kabuki*   or female only
as the lost heroes womanized in the Ladies' Opera
Where in these alleys jammed with competing waves
of signs in two tongues and three scripts
can the simple song of a man be heard?

By the shoguns' palace   the Important Cultural Property
stripped for tiptoeing schoolgirls   I stare at the staring
penned carp that flail on each other's backs
to the shrunk pool's edge for the crumb this non-fish
tossed   Is this the Day's one parable?

Or under that peeling pagoda the five hundred tons
of hermaphrodite Word?

At the inn I prepare to surrender again my defeated
shoes to the bending maid   But suddenly the closed
lotus opens to a smile and she points
over my shoulder   above the sagging tiles   to where
tall in the bare sky and huge as Gulliver
a carp is rising   golden and fighting
thrusting its paper body up from the fist
of a small boy on an empty roof   higher
and higher   into the endless winds of the world

Kyoto & Hong Kong 1958

The Bear on the Delhi Road

Unreal   tall as a myth
by the road the Himalayan bear
is beating the brilliant air
with his crooked arms
About him two men   bare
spindly as locusts   leap

One pulls on a ring
in the great soft nose   His mate
flicks   flicks with a stick
up at the rolling eyes

They have not led him here
down from the fabulous hills
to this bald alien plain
and the clamorous world   to kill
but simply to teach him to dance

They are peaceful both   these spare
men of Kashmir   and the bear

alive is their living   too
If   far on the Delhi way
around him galvanic they dance
it is merely to wear   wear
from his shaggy body the tranced
wish forever to stay
only an ambling bear
four-footed in berries

It is no more joyous for them
in this hot dust to prance
out of reach of the praying claws
sharpened to paw for ants
in the shadows of deodars
It is not easy to free
myth from reality
or rear this fellow up
to lurch   lurch with them
in the tranced dancing of men

Srinagar 1958—Île des Porquerolles 1959

El Greco: *Espolio* *painting of Christ's stripped of garments*

The carpenter is intent on the pressure of his hand

on the awl   and the trick of pinpointing his strength
through the awl to the wood   which is tough
He has no effort to spare for despoilings
or to worry if he'll be cut in on the dice
His skill is vital to the scene   and the safety of the state
Anyone can perform the indignities   It's his hard arms
and craft that hold the eyes of the convict's women
There is the problem of getting the holes exact
(in the middle of this elbowing crowd)
and deep enough to hold the spikes

after they've sunk through those bared feet
and inadequate wrists he knows are waiting behind him

He doesn't sense perhaps that one of the hands
is held in a curious gesture over him—
giving   or asking   forgiveness?—
but he'd scarcely take time to be puzzled by poses
Criminals come in all sorts
as anyone knows who makes crosses
are as mad or sane as those who decide on their killings
Our one at least has been quiet so far
though they say he talked himself into this trouble
a carpenter's son who got notions of preaching

Well heres a carpenter's son who'll have carpenter sons
God willing   and build what's wanted
temples or tables   mangers or crosses
and shape them decently
working alone in that firm and profound abstraction
which blots out the bawling of rag-snatchers
To construct with hands   knee-weight   braced thigh
keeps the back turned from death

But it's too late now for the other carpenter's boy
to return to this peace before the nails are hammered

Point Grey 1960

For George Lamming

to you
      I can risk words about this

Mastering them   you know
      they are dull
            servants

who say less
    and worse
        than we feel

That party above Kingston Town
    we stood   five (six?) couples

linked singing
    more than rum happy

I was giddy
    from sudden friendship
wanted   undeserved

    black tulip faces
self swaying forgotten
    laughter in dance

Suddenly on a wall mirror
    my face assaulted me
stunned to see itself
    like a white snail
        in the supple dark flowers

Always now I move grateful
    to all of you
who let me walk thoughtless
    and unchallenged
in the gardens
    in the castles
        of your skins

Kingston, Jamaica 1962

ARRIVALS Wolfville
Locals
From Halifax   30 mins L

It was the hand that caught in me

Sudden as a beast the blizzard
had whirled on us   was gone
as quick over the hill and howling
through the next village   whose spire
could be glimpsed blotting out now
in a grey fury

And we are wading   a straggle of passengers
in town shoes   through a snowscape
clean and cosy as any Christmas card
the small firs like spunwhite candy
spaced on the ice-cream hillocks

Already the sunlight quivers down
burning on the narrow tracks at the crossing
and fires the sleet that sheathes one flank
and the bland diesel-face of our train
so small and innocent now it has stopped

You wouldnt think from that little jolt we got!
... Speedin ... Naw, in that storm he jes couldn see

   Green as a great bruise
   where the smooth flesh of the drifts
   has been savaged   the auto lies
   crumpled and akimbo
   like a beetle battered by catspaw

Flung it fifty feet ... Yeah an him further ...
This year's chevvy ... Well we stopped fast enough

We stand   the unsilent   stamping
staring   to reduce to livable size
what is casually spreadeagled here in the snow

Should be a law about level cross—
Sure but we oughta wistled wen—Hell we did!
. . . Anybody know who he is?

We too anonymous   one to the other
but our breaths write on the air
the kinship of being alive
surrounding the perfect stranger

Christ it's too cold I'm gittin back . . .
Yep ain't nothin we kin do . . . Hey look
he's only gone three hundred . . .

A thin man unprompted is gathering papers
slewed from a briefcase over the raddled banks
He slaps them free of flakes
and packs them carefully back in the case
Now he teeters   not knowing what to do with it
The brakeman plods up with a plaid blanket

Train gonna be held up till police come?
. . . No I'm stayin
Conductor was up to that farm phonin em

The man with the case silently lays it
next to the open palm
the blanket has failed to cover
He offers his only remark

Assizes is on up to Wolfville
Them's law papers

The halfburied engine continues to tick
with cooling   something live under the snow
Each time we are startled

Lawyer eh?... Musta stalled on the track
grabbed his case   got half out his door...
Yep   nearly made it... Young feller too

    The sun has given way again to a black sky
    Most have tramped back to the train
    The rest of us circle about
    as if for somewhere to put down the guilt

Yer all lucky we dint go offa the tracks
... He's right   Can't blame the crew none

    Diesel shrieks and we jump
    The brakeman gestures   Turning at once
    we leave him beating his arms for warmth
    turn in a pleasure of hurry   to hop
    like schoolboys back in the steps we made
    eager for heat and motion   arrivals
    and shaping already what happened

    The train moves to its goal
    and scatters us from the scene forever
    The manner of hills   words   faces
    slides from the gloss protecting each mind
    We will forget even that scotched face perhaps
    waiting till the gay rug came down
    in a Christmas world

    But not surely the longfingered hand
    stretched in some arresting habit of eloquence
    to the last irrational judgement
    roaring in from the storm

    Or is it only in me that the hand hooked
    and I who must manage it now like a third?

1962

Cartagena de Indias

'Ciudad triste, ayer reina de la mar.'—HEREDIA

Each face its own phantom
its own formula of breed and shade
but all the eyes accuse me back and say

> There are only two races here:
> we human citizens
> who are poor but have things to sell
> and you   from outer space
> unseasonable   our one tourist
> but plainly able to buy

This arthritic street
where Drake's men and Cole's ran
swung cutlasses   where wine and sweet blood
snaked in the cobble's joints
>   leaps now in a sennet of taxi horns
>   to betray my invasion
All watch my first retreat
to barbizans patched from Morgan's grapeshot
and they rush me
>   three desperate tarantula youths
>   waving Old Golds unexcised

By an altar blackened
where the Indian silver was scratched away
in sanctuary leaning   on lush cool marble
>   I am hemmed by a Congo drum man in jeans
> He bares a brace of Swiss watches
>   whispers in husky Texan

Where gems and indigo were sorted
>   in shouting arcades
>   I am deftly shortchanged
and slink to the trees that lean
and flower tall in the Plaza

Nine shoeboys wham their boxes
slap at my newshined feet

Only in the Indio market
mazed on the sodden quais
I am granted uneasy truce
Around the ritual braidings of hair
the magical arrangements of fish
the piled rainbows of rotting fruit
I cast a shadow of silence
  blue-dreaded eyes
  corpse face
  hidalgo clothes
  tall one   tall as a demon
  pass O pass us quickly

Behind me the bright blaze of patois
  leaps again

I step to the beautiful slave-built bridge
and a mestiza girl
  levels Christ's hands at me
  under a dangling goitre

Past the glazed-eyed screamers of *dulces*
swing to a pink lane
where a poxed and slit-eyed savage
  pouts an obscenity
  offering a sister
  as he would spit me
  a dart from a blowpipe

Somewhere there must be another bridge
from my stupid wish
to their human acceptance
but what can I offer—
my tongue half-locked in the cell
of its language—other than pesos
  to these old crones of thirty

whose young sink in pellagra
as I clump unmaimed
in the bright shoes
that keep me from hookworm
lockjaw and snakebite

It's written in the cut of my glasses
I've a hotelroom all to myself
with a fan   and a box of Vitamin C
It can be measured
in my unnatural stride
that my life expectation
is more than forty
especially now that I'm close to sixty

older than ever bankrupt Bolivar was
who sits now in a frozen prance
high over the coconut trays
quivering on the heads
     of three gaunt mulatto ladies
     circling in a pavane of commerce
     down upon spotlit me

Out of the heaving womb of independence
Bolívar rode   and over the bloody afterbirth
into coffee and standard oil
     from inquisitional baroque
     to armed forces corbusier
He alone has nothing more   to sell me

I come routed now   scuffling
through dust in a nameless square
treeless   burning   deserted
come lost and guiltily wakeful
in the hour of siesta
     at last to a message

     to a pair of shoes
     in a circle of baked mud

40 | Earle Birney

        worn   out of shape   one on its side
For a second I am shaken by panic
heat? humidity? something has got me
        the shoes are concrete
        and ten feet long

        the sight of a plaque calms
        without telling me much

                    En homenaje de la memoria de
                            LUIS LOPEZ
                    se erigió este monumento
                    a los zapatos viejos
                    el día 10 de febrero de 1957

Luis Lopez?   Monument to his old shoes?
What???   There was nothing else

Back through the huckster streets
the sad taxi men still awake and horn-happy

        Si señor   Luis Lopez el poeta
        Here is his book
        Unamuno praised it   *si si*
        You have seen *los zapatos*?   Ah?
        But they are us, *señor*
        It was about us he wrote
        about Cartagena where he was born
        and died   See here this sonnet
        always he made hard words
        Said we were lazy except to make noise
        we only shout to get money
        ugly too, backward ... why not?
        It is for a poet to write these things
        Also *plena*—how say it?—
        plena de rancio desaliño
Full of rancid disarray!
        Si si but look, at the end, when old
        he come to say one nice thing

only one ever about us
He say we inspire that love a man has
for his old shoes—*Entonces*
we give him a monument to the shoes

I bought the book   walked back
sat on the curb happier than Wordsworth
gazing away at his daffodils
Discarded queen   I thought   I love you too
Full of rancid disarray
city like any city
full of the stench of human indignity
and disarray of the human proportion
full of the noisy always poor
and the precocious dying
stinking with fear   the stale of ignorance
I love you first for giving birth
to Luis Lopez   suffering him
honouring him at last
in the grand laconic manner
he taught you

—and him I envy
I who am seldom read by my townsmen

Descendants of pirates   grandees
galleyslaves and cannibals
I love the whole starved cheating
poetry-reading lot of you   most of all
for throwing me the shoes of deadman Luis
to walk me back into your brotherhood

Colombia 1962—Greece 1963

November Walk Near False Creek Mouth

The time is the last of warmth
and the fading of brightness
    before the final flash and the night

I walk as the earth turns
from its burning father
here on this lowest edge of mortal city
where windows flare on faded flats
and the barren end of the ancient English
    who tippled mead in Alfred's hall
    and took tiffin in lost Lahore
drink now their fouroclock chainstore tea
sighing like old pines as the wind turns

The beat is the small   slap   slapping
of the tide sloping   slipping
its long soft fingers into the tense
joints of the trapped seawall

More ones than twos on the beaches today
strolling   or stranded as nations
woolly mermaids   dazed on beachlogs
a kept dog   sniffing   leading his woman
Seldom the lovers   seldom as reason
They will twine indoors from now to May
or ever to never   except the lovers
of what is not city   the refugees
    from the slow volcano
    the cratered rumbling   sirening vents
    the ashen air   the barren spilling
    compulsive rearing of glassy cliff
    from city
they come to the last innocent warmth
and the fading
before the unimaginable brightness

The theme lies in the layers
made and unmade by the nudging   lurching
spiralling down from nothing

down through the common explosion of time
through the chaos of suns
to the high seas of the spinning air
where the shelves form   and re-form down
through cirrus to clouds on cracking peaks
to the terraced woods and the shapeless town
and its dying shapers

The act is the sliding out
to the shifting rotting
folds of the sands that lip
slipping to reefs and sinking cliffs
that ladder down to the ocean's abyss
and farther down through a thousand seas
of the mantling rock
to the dense unbeating black unapproachable
heart of this world

Lanknosed lady sits on a seawall
not alone   she sits with an older book
Who is it?   Shakespeare   Sophocles   Simenon?
They are tranced as sinners unafraid
in the common gaze to pursue
under hard covers their private quaint barren
affair   though today there is no unbusy body
but me to throw them a public look

   not this wrinkled triad of tourists
   strayed off the trail from the rank zoo
   peering away from irrelevant sea
   seeking a starred sign for the bus-stop
   They dangle plastic totems   a kewpie
   a Hong Kong puzzle for somebody's child
   who waits to be worshipped
   back on the prairie farm

No nor the two manlings
all muscles and snorkels and need to shout
with Canadian voices   Nipponese bodies
racing each other into the chilling waters
last maybe of whatever summer's swimmers

Nor for certain the gamey old gaffer
asleep on the bench like a local Buddha
above them   buttonedup mackinaw
Sally Ann trousers   writing in stillness
his own last book   under the squashed
cock of his hat   with a bawdy plot
she never will follow

A tremor only of all his dream
runs like fear from under the hat
through the burned face to twitch
one broken boot   at the other end
of the bench as I pass

dreaming my own unraveled plots
between eating water and eaten shore
    in this hour of the tired and homing
    retired   dissolving
    in the days of the separate wait
    for the mass dying

and I   having clambered down to the last
shelf of the gasping world of lungs
do not know why I too wait   and stare
before descending the final step
into the clouds of the sea

The beat beating   is the soft cheek
nudging of the sly   shoving   almost
immortal ocean at work
on the earth's liquidation

Outward the sun   explodes light

like a mild rehearsal of light to come
over the vitreous waters
At this edge of the blast
a young girl sits on a granite bench
so still as if already only
silhouette burned in the stone

Two women pass in a cloud of words
    ... so I said   You're *not*!?
    and she said   I *am*!
    I'm one of the Lockeys!
    Not the Lockeys of *Out*garden surely
    I said   *Yes*   she said   but I live
    in Winnipeg now   Why for heaven's *sake*
    I said   then you *must* know Carl *Thorson*?
    Carl?   she said   he's my cousin by marriage
    He is   I said   why he's *mine* too! So ...

Born from the glare come the freakish forms
of tugs   all bows and swollen funnels
straining to harbor in False Creek
and blindly followed by mute scows
    with islets of gravel to thicken the city
    and square bowls of saffron sawdust
    the ground meal of the manstruck forest
or towing shining grids of the trees stricken

At the edge of knowledge the *Prince Apollo*
    (or is it the *Princess Helen*?)
floats in a paperblue fusion of air
gulf   Mykenean islands
and crawls with its freight of flesh
toward the glare and the night waiting
behind the hidden Gate of the Lions

The beat is the slap slip   nudging
as the ledges are made   unmade
by the lurching swaying of all the world
that lies under the spinning air

from the dead centre and the fiery circles
up through the ooze to black liquidities
up to the vast moats
where the doomed whales are swimming
by the weedy walls of sunless Carcassonnes
rising   rising   to the great eels waiting
in salt embrasures   and swirling up
to the twilit roofs that floor the Gulf
up to the crab-scratched sands
of the dappled Banks
into the sunblazed living mud
and the radiant mussels
that armor the rocks

    and I on the path at the high-tide edge
    wandering under the leafless maples
    between the lost salt home
    and the asphalt ledge where carhorns call
    call in the clotting air by a shore
    where shamans never again will sound
    with moon-snail conch the ritual plea
    to brother salmon or vanished seal
    and none ever heard
    the horn of Triton or merman

The beat is the bob   dip   dipping
in the small waves   of the ducks shoring
and the shored rocks that seem to move
from turning earth or breathing ocean
in the dazzling slant of the cooling sun

Through piled backyards of the sculptor sea
I climb   over discarded hemlock saurians
    Medusae cedar-stumps   muscled horsemen
    Tartars or Crees   sandsunk forever
and past the raw sawed butt
    telltale with brands
of a buccaneered boom-log
    whisked away to a no-question mill

all the swashing topmost reach of the sea
   that is also the deepest
   reach of wrens   the vanishing squirrel
   and the spilling city
the stinking ledge disputed by barnacles
waiting for tiderise to kick in their food
contested by jittery sandfleas
and hovering gulls that are half-sounds only
traced overhead   lone as my half-thoughts
   wheeling too with persistence of hunger
   or floating on scraps of flotsam

Slowly   scarcely sensed   the beat
has been quickening now as the air
from the whitened peaks is falling
faraway sliding   pouring down
through the higher canyons and over
knolls and roofs to a oneway urgent
procession of rhythms

blowing the haze from False Creek's girders
where now I walk as the waves stream
from my feet to the bay to the far shore
Where they lap like dreams that never reach

The tree-barbed tip of Point Grey's lance
has failed again to impale the gone sun
Clouds and islands float together
out from the darkening bandsaw of suburbs
and burn like sodium over the sunset waters

Something   is it only the wind?
above a jungle of harbor masts
is playing paperchase with the persons
of starlings   They sift and fall
stall and soar   turning
   as I too turn   with the need to feel
   once more the yielding of moist sand
   and thread the rocks back to the seawall

shadowed and empty now
of booklost ladies or flickering wrens

and beyond to the Boats for Hire
where a thin old Swede clings in his chair
like hope to the last light
eyeing bluely the girls with rackets
padding back from belated tennis
while herring gulls make civic statues
of three posts on the pier
and all his child-bright boats
heave unwanted to winter sleep

Further the shore dips   and the sea   sullen
with sludge from floors of barges   spits
arrogantly over the Harbour Board's wall
and only the brutish prow of something
a troller perhaps   lies longdrowned
on an Ararat of broken clamshells
and the flakings of dead crabs

The shore snouts up again
spilling beachlogs glossy and dry
as sloughed snakeskins
but with sodden immovable hearts
heigh ho the logs that no one wants
and the men that sit on the logs
that no one wants
while the sea repeats what it said
to the first unthinking frogs
and the green wounds of the granite stones

By cold depths and by cliffs
whose shine will pass any moment now
the shore puts an end to my ledge
and I climb past the dried shell
of the children's pool   waiting like faith
for summer   to where the last leaves
of the shore's alders   glistening with salt

have turned the ragged lawns
to a battlefield bright with their bodies

For the time is after the scarring of maples
torn by the fall's first fury of air
on the nearest shelf above brine and sand
where the world of the dry troubling begins

   the first days of the vitreous fusing
   of deserts   the proud irradiations of air
   in the time when men rise
   and fall   from the moon's ledge

   while the moon sends   as before
   the waters swirling up and back
   from the bay's world
   to this darkening bitten shore

   I turn to the terraced road
   the cold steps to the bland new block
   the human-encrusted reefs
   that rise here higher than firs or singing
   up to aseptic penthouse hillforts
   to antennae above the crosses
   pylons marching over the peaks
   of mountains without Olympus

Higher than clouds and strata of jetstreams
the air-roads wait the two-way traffic
And beyond?   The desert planets
What else?   a galaxy-full perhaps
of suns and penthouses waiting

But still on the highest shelf of ever
washed by the curve of timeless returnings
lies the unreached unreachable nothing
whose winds wash down to the human shores
and slip   shoving

into each thought nudging my footsteps now
as I turn to my brief night's ledge

in the last of warmth
and the fading of brightness
on the sliding edge of the beating sea

Vancouver 1961—Ametlla, Spain 1963

There Are Delicacies

there are delicacies in you
    like the hearts of watches
there are wheels that turn
    on the tips of rubies
& tiny intricate locks

i need your help
    to contrive keys
there is so little time
    even for the finest
        of watches

Scarborough 1965

Al Purdy

The Cariboo Horses

At 100 Mile House the cowboys ride in rolling
stagey cigarettes with one hand reining
half-tame bronco rebels on a morning grey as stone
—so much like riding dangerous women
              with whiskey coloured eyes—
such women as once fell dead with their lovers
with fire in their heads and slippery froth on thighs
—Beaver and Carrier women maybe or
              Blackfoot squaws far past the edge of this valley
on the other side of those two toy mountain ranges
              from the sunfierce plains beyond—

But only horses
                        waiting in stables
hitched at taverns
                        standing at dawn
pastured outside the town with
jeeps and fords and chevvys and
busy muttering stake trucks rushing
importantly over roads of man's devising
over the safe known roads of the ranchers
families and merchants of the town—
              On the high prairie
are only horse and rider
              wind in dry grass
clopping in silence under the toy mountains
dropping sometimes and
              lost in the dry grass
              golden oranges of dung—

Only horses
              no stopwatch memories or palace ancestors
not Kiangs hauling undressed stone in the Nile Valley
and having stubborn Egyptian tantrums or
Onagers racing thru Hither Asia and
the last Quagga screaming in African highlands
              lost relatives of these

            whose hooves were thunder
the ghosts of horses battering thru the wind
whose names were the wind's common usage
whose life was the sun's
            arriving here at chilly noon
            in the gasoline smell of the
            dust and waiting 15 minutes
            at the grocer's—

mundane situation

Song of the Impermanent Husband

Oh I would
            I would in a minute
if the cusswords and bitter anger couldn't—
if the either/or quarrel didn't—
and the fat around my middle wasn't—
if I was young if
            I wasn't so damn sure
I couldn't find another maddening bitch
like you holding on for dear life to
all the different parts of me for
twenty or twenty
            thousand years
I'd leave in the night like
a disgraced caviar salesman
            descend the moonlight
stairs to Halifax
      (uh—no—not Halifax)
well then Toronto
            uh
I guess not Toronto either/or
nouveau riche Vancouver down
                  down
                        down
the dark stairs to

the South Seas' sunlit milky reefs and
    the jungle's green
        unending bank account with
all the brown girls being brown
      as they can be and all
the one piece behinds stretched tight tonight
in small sarongs not to be touched tho Oh
beautiful as an angel's ass without the genitals
and me
      in Paris like a smudged Canadian postcard and
(dear me)
      all the importuning white and lily girls
of Rue Pigalle
      and stroll
the sodden London streets and
      find a sullen foggy woman who
enjoyed my odd colonial ways and send
a postcard back to you about my faithfulness and
talk about the lovely beastly English weather
I'd be the slimiest most uxorious wife deserter
      my shrunk amoeba self absurd inside
a saffron girl's geography and
hating me between magnetic nipples
but
    fooling no one in all the sad
    and much emancipated world
Why then I'll stay at least for tea for
all the brownness is too brown and
all the whiteness too damned white
and I'm afraid
      afraid of being
any other woman's man who
might be me
      afraid
the unctuous and uneasy self I glimpse
sometimes might lose my faint and yapping cry for
being anything was never quite what I intended
And you you
      bitch no irritating

questions re love and permanence only
                an unrolling lifetime here
between your rocking thighs and
                the semblance of motion

Transient

Riding the boxcars out of Winnipeg in a
morning after rain so close to
the violent sway of fields it's
like running and running
naked with summer in your mouth and
the guy behind you grunts and says
'Got a smoke?'

Being a boy scarcely a moment and you
hear the rumbling iron roadbed singing
under the wheels at night and a door jerking open
mile after dusty mile riding into Regina with
the dust storm crowding behind you and
a guy you hardly even spoke to
nudges your shoulder chummily and says
'Got a smoke?'

Riding into the Crow's Nest mountains with
your first beard itching and a
hundred hungry guys fanning out thru
the shabby whistlestops for handouts and
not even a sandwich for two hundred miles
only the high mountains and knowing
what it's like to be not quite a child
any more and listening to the tough men
talk of women and talk of the way things are
in 1937

Riding down in the spit-grey sea level morning
thru dockyard streets and dingy dowager houses

with ocean a jump away and the sky beneath you
in puddles on Water Street and an old Indian woman
pushing her yawning scratching daughter
onto a balcony to yell at the boy-man passing
'Want some fun?—come on up' and the girl just
come from riding the shrieking bedspring bronco
all the up and down night to a hitchpost morning
full of mothers and dirt and lice and
      hardly the place for a princess
      of the Coast Salish
            (My dove my little one
tonight there will be wine and the loins of a dozen men
to pin you down in the outlying lands of sleep
innocent as a child
      awaiting the last of all your bridegrooms)

Stand in the swaying boxcar doorway
moving east away from the sunset and
after a while the eyes digest a country and
the belly perceives a mapmaker's vision
in dust and dirt on the face and hands here
its smell drawn deep thru the nostrils down
to the lungs and spurts thru blood stream
campaigns in the lower intestine
      and chants love songs to the kidneys
After a while there is no arrival and
no departure possible any more
you are where you were always going
and the shape of home has planted itself in your loins
the identity of forests that were always nameless
the selfhood of rivers that are changing always
the nationality of riding a boxcar thru the depression
over long green plains and high mountain country
with the best and worst of a love that's not to be spoken
and a guy right behind you says then
'Got a smoke?'
You give him one and stand in the boxcar doorway
or looking out the window of a Montreal apartment
or running the machines in a Vancouver factory
—you stand there growing older

Eskimo Graveyard

Walking in glacial litter
frost boils and boulder pavements
of an old river delta
where angry living water
changes its mind every half century
and takes a new direction
to the blue fiord
The Public Works guy I'm with
says you always find good gravel
for concrete near a graveyard
where digging is easy maybe
a footnote on human character
But wrapped in blankets
above ground a dead old woman
(for the last few weeks I'm told)
without a grave marker
And a hundred yards away
the Anglican missionary's grave
with whitewashed cross
that means equally nothing
The river's soft roar
drifts to my ears and changes
tone when the wind changes
ice debris melts at low tide
& the Public Works guy is mildly pleased
with the good gravel we found
for work on the schoolhouse
which won't have to be shipped in
from Montreal
and mosquitoes join happily
in our conversation   Then
he stops to consult
with the construction foreman
I walk on
toward the tents of The People
half a mile away
at one corner of the picture
Mothers with children on their backs

in the clean white parkas
they take such pride in
buying groceries at H.B.C.
boys lounging under the store
in space where timber stilts
hold it above the permafrost
with two of them arm in arm
in the manner of Eskimo friends
After dinner
I walk down among the tents
and happen to think of the old woman
neither wholly among the dead
nor quite gone from the living
and wonder how often
a thought of her enters the minds
of people she knew before
and what kind of flicker it is
as lights begin to come on
in nightlong twilight
and thoughts of me
occur to the mosquitoes
I keep walking
as if something ought to happen
(I don't know what)
with the sun stretching
a yellow band across the water
from headland to black headland
at high tide in the fiord
sealing in the settlement
as if there was no way out
and indeed there isn't
until the looping Cansos come
dropping thru the mountain doorway
That old woman?
it occurs to me
I might have been thinking
about human bookkeeping
debits and credits that is
or profit and loss

(and laugh at myself)
among the sealed white tents
like glowing swans
hoping
for a most improbable
birth

Pangnirtung

Arctic Rhododendrons

They are small purple surprises
in the river's white racket
and after you've seen them
a number of times
in water-places
where their silence seems
related to river-thunder
you think of them as 'noisy flowers'
Years ago
it may have been
that lovers came this way
stopped in the outdoor hotel
to watch the water floorshow
and lying prone together
where the purged green
boils to a white heart
and the shore trembles
like a stone song
with bodies touching
flowers were their conversation
and love the sound of a colour
that lasts two weeks in August
and then dies
except for the three or four
I pressed in a letter
and sent whispering to you

Pangnirtung

Detail

The ruined stone house
has an old apple tree
left there by the farmer
whatever else he took with him
It bears fruit every year
gone wild and wormy
with small bitter apples
nobody eats
even children know better
I passed that way on the road
to Trenton twice a month
all winter long
noticing how the apples clung
in spite of hurricane winds
sometimes with caps of snow
little golden bells
And perhaps none of the other
travellers looked that way
but I make no parable of them
they were there and that's all
For some reason I must remember
and think of the leafless tree
and its fermented fruit
one week in late January
when wind blew down the sun
and earth shook like a cold room
no one could live in
with zero weather
soundless golden bells
alone in the storm

Interruption

When the new house was built
callers came:

black squirrels on the roof every morning
between sleep and wakefulness,
and a voice saying 'Hello dead man.'
A chipmunk looks in the window
and I look out,
the small face and the large one
waver together in glass,
but neither moves
while the leaves turn into shadows.
Orioles, robins and red-winged blackbirds
are crayons that colour the air;
something sad and old
cries down in the swamp.
Moonlight in the living room,
a row of mice single file
route marching across the empty lunar plain
until they touch one of my thoughts
and jump back frightened,
but I don't wake up.
Pike in the lake pass and re-pass the windows
with clouds in their mouth.
For 20 minutes every night
the sun slaps a red paint brush
over dinner dishes and leftovers,
but we keep washing it off.
Birds can't take a short cut home,
they have to fly around the new house;
and cedars grow pale green candles
to light their way thru the dark.
Already the house is old:
a drowned chipmunk (the same one?)
in the rain barrel this morning,
dead robins in the roof overhang,
and the mice are terrified—
We have set traps,
and must always remember
to avoid them ourselves.

Lament for the Dorsets

(Eskimos extinct in the 14th century A.D.)

Animal bones and some mossy tent rings
scrapers and spearheads   carved ivory swans
all that remains of the Dorset giants
who drove the Vikings back to their long ships
talked to spirits of earth and water
—a picture of terrifying old men
so large they broke the backs of bears
so small they lurk behind bone rafters
in the brain of modern hunters
among good thoughts and warm things
and come out at night
to spit on the stars

The big men with clever fingers
who had no dogs and hauled their sleds
over the frozen northern oceans
awkward giants
                          killers of seal
they couldn't compete with little men
who came from the west with dogs
Or else in a warm climatic cycle
the seals went back to cold waters
and the puzzled Dorsets scratched their heads
with hairy thumbs around 1350 A.D.
—couldn't figure it out
went around saying to each other
plaintively
              'What's wrong? What happened?
              Where are the seals gone?'
And died

Twentieth century people
apartment dwellers
executives of neon death
warmakers with things that explode
—they have never imagined us in their future
how could we imagine them in the past

squatting among the moving glaciers
six hundred years ago
with glowing lamps?
As remote or nearly
as the trilobites and swamps
when coal became
or the last great reptile hissed
at a mammal the size of a mouse
that squeaked and fled

Did they ever realize at all
what was happening to them?
Some old hunter with one lame leg
a bear had chewed
sitting in a caribou skin tent
—the last Dorset?
Let's say his name was Kudluk
carving 2-inch ivory swans
for a dead grand-daughter
taking them out of his mind
the places in his mind
where pictures are
He selects a sharp stone tool
to gouge a parallel pattern of lines
on both sides of the swan
holding it with his left hand
bearing down and transmitting
his body's weight
from brain to arm and right hand
and one of his thoughts
turns to ivory
The carving is laid aside
in beginning darkness
at the end of hunger
after a while wind
blows down the tent and snow
begins to cover him
After 600 years
the ivory thought   } culture still live
is still warm

The Runners

'It was when Leif was with King Olaf Tryggvason, and he bade him proclaim Christianity to Greenland, that the king gave him two Gaels; the man's name was Haki, and the woman's Haekia. The king advised Leif to have recourse to these people, if he should stand in need of fleetness, for they were swifter than deer. Erick and Leif had tendered Karlsefni the services of this couple. Now when they had sailed past Marvel-Strands (to the New World) they put the Gaels ashore, and directed them to run to the southward, and investigate the nature of the country, and return again before the end of the third half-day.'

—From ERICK THE RED'S SAGA

Brother, the wind of this place is cold,
and hills under our feet tremble,
the forests are making magic against us—
I think the land knows we are here,
I think the land knows we are strangers.
Let us stay close to our friend the sea,
or cunning dwarves at the roots of darkness
shall seize and drag us down—

Sister, we must share our strength between us,
until the heat of our bodies makes a single flame,
and one that we are is more than two that we were:
while the moon sees only one shadow,
and the sun knows only our double heartbeat,
and the rain does not come between—

Brother, I am afraid of this dark place,
I am hungry for the home islands,
and wind blowing the waves to coloured spray,
I am sick for the sun—

Sister, we must not think those thoughts again,
for three half-days have gone by,
and we must return to the ship.
If we are away longer,
the Northmen will beat us with thongs,
until we cry for death—
Why do you stare at nothing?

Brother, a cold wind touched me,
tho I stand in your arms' circle:

perhaps the Northmen's runes have found us,
the runes they carve on wood and stone.
I am afraid of this dark land,
ground mist that makes us half ghosts,
and another silence inside silence . . .
But there are berries and fish here,
and small animals by the sea's edge
that crouch and tremble and listen . . .
If we join our words to the silence,
if our trails cross the trails we made,
and the sun remembers what the moon forgets . . .
Brother, it comes to me now,
the long ship must sail without us,
we stay here—

Sister, we should die slowly,
the beasts would gnaw at our bodies,
the rains whiten our bones.
The Northmen's runes are strong magic,
the runes would track us down,
tho we keep on running
past the Land of Flat Stones
over the Marvel-Strands
beyond the land of great trees . . .
Tho we ran to the edge of the world,
our masters would track us down—

Brother, take my hand in your hand,
this part of ourselves between us
while we run together,
over the stones of the sea-coast,
this much of ourselves is our own:
while rain cries out against us,
and darkness swallows the evening,
and morning moves into stillness,
and mist climbs to our throats,
while we are running,
while we are running—

Sister—

The Beavers of Renfrew

By day
chain saws stencil the silence in my head,
black quotes appear on the red brain—
Across glacial birth marks old Jake
Loney is cutting his winter wood,
tongue drowned in a chaw of tobacco—
The belly button pond at one
end of the farm brims
full its cockleshell three acres:
—tonight the beaver are back,
and work their swing shift
under the moon.
Sometimes at low earthen dams
where the pouring spillway empties,
they stand upright in a pride of being,
holding rainbow trout like silver thoughts,
or pale gold Indian girls
arriving here intact from bone cameras
ten thousand ancestors ago,
before letting them spin down the moonlight
rapids as mortal lures
for drowned fishermen—
Among the beaver lodges
I stand unable to sleep,
but cannot stay awake
while poplar and birch fall around me.
I am not mistaken for a tree,
but almost totally ignored,
pissed on by mistake occasionally—
Standing here long enough,
seeing the gentle bodies moving
close to what they truly are,
I wonder what screwed-up philosophy,
what claim to a god's indulgence,
made men decide their own importance?
And what is great music and art
but an alibi for murderers?

Perhaps in the far-off beginnings
of things they made a pact with men,
dammed the oceans for us,
chewed a hole in the big log bridge
wedged between Kamchatka and Alaska,
tore open the Mediterranean,
parted the Red Sea for Moses,
drowned Atlantis and the Eden-myth,
original sin and all that,
in the great salt womb of the sea—
And why?
Because they pitied men.
To the wet animal shivering in a tree
they said,
       'Come on down—
               It's all right.'
And he shinnied down with hairless
purple behind pointed east for heat,
tail between hind legs,
humbly standing on all fours,
touching his forelock muttering,
'Yessir yessir thank'ee kindly,'
but not knowing how to speak yet of course—
Beaver looked at this dripping creature,
a miserable biological dead end:
but every failure has flashes of genius
exploding out of death:
and the man listened
to an agreement of the water beings
and land beings together
which men have forgotten since:
the secret of staying completely still,
allowing ourselves to catch up
with the shadow just ahead of us
we have lost,
when the young world was a cloudy room
drifting thru morning stillness—
But the rest of it
I have forgotten,

and the gentle beaver will not remind us:
standing upright at their earthen dams
holding the moonlit reins of water,
at peace with themselves—

'Why not make a left turn
and just stay here,'
I said next day to old Jake Loney,
'instead of going forward to the planets?'
The chain saw bucked in his hands,
chewing out chunks of pine that toppled
and scarred the air with green absence.
Far off a beaver tail slapped water,
a bird looked for the tree that was gone—
Old Jake's cheek bulged its chaw of tobacco—
'Well, why not?' I said argumentatively,
before he could spit,
                    'Why not?'
And the log bridge across the Bering
burst with a roar around
me again nothing but water,
brown water—
                    'Why not?'

Alive or Not

It's like a story
because it takes so long to happen:

a block away on an Ottawa street
I see this woman about to fall
and she collapses slowly
in sections the way you read about
and there just might be time
for me to reach her
running as fast as I can
before her head hits the sidewalk

Of course it's my wife
I am running toward her now
and there is a certain amount of horror
a time lag in which other things happen
I can almost see flowers break into blossom
while I am running toward the woman
my wife it seems
orchids in the Brazilian jungle
exist like unprovable ideas
until a man in a pith helmet
steps on one and yells Eureka or something
—and while I am thinking about this
her body splashes on the street
her glasses fall broken beside her
with a musical sound under the traffic
and she is probably dead too
Of course I cradle her in my arms
a doll perhaps without life
while someone I do not know
signals a taxi
as the bystanders stare
What this means years later
as I grow older and older
is that I am still running toward her:
the woman falls very slowly
she is giving me more and more time
to reach her and make the grab
and each time each fall she may die
or not die and this will go on forever
this will go on forever and ever
As I grow older and older
my speed afoot increases
each time I am running and reach
the place before she falls every time
I am running too fast to stop
I run past her farther and farther
it's almost like a story
as an orchid dies in the Brazilian jungle
and there is a certain amount of horror

A Handful of Earth:
To René Lévesque

Proposal:
let us join Quebec
if Quebec won't join us
I don't mind in the least
being governed from Quebec City
by Canadiens instead of Canadians
in fact the fleur-de-lis
               and maple leaf
are only symbols
and our true language
speaks from inside
the country itself

Listen:
you can hear soft wind blowing
among tall fir trees on Vancouver Island
it is the same wind we knew
whispering along Côte des Neiges
on the island of Montreal
when we were lovers and had no money
Once flying in a little Cessna 180
above that great spine of mountains
where a continent attempts the sky
I wondered who owns this land
and knew that no one does
for we are tenants only

Go back a little:
to hip-roofed houses on the Ile d'Orléans
and scattered along the road to Chicoutimi
the remaining few log houses in Ontario
sod huts of sunlit prairie places
dissolved in rain long since
the stones we laid atop of one another
a few of which still stand
those origins

in which children were born
in which we loved and hated
in which we built a place to stand on
and now must tear it down?
—and here I ask all the oldest questions
of myself
the reasons for being alive
the way to spend this gift and thank the giver
but there is no way

I think of the small dapper man
chain-smoking at PQ headquarters
Lévesque
on Avenue Christophe Colombe in Montreal
where we drank coffee together six years past
I say to him now: my place is here
whether Côte des Neiges Avenue Christophe Colombe
Yonge Street Toronto Halifax or Vancouver
this place is where I stand
where all my mistakes were made
when I grew awkwardly and knew what I was
and that is Canadian or Canadien
it doesn't matter which to me

Sod huts break the prairie skyline
then melt in rain
the hip-roofed houses of New France as well
but French no longer
nor are we any longer English
—limestone houses
lean-tos and sheds our fathers built
in which our mothers died
before the forests tumbled down
ghost habitations
only this handful of earth
for a time at least
I have no other place to go

Irving Layton

Against This Death

I have seen respectable
death
served up like bread and wine
in stores and offices,
in club and hostel,
and from the streetcorner
church
that faces
two-ways;
I have seen death
served up
like ice.

Against this death,
slow, certain:
the body,
this burly sun,
the exhalations
of your breath,
your cheeks
rose and lovely,
and the secret
life
of the imagination
scheming freedom
from labour
and stone.

Look, the Lambs
Are All Around Us!

Your figure, love,
curves itself
into a man's memory;
or to put it the way
a junior prof
at Mount Allison might,
Helen with her thick
absconding limbs
about the waist
of Paris
did no better.

Hell, my back's sunburnt
from so much love-making
in the open air.
The Primate (somebody
made a monkey of him)
and the Sanhedrin
(long on the beard, short
on the brain)
send envoys to say
they don't approve.
You never see them, love.
You toss me in the air
with such abandon,
they take to their heels and run.
I tell you
each kiss of yours
is like a blow on the head!

What luck, what luck to be loved
by the one girl
in this Presbyterian
country
who knows how to give
a man pleasure.

The Cold Green Element

At the end of the garden walk
the wind and its satellite wait for me;
their meaning I will not know
              until I go there,
but the black-hatted undertaker

who, passing, saw my heart beating in the grass,
is also going there. Hi, I tell him,
a great squall in the Pacific blew a dead poet
              out of the water,
who now hangs from the city's gates.

Crowds depart daily to see it, and return
with grimaces and incomprehension;
if its limbs twitched in the air
              they would sit at its feet
peeling their oranges.

And turning over I embrace like a lover
the trunk of a tree, one of those
for whom the lightning was too much
              and grew a brilliant
hunchback with a crown of leaves.

The ailments escaped from the labels
of medicine bottles are all fled to the wind;
I've seen myself lately in the eyes
              of old women,
spent streams mourning my manhood,

in whose old pupils the sun became
a bloodsmear on broad catalpa leaves
and hanging from ancient twigs,
              my murdered selves
sparked the air like the muted collisions

of fruit. A black dog howls down my blood,

a black dog with yellow eyes;
he too by someone's inadvertence
        saw the bloodsmear
on the broad catalpa leaves.

But the furies clear a path for me to the worm
who sang for an hour in the throat of a robin,
and misled by the cries of young boys
        I am again
a breathless swimmer in that cold green element.

The Fertile Muck

There are brightest apples on those trees
    but until I, fabulist, have spoken
they do not know their significance
or what other legends are hung like garlands
    on their black boughs twisting
like a rumour. The wind's noise is empty.

Nor are the winged insects better off
    though they wear my crafty eyes
wherever they alight. Stay here, my love;
you will see how delicately they deposit
    me on the leaves of elms
or fold me in the orient dust of summer.

And if in August joiners and bricklayers
    are thick as flies around us
building expensive bungalows for those
who do not need them, unless they release
    me roaring from their moth-proofed cupboards
their buyers will have no joy, no ease.

I could extend their rooms for them without cost

and give them crazy sundials
to tell the time with, but I have noticed
how my irregular footprint horrifies them
    evenings and Sunday afternoons:
they spray for hours to erase its shadow.

How to dominate reality? Love is one way;
    imagination another. Sit here
beside me, sweet; take my hard hand in yours.
We'll mark the butterflies disappearing over the hedge
    with tiny wristwatches on their wings:
our fingers touching the earth, like two Buddhas.

On Seeing the Statuettes
of Ezekiel and Jeremiah in the
Church of Notre Dame

They have given you French names
    and made you captive, my rugged
troublesome compatriots;
    your splendid beards, here, are epicene,
plaster white
            and your angers
unclothed with Palestinian hills quite lost
in this immense and ugly edifice.

You are bored—I see it—sultry prophets
    with priests and nuns
(What coarse jokes must pass between you!)
    and with those morbidly religious
i.e. my prize brother-in-law
                    ex-Lawrencian
pawing his rosary, and his wife
sick with many guilts.

Believe me I would gladly take you
    from this spidery church
its bad melodrama, its musty smell of candle
    and set you both free again
in no make-believe world
              of sin and penitence
but the sunlit square opposite
alive at noon with arrogant men.

Yet cheer up Ezekiel and you Jeremiah
    who were once cast into a pit;
I shall not leave you here incensed, uneasy
    among alien Catholic saints
but shall bring you from time to time
            my hot Hebrew heart
as passionate as your own, and stand
with you here awhile in aching confraternity.

Sacrament by the Water

How shall I sing the accomplished waters
Whose teeming cells make green my hopes
How shall the Sun at daybreak marry us
Twirling these waters like a hoop.

Gift of the waters that sing
Their eternal passion for the sky,
Your cunning beauty in a wave of tumult
Drops an Eden about your thighs.

Green is the singing singing water
And green is every joyous leaf
White myrtle's in your hand and in the other
The hairy apple bringing life.

Whatever Else Poetry Is Freedom

Whatever else poetry is freedom.
Forget the rhetoric, the trick of lying
All poets pick up sooner or later. From the river,
Rising like the thin voice of grey castratos—the mist;
Poplars and pines grow straight but oaks are gnarled;
Old codgers must speak of death, boys break windows;
Women lie honestly by their men at last.

And I who gave my Kate a blackened eye
Did to its vivid changing colours
Make up an incredible musical scale;
And now I balance on wooden stilts and dance
And thereby sing to the loftiest casements.
See how with polish I bow from the waist.
Space for these stilts! More space or I fail!

And a crown I say for my buffoon's head.
Yet no more fool am I than King Canute,
Lord of our tribe, who scanned and scorned;
Who half-deceived, believed; and, poet, missed
The first white waves come nuzzling at his feet;
Then damned the courtiers and the foolish trial
With a most bewildering and unkingly jest.

It was the mist. It lies inside one like a destiny.
A real Jonah it lies rotting like a lung.
And I know myself undone who am a clown
And wear a wreath of mist for a crown;
Mist with the scent of dead apples,
Mist swirling from black oily waters at evening,
Mist from the fraternal graves of cemeteries.

It shall drive me to beg my food and at last
Hurl me broken I know and prostrate on the road;
Like a huge toad I saw, entire but dead,
That Time mordantly had blacked; O pressed
To the moist earth it pled for entry.

I shall be I say that stiff toad for sick with mist
And crazed I small the odour of mortality.

And Time flames like a paraffin stove
And what it burns are the minutes I live.
At certain middays I have watched the cars
Bring me from afar their windshield suns;
What lay to my hand were blue fenders,
The suns extinguished, the drivers wearing sunglasses.
And it made me think I had touched a hearse.

So whatever else poetry is freedom. Let
Far off the impatient cadences reveal
A padding for my breathless stilts. Swivel,
O hero, in the fleshy groves, skin and glycerine,
And sing of lust, the sun's accompanying shadow
Like a vampire's wing, the stillness in dead feet—
Your stave brings resurrection, O aggrievèd king.

Berry Picking

Silently my wife walks on the still wet furze
Now darkgreen the leaves are full of metaphors
Now lit up is each tiny lamp of blueberry.
The white nails of rain have dropped and the sun is free.

And whether she bends or straightens to each bush
To find the children's laughter among the leaves
Her quiet hands seem to make the quiet summer hush—
Berries or children, patient she is with these.

I only vex and perplex her; madness, rage
Are endearing perhaps put down upon the page;
Even silence daylong and sullen can then
Enamour as restraint or classic discipline.

So I envy the berries she puts in her mouth,
The red and succulent juice that stains her lips;
I shall never taste that good to her, nor will they
Displease her with a thousand barbarous jests.

How they lie easily for her hand to take,
Part of the unoffending world that is hers;
Here beyond complexity she stands and stares
And leans her marvellous head as if for answers.

No more the easy soul my childish craft deceives
Nor the simpler one for whom yes is always yes;
No, now her voice comes to me from a far way off
Though her lips are redder than the raspberries.

Cain

Taking the air rifle from my son's hand,
I measured back five paces, the Hebrew
In me, narcissist, father of children,
Laid to rest. From there I took aim and fired.

The silent ball hit the frog's back an inch
Below the head. He jumped at the surprise
Of it, suddenly tickled or startled
(He must have thought) and leaped from the wet sand
Into the surrounding brown water. But
The ball had done its mischief. His next spring
Was a miserable flop, the thrust all gone
Out of his legs. He tried—like Bruce—again,
Throwing out his sensitive pianist's
Hands as a dwarf might or a helpless child.
His splash disturbed the quiet pondwater
And one old frog behind his weedy moat
Blinking, looking self-complacently on.
The lin's surface at once became closing

Eyelids and bubbles like notes of music
Liquid, luminous, dropping from the page
White, white-bearded, a rapid crescendo
Of inaudible sounds and a crones' whispering
Backstage among the reeds and bulrushes
As for an expiring Lear or Oedipus.

But Death makes us all look ridiculous.
Consider this frog (dog, hog, what you will)
Sprawling, his absurd corpse rocked by the tides
That his last vain spring had set in movement.
Like a retired oldster, I couldn't help sneer,
Living off the last of his insurance:
Billows—now crumbling—the premiums paid.
Absurd, how absurd. I wanted to kill
At the mockery of it, kill and kill
Again—the self-infatuate frog, dog, hog,
Anything with the stir of life in it,
Seeing the dead leaper, Chaplin-footed,
Rocked and cradled in this afternoon
Of tranquil water, reeds, and blazing sun,
The hole in his back clearly visible
And the torn skin a blob of shadow
Moving when the quiet poolwater moved.

O Egypt, marbled Greece, resplendent Rome,
Did you also finally perish from a small bore
In your back you could not scratch? And would
Your mouths open ghostily, gasping out
Among the murky reeds, the hidden frogs,
We climb with crushed spines toward the heavens?

When the next morning I came the same way
The frog was on his back, one delicate
Hand on his belly, and his white shirt front
Spotless. He looked as if he might have been
A comic; tapdancer apologizing
For a fall, or an Emcee, his wide grin
Coaxing a laugh from us for an aside
Or perhaps a joke we didn't quite hear.

Keine Lazarovitch 1870-1959

When I saw my mother's head on the cold pillow,
Her white waterfalling hair in the cheeks' hollows,
I thought, quietly circling my grief, of how
She had loved God but cursed extravagantly his creatures.

For her final mouth was not water but a curse,
A small black hole, a black rent in the universe,
Which damned the green earth, stars and trees in its stillness
And the inescapable lousiness of growing old.

And I record she was comfortless, vituperative,
Ignorant, glad, and much else besides; I believe
She endlessly praised her black eyebrows, their thick weave,
Till plagiarizing Death leaned down and took them for his
    mould.

And spoiled a dignity I shall not again find,
And the fury of her stubborn limited mind;
Now none will shake her amber beads and call God blind,
Or wear them upon a breast so radiantly.

O fierce she was, mean and unaccommodating;
But I think now of the toss of her gold earrings,
Their proud carnal assertion, and her youngest sings
While all the rivers of her red veins move into the sea.

A Tall Man Executes a Jig

I

So the man spread his blanket on the field
And watched the shafts of light between the tufts
And felt the sun push the grass towards him;
The noise he heard was that of whizzing flies,
The whistlings of some small imprudent birds,

And the ambiguous rumbles of cars
That made him look up at the sky, aware
Of the gnats that tilted against the wind
And in the sunlight turned to jigging motes.
Fruitflies he'd call them except there was no fruit
About, spoiling to hatch these glitterings,
These nervous dots for which the mind supplied
The closing sentences from Thucydides,
Or from Euclid having a savage nightmare.

II

Jig jig, jig jig. Like minuscule black links
Of a chain played with by some playful
Unapparent hand or the palpitant
Summer haze bored with the hour's stillness.
He felt the sting and tingle afterwards
Of those leaving their orthodox unrest,
Leaving their undulant excitation
To drop upon his sleeveless arm. The grass,
Even the wildflowers became black hairs
And himself a maddened speck among them.
Still the assaults of the small flies made him
Glad at last, until he saw purest joy
In their frantic jiggings under a hair,
So changed from those in the unrestraining air.

III

He stood up and felt himself enormous.
Felt as might Donatello over stone,
Or Plato, or as a man who has held
A loved and lovely woman in his arms
And feels his forehead touch the emptied sky
Where all antinomies flood into light.
Yet jig jig jig, the haloing black jots
Meshed with the wheeling fire of the sun:
Motion without meaning, disquietude
Without sense or purpose, ephemerides

That mottled the resting summer air till
Gusts swept them from his sight like wisps of smoke.
Yet they returned, bringing a bee who, seeing
But a tall man, left him for a marigold.

IV

He doffed his aureole of gnats and moved
Out of the field as the sun sank down,
A dying god upon the blood-red hills.
Ambition, pride, the ecstasy of sex,
And all circumstance of delight and grief,
That blood upon the mountain's side, that flood
Washed into a clear incredible pool
Below the ruddied peaks that pierced the sun.
He stood still and waited. If ever
The hour of revelation was come
It was now, here on the transfigured steep.
The sky darkened. Some birds chirped. Nothing else.
He thought the dying god had gone to sleep:
An Indian fakir on his mat of nails.

V

And on the summit of the asphalt road
Which stretched towards the fiery town, the man
Saw one hill raised like a hairy arm, dark
With pines and cedars against the stricken sun
—The arm of Moses or of Joshua.
He dropped his head and let fall the halo
Of mountains, purpling and silent as time,
To see temptation coiled before his feet:
A violated grass snake that lugged
Its intestine like a small red valise.
A cold-eyed skinflint it now was, and not
The manifest of that joyful wisdom,
The mirth and arrogant green flame of life;
Or earth's vivid tongue that flicked in praise of earth.

VI

And the man wept because pity was useless.
'Your jig's up; the flies come like kites,' he said
And watched the grass snake crawl towards the hedge,
Convulsing and dragging into the dark
The satchel filled with curses for the earth,
For the odours of warm sedge, and the sun,
A blood-red organ in the dying sky.
Backwards it fell into a grassy ditch
Exposing its underside, white as milk,
And mocked by wisps of hay between its jaws;
And then it stiffened to its final length.
But though it opened its thin mouth to scream
A last silent scream that shook the black sky,
Adamant and fierce, the tall man did not curse.

VII

Beside the rigid snake the man stretched out
In fellowship of death; he lay silent
And stiff in the heavy grass with eyes shut,
Inhaling the moist odours of the night
Through which his mind tunnelled with flicking tongue
Backwards to caves, mounds, and sunken ledges
And desolate cliffs where come only kites,
And where of perished badgers and racoons
The claws alone remain, gripping the earth.
Meanwhile the green snake crept upon the sky,
Huge, his mailed coat glittering with stars that made
The night bright, and blowing thin wreaths of cloud
Athwart the moon; and as the weary man
Stood up, coiled above his head, transforming all.

If I Lie Still

If I lie still
the light from the leaves
will drop on my hands and knees

Fire will envelop me
yet I won't burn

I shall hear the silence plainly
while the stream flows into my veins
and out again

Small wild animals will no longer fear me,
but bring their young
to tickle my heels,
nuzzle in my armpits

I shall know love without disquiet
—without passion

For a thousand years
I shall lie like this
with my head toward the sun

Till knowledge and power
have become one;
then I shall write a single verse,
achieve one flawless deed

Then lie down again
to become like this shallow
stone under my hand,
and let my face
be covered with grass

To be pulled out by the roots
by what raging hermit,
his breast torn apart as mine now?

Marché Municipale

FOR DESMOND PACEY

In the empty market
    coolness spills out
from vineyards
    gathered in boxes of grapes;
the rumour of orchards,
and pears full of an indisputable dignity
that lie like jaundiced dowagers
    in their white wrappers;
and from freshly washed tomatoes
that flash in the surrounding gloom
like the neon signs of lost American towns
you speed past on rainy nights
    on the way to nowhere.

It is a coolness
    making herrings smell more rank;
in which the ripe colour of bananas astounds;
potatoes, a visible skin affliction of air,
lie mute, lie sullen in their earthy bags;
and the slow mysterious decay of olives
    filling the deserted aisles
with its black sensual irony discomfits
the pragmatic vegetables in their stands,
    countermands
the imperial fiats of pineapples.

And the stillness is such
    that waits for iron weights or a box
to shatter; or a child hidden
in a cupboard expelling his breath
and saying, 'Ah, Ah' making it appear
    silence had spoken;
or a film with no commentary
showing machine guns and rifles
    fallen out of

the huge blistered hands of destiny
sands are burying; even the muzzles
that with a last malevolent squint
   at the sun
sink into a darkness and silence
more vast, more final than Pharaoh's kingdom.

Rhine Boat Trip

The castles on the Rhine
are all haunted
by the ghosts of Jewish mothers
looking for their ghostly children

And the clusters of grapes
in the sloping vineyards
are myriads of blinded eyes
staring at the blind sun

The tireless Lorelei
can never comb from their hair
the crimson beards
of murdered rabbis

However sweetly they sing
one hears only
the low wailing of cattle-cars
moving invisibly across the land

Israelis

It is themselves they trust and no one else;
Their fighter planes that screech across the sky,
Real, visible as the glorious sun;
Riflesmoke, gunshine, and rumble of tanks.

Man is a fanged wolf, without compassion
Or ruth: Assyrians, Medes, Greeks, Romans,
And devout pagans in Spain and Russia
—Allah's children, most merciful of all.

Where is the Almighty if murder thrives?
He's dead as mutton and they buried him
Decades ago, covered him with their own
Limp bodies in Belsen and Babi Yar.

Let the strong compose hymns and canticles,
Live with the Lord's radiance in their hard skulls
Or make known his great benevolences;
Stare at the heavens and feel glorified

Or humbled and awestruck buckle their knees:
They are done with him now and forever.
Without a whimper from him they returned,
A sign like an open hand in the sky.

The pillar of fire: Their flesh made it;
It burned briefly and died—you all know where.
Now in their own blood they temper the steel,
God being dead and their enemies not.

P.K.Page

The Stenographers

After the brief bivouac of Sunday,
their eyes, in the forced march of Monday to Saturday,
hoist the white flag, flutter in the snow-storm of paper,
haul it down and crack in the mid-sun of temper.

In the pause between the first draft and the carbon
they glimpse the smooth hours when they were children—
the ride in the ice-cart, the ice-man's name,
the end of the route and the long walk home;

remember the sea where floats at high tide
were sea marrows growing on the scatter-green vine
or spools of grey toffee, or wasps' nests on water;
remember the sand and the leaves of the country.

Bell rings and they go and the voice draws their pencil
like a sled across snow; when its runners are frozen
rope snaps and the voice then is pulling no burden
but runs like a dog on the winter of paper.

Their climates are winter and summer—no wind
for the kites of their hearts—no wind for a flight;
a breeze at the most, to tumble them over
and leave them like rubbish—the boy-friends of blood.

In the inch of the noon as they move they are stagnant.
The terrible calm of the noon is their anguish;
the lip of the counter, the shapes of the straws
like icicles breaking their tongues, are invaders.

Their beds are their oceans—salt water of weeping
the waves that they know—the tide before sleep;
and fighting to drown they assemble their sheep
in columns and watch them leap desks for their fences

and stare at them with their own mirror-worn faces.
In the felt of the morning the calico-minded,

sufficiently starched, insert papers, hit keys,
efficient and sure as their adding machines;

yet they weep in the vault, they are taut as net curtains
stretched upon frames. In their eyes I have seen
the pin men of madness in marathon trim
race round the track of the stadium pupil.

The Landlady

Through sepia air the boarders come and go,
impersonal as trains. Pass silently
the craving silence swallowing her speech;
click doors like shutters on her camera eye.

Because of her their lives become exact:
their entrances and exits are designed;
phone calls are cryptic. Oh, her ticklish ears
advance and fall back stunned.

Nothing is unprepared. They hold the walls
about them as they weep or laugh. Each face
is dialled to zero publicly. She peers
stippled with curious flesh;

pads on the patient landing like a pulse,
unlocks their keyholes with the wire of sight,
searches their rooms for clues when they are out,
pricks when they come home late.

Wonders when they are quiet, jumps when they move,
dreams that they dope or drink, trembles to know
the traffic of their brains, jaywalks their street
in clumsy shoes.

Yet knows them better than their closest friends:
their cupboards and the secrets of their drawers,
their books, their private mail, their photographs
are theirs and hers.

Knows when they wash, how frequently their clothes
go to the cleaners, what they like to eat,
their curvature of health, but even so
is not content.

And like a lover must know all, all, all.
Prays she may catch them unprepared at last
and palm the dreadful riddle of their skulls—
hoping the worst.

Stories of Snow

Those in the vegetable rain retain
an area behind their sprouting eyes
held soft and rounded with the dream of snow
precious and reminiscent as those globes—
souvenir of some never-nether land—
which hold their snow-storms circular, complete,
high in a tall and teakwood cabinet.

In countries where the leaves are large as hands
where flowers protrude their fleshy chins
and call their colours,
an imaginary snow-storm sometimes falls
among the lilies.
And in the early morning one will waken

to think the glowing linen of his pillow
a northern drift, will find himself mistaken
and lie back weeping.
And there the story shifts from head to head,
of how in Holland, from their feather beds
hunters arise and part the flakes and go
forth to the frozen lakes in search of swans—
the snow-light falling white along their guns,
their breath in plumes.
While tethered in the wind like sleeping gulls
ice-boats wait the raising of their wings
to skim the electric ice at such a speed
they leap jet strips of naked water,
and how these flying, sailing hunters feel
air in their mouths as terrible as ether.
And on the story runs that even drinks
in that white landscape dare to be no colour;
how flasked and water clear, the liquor slips
silver against the hunters' moving hips.
And of the swan in death these dreamers tell
of its last flight and how it falls, a plummet,
pierced by the freezing bullet
and how three feathers, loosened by the shot,
descend like snow upon it.
While hunters plunge their fingers in its down
deep as a drift, and dive their hands
up to the neck of the wrist
in that warm metamorphosis of snow
as gentle as the sort that woodsmen know
who, lost in the white circle, fall at last
and dream their way to death.

And stories of this kind are often told
in countries where great flowers bar the roads
with reds and blues which seal the route to snow—
as if, in telling, raconteurs unlock
the colour with its complement and go
through to the area behind the eyes
where silent, unrefractive whiteness lies.

Photos of a Salt Mine

How innocent their lives look,
how like a child's
dream of caves and winter, both combined;
the steep descent to whiteness
and the stope
with its striated walls
their folds all leaning as if pointing to
the greater whiteness still,
that great white bank
with its decisive front,
that seam upon a slope,
salt's lovely ice.

And wonderful underfoot the snow of salt
the fine
particles a broom could sweep,
one thinks
muckers might make angels in its drifts
as children do in snow,
lovers in sheets,
lie down and leave imprinted where they lay
a feathered creature holier than they.

And in the outworked stopes
with lamps and ropes
up miniature matterhorns
the miners climb
probe with their lights
the ancient folds of rock—
syncline and anticline—
and scoop from darkness an Aladdin's cave:
rubies and opals glitter from its walls.

But hoses douse the brilliance of these jewels,
melt fire to brine.
Salt's bitter water trickles thin and forms,

slow fathoms down,
a lake within a cave,
lacquered with jet—
white's opposite.
There grey on black the boating miners float
to mend the stays and struts of that old stope
and deeply underground
their words resound,
are multiplied by echo, swell and grow
and make a climate of a miner's voice.

So all the photographs like children's wishes
are filled with caves or winter,
innocence
has acted as a filter,
selected only beauty from the mine.
Except in the last picture,
it is shot
from an acute high angle. In a pit
figures the size of pins are strangely lit
and might be dancing but you know they're not.
Like Dante's vision of the nether hell
men struggle with the bright cold fires of salt,
locked in the black inferno of the rock:
the filter here, not innocence but guilt.

The Permanent Tourists

Somnolent through landscapes and by trees
nondescript, almost anonymous,
they alter as they enter foreign cities—
the terrible tourists with their empty eyes
longing to be filled with monuments.

Verge upon statues in the public squares
remembering the promise of memorials
yet never enter the entire event
as dogs, abroad in any kind of weather,
move perfectly within their rainy climate.

Lock themselves into snapshots on the steps
of monolithic bronze as if suspecting
the subtle mourning of the photograph
might later conjure in the memory
all they are now incapable of feeling.

And search all heroes out: the boy who gave
his life to save a town; the stolid queen;
forgotten politicians minus names
and the plunging war dead, permanently brave,
forever and ever going down to death.

Look, you can see them nude in any café
reading their histories from the bill of fare,
creating futures from a foreign teacup.
Philosophies like ferns bloom from the fable
that travel is broadening at the café table.

Yet somehow beautiful, they stamp the plaza.
Classic in their anxiety they call
all sculptured immemorial stone
into their passive eyes, as rivers
draw ruined columns to their placid glass.

Cook's Mountains

By naming them he made them.
They were there
before he came
but they were not the same.
It was his gaze
that glazed each one.
He saw
the Glass House Mountains in his glass.
They shone.

And still they shine.
We saw them as we drove—
sudden, surrealist, conical
they rose
out of the rain forest.
The driver said,
'Those are the Glass House Mountains up ahead.'

And instantly they altered to become
the sum of shape and name.
Two strangenesses united into one
more strange than either.
Neither of us now
remembers how they looked before they broke
the light to fragments as the driver spoke.

Like mounds of mica,
hive-shaped hothouses,
mountains of mirror glimmering
they form
in diamond panes behind the tree ferns of
the dark imagination,
burn and shake
the lovely light of Queensland like a bell
reflecting Cook upon a deck
his tongue
silvered with paradox and metaphor.

Arras

Consider a new habit—classical,
and trees espaliered on the wall like candelabra.
How still upon that lawn our sandalled feet.

But a peacock rattling his rattan tail and screaming
has found a point of entry. Through whose eye
did it insinuate in furled disguise
to shake its jewels and silk upon that grass?

The peaches hang like lanterns. No one joins
those figures on the arras.
                              Who am I
or who am I become that walking here
I am observer, other, Gemini,
starred for a green garden of cinema?

I ask, what did they deal me in this pack?
The cards, all suits, are royal when I look.
My fingers slipping on a monarch's face
twitch and grow slack.
I want a hand to clutch, a heart to crack.

No one is moving now, the stillness is
infinite. If I should make a break....
take to my springy heels....? But nothing moves.
The spinning world is stuck upon its poles,
the stillness points a bone at me. I fear
the future on this arras.
                              I confess:

It was my eye.

Voluptuous it came.
Its head the ferrule and its lovely tail
folded so sweetly; it was strangely slim
to fit the retina. And then it shook
and was a peacock—living patina,

eye-bright, maculate!
Does no one care?

I thought their hands might hold me if I spoke.
I dreamed the bite of fingers in my flesh,
their poke smashed by an image, but they stand
as if within a treacle, motionless,
folding slow eyes on nothing. While they stare
another line has trolled the encircling air,
another bird assumes its furled disguise.

After Rain

The snails have made a garden of green lace:
broderie anglaise from the cabbages,
chantilly from the choux-fleurs, tiny veils—
I see already that I lift the blind
upon a woman's wardrobe of the mind.

Such female whimsy floats about me like
a kind of tulle, a flimsy mesh,
while feet in gum boots pace the rectangles—
garden abstracted, geometry awash—
an unknown theorem argued in green ink,
dropped in the bath.
Euclid in glorious chlorophyl, half drunk.

I none too sober slipping in the mud
where rigged with guys of rain
the clothes-reel gauche
as the rangey skeleton of some
gaunt delicate spidery mute
is pitched as if
listening;

while hung from one thin rib
a silver web—
its infant, skeletal, diminutive,
now sagged with sequins, pulled ellipsoid,
glistening.

I suffer shame in all these images.
The garden is primeval, Giovanni
in soggy denim squelches by my hub
over his ruin,
shakes a doleful head.
But he so beautiful and diademmed,
his long Italian hands so wrung with rain
I find his ache exists beyond my rim
and almost weep to see a broken man
made subject to my whim.

O choir him, birds, and let him come to rest
within this beauty as one rests in love,
till pears upon the bough
encrusted with
small snails as pale as pearls
hang golden in
a heart that knows tears are a part of love.

And choir me too to keep my heart a size
larger than seeing, unseduced by each
bright glimpse of beauty striking like a bell,
so that the whole may toll,
its meaning shine
clear of the myriad images that still—
do what I will—encumber its pure line.

Brazilian Fazenda

That day all the slaves were freed
their manacles, anklets
left on the window ledge to rust in the moist air

and all the coffee ripened
like beads on a bush or balls of fire
as merry as Christmas

and the cows all calved and the calves all lived
such a moo.
On the wide verandah where birds in cages
sang among the bell flowers
I in a bridal hammock
white and tasselled
whistled

and bits fell out of the sky near Nossa Senhora
who had walked all the way in bare feet from Bahia

and the chapel was lit by a child's
fistful of marigolds on the red velvet altar
thrown like a golden ball.

Oh let me come back on a day
when nothing extraordinary happens
so I can stare
at the sugar white pillars
and black lace grills
of this pink house.

Cry Ararat!

I

In the dream the mountain near
but without sound.
A dream through binoculars
seen sharp and clear:
the leaves moving, turning
in a far wind
no ear can hear.

First soft in the distance,
blue in blue air
then sharpening, quickening
taking on green.
Swiftly the fingers
seek accurate focus
(the bird
has vanished so often
before the sharp lens
could deliver it)
then as if from the sea
the mountain appears
emerging new-washed
growing maples and firs.
The faraway, here.

Do not reach to touch it
nor labour to hear.
Return to your hand
the sense of the hand;
return to your ear
the sense of the ear.
Remember the statue,
that space in the air
which with nothing to hold
what the minute is giving
is through each point
where its marble touches air.

Then will each leaf and flower
each bird and animal
become as perfect as
the thing its name evoked
when busy as a child
the world stopped at the Word
and Flowers more real than flowers
grew vivid and immense;
and Birds more beautiful
and Leaves more intricate
flew, blew and quilted all
the quick landscape.

So flies and blows the dream
embracing like a sea
all that in it swims
when dreaming, you desire
and ask for nothing more
than stillness to receive
the I-am animal,
the We-are leaf and flower,
the distant mountain near.

II

So flies and blows the dream that haunts us when we wake
to the unreality of bright day:
the far thing almost sensed by the still skin
and then the focus lost, the mountain gone.
This is the loss that haunts our daylight hours
leaving us parched at nightfall
blowing like last year's leaves
sibilant on blossoming trees
and thirsty for the dream of the mountain
more real than any event:
more real than strangers passing on the street
in a city's architecture white as bone
or the immediate companion.

But sometimes there is one
raw with the dream of flying:
'I, a bird,
landed that very instant
and complete—
as if I had drawn a circle in my flight
and filled its shape—
find air a perfect fit.
But this my grief,
that with the next tentative lift
of my indescribable wings
the ceiling looms
heavy as a tomb.

'Must my most exquisite and private dream
remain unleavened?
Must this flipped and spinning coin that sun
could gild and make miraculous become
so swiftly pitiful?
The vision of the flight it imitates
burns brightly in my head as if a star
rushed down to touch me where I stub against
what must forever be my underground.'

III

These are the dreams that haunt us,
these the fears.
Will the grey weather wake us,
toss us twice in the terrible night to tell us
the flight is cancelled
and the mountain lost?

O, then cry Ararat!

The dove believed
in her sweet wings and in the rising peak
with such a washed and easy innocence

that she found rest on land for the sole of her foot
and, silver, circled back,
a green twig in her beak.

The leaves that make the tree by day,
the green twig the dove saw fit
to lift across a world of water
break in a wave about our feet.
The bird in the thicket with his whistle
the crystal lizard in the grass
the star and shell
tassel and bell
of wild flowers blowing where we pass,
this flora-fauna flotsam, pick and touch,
requires the focus of the total I.

A single leaf can block a mountainside;
all Ararat be conjured by a leaf.

A Grave Illness

Someone was shovelling gravel all that week.
The flowering plums came out.
Rose-colored streets
branched in my head—
spokes of a static wheel
spinning and whirring only when I coughed.
And sometimes, afterwards, I couldn't tell
if I had coughed or he had shovelled.   Which.

Someone was shovelling until it hurt.
The rasp of metal on cement, the scrape
and fall
of all that broken rock—
such industry day after day. For what?
My cough's accompanist?

The flowering trees
blossomed behind my eyes in drifts of red
delicate petals. I was hot.
The shovel grated in my breaking chest.

Someone was shovelling gravel. Was it I?
Burying me in shifts and shards of rock
up to my gasping throat. My head was out
dismembered, sunken-eyed
as John the Baptist's on its plate.
Meanwhile the plum
blossoms trickling from above
through unresistant air
fell on my eyes and hair
vermilion as my blood.

Sestina for Pat Lane after Reading 'Albino Pheasants'

Pale beak . . . pale eye . . . the dark imagination
flares like magnesium.   Add but, *pale flesh*
and I am lifted to a weightless world:
watered cerulean, chrome-yellow, light,
and green, veronese—if I remember—a soft wash
recalls a summer evening sky.

At Barro de Navidad we watched the sky
fade softly like a bruise.   Was it imagination
that showed us Venus phosphorescent in a wash
of air and ozone?—a phosphorescence flesh
wears like a mantle in bright moonlight,
a natural skin-tone in that other world.

Why do I wish to escape this world?
Why do three phrases alter the color of the sky

the clarity, texture even, of the light?
What is there about the irrepressible imagination
that the adjective *pale* modifying *beak*, *eye* and *flesh*
can set my sensibilities awash?

If with my thickest brush I were to lay a wash
of thinnest water-color I could make a world
as unlike my own dense flesh
as the high-noon midsummer sky;
but it would not catch at my imagination
or change the waves or particles of light

yet *pale* can tip the scales, make light
this heavy planet.   If I were to wash
everything I own in mercury, would imagination
run rampant in that suddenly silver world—
free me from gravity, set me floating sky-
ward—thistledown—permanently disburdened of my flesh?

Like cygnets hatched by ducks, our minds and flesh
are imprinted early—what to me is light
may be dark to one born under a sunny sky.
And however cool the water my truth won't wash
without shrinking except in my own world
which is one part matter, nine parts imagination.

I fear flesh which blocks imagination,
the light of reason which constricts the world.
Pale beak ... pale eye ... pale flesh ... My sky's awash.

Raymond Souster

The Nest

It will have to be near some water
so there can be moonlight like a pool
to bathe our tired, sleep-returning eyes. *end of day*

There must be a high, strong roof
so the rain children will not break
the step of their marching above us.

White sheets to lull our flesh asleep
after we've squeezed all the love from our bodies,
with God's hand on the door
so none can touch the slightest scattered hair
of your head on its pillow, that none
will hand me a gun again and say,
leave her, there's new blood to be spilled
in the name of our latest lie.

Young Girls

With the night full of spring and stars we stand
here in this dark doorway and watch the young
girls pass, two, three together, hand in hand.
Like flowers they are whose fragrance has not sprung
or awakened, whose bodies dimly feel
the flooding upward welling of the trees;
whose senses, caressed by the wind's soft fingers, reel
with a delirium that makes them ill at ease.

They lie awake at night unable to sleep
and walk the streets kindled by strange desires;
they steal glances at us, unable to keep
control upon those subterranean fires.
We whistle after them, then laugh, for they
stiffen, not knowing what to do or say.

Lagoons, Hanlan's Point

Mornings
before the sun's liquid
spilled gradually, flooding
the island's cool cellar,
there was the boat
and the still lagoons,
with the sound of my oars
the only intrusion
over cries of birds
in the marshy shallows,
or the loud thrashing
of the startled crane
rushing the air.

And in one strange
dark, tree-hung entrance,
I followed the sound
of my heart all the way
to the reed-blocked ending,
with the pads of the lily
thick as green-shining film
covering the water.

And in another
where the sun came
to probe the depths
through a shaft of branches,
I saw the skeletons
of brown ships rotting
far below in their burial-ground,
and wondered what strange fish
with what strange colours
swam through these palaces
under the water....

A small boy

with a flat-bottomed punt
and an old pair of oars
moving with wonder
through the antechamber
of a waking world.

The Lilac Poem

Before the lilacs are over and they are only
shrunken stalks at the ends of drooping branches,
I want to write a poem about them and their beauty
brief and star-shining as a young girl's promise. —

Because there is so much made of strength and wealth and power,
because the little things are lost in this world,
I write this poem about lilacs knowing that both
are this day's only: tomorrow they will lie forgotten.

Downtown Corner News Stand

It will need all of death to take you from this corner.
It has become your world, and you its unshaved
bleary-eyed, foot-stamping king. In winter
you curse the cold, huddled in your coat from the wind,
you fry in summer like an egg hopping on a griddle;
and always the whining voice, the nervous-flinging arms,
the red face, shifting eyes watching, waiting
under the grimy cap for God knows what
to happen. (But nothing ever does, downtown Toronto
goes to sleep and wakes the next morning
always the same, except a little dirtier.)
And you stand with your armful of *Stars* and *Telys*,
the peak of your cap well down against the sun,
and all the city's restless seething river

surges beside you, but not once do you plunge
into its flood, are carried or tossed away:
but reappear always, beard longer than ever, nose running,
to catch the noon editions at King and Bay.

Study: The Bath

In the almost dim light
of the bathroom a woman
steps from white tub
towel around her shoulders.

Drops of water glisten
on her body, slight buttocks,
neck, tight belly,
fall at intervals
from the slightly plumed
oval of crotch.

Neck bent forward
eyes collected
her attention gathered
at the ends of fingers

as she removes
dead skin from her nipples.

Flight of the Roller-Coaster

Once more around should do it, the man confided . . .

and sure enough, when the roller-coaster reached the peak
of the giant curve above me, screech of its wheels

almost drowned out by the shriller cries of the riders,

instead of the dip and plunge with its landslide of screams,
it rose in the air like a movieland magic carpet,
    some wonderful bird,

and without fuss or fanfare swooped slowly across
    the amusement-park,
over Spook's Castle, ice-cream booths, shooting-gallery.
    And losing no height

made the last yards above the beach, where the cucumber-cool
brakeman in the last seat saluted
a lady about to change from her bathing-suit.

Then, as many witnesses reported, headed leisurely
    out over the water,
disappearing all too soon behind a low-flying flight of clouds.

All This Slow Afternoon

All this slow afternoon
the May winds blowing
honey of the lilacs,
sounds of waves washing
through the highest branches
of my poplar tree.

Enough in such hours
to be simply alive;
I will take death tomorrow
without bitterness.

Today all I ask
is to be left alone
in the wind

in the sunshine,
with the honey of lilacs
down the garden;

to fall asleep tired
of small birds' gossip,
of so much greenness
pushed behind my eyes.

The Six-Quart Basket

The six-quart basket
one side gone
half the handle torn off

sits in the centre of the lawn
and slowly fills up
with the white fruits of the snow.

The Death of the Grenadiers

It was over the ice
of this bottomless pond
(so the story goes)
that the Grenadiers
chased those Indians,
and the ice that gave way
to the marching step
of the English held up
for the braves' single file. . . .

And girls have told me
they've felt that someone
was looking up their legs
as they skated the pond,
and looking down they've seen
(noses close to the ice
on the underneath side),
the white-bearded faces
of lonely soldiers
looking up at them
with lascivious winks
in their socketless eyes.

A Morning in Brussels

—Granted the most subtle torture that in which the victim
knows each step of his pain but is powerless to change
it in any way—

Then become this moment the young French-Canadian airman
of twenty, who, having watched in the cellar of the Rue
Royale the most expert monsters of the Gestapo stalk
round on cat-silent shoes behind the line of prisoners
(faces held six inches back from dripping walls), lashing
out with rubber truncheons now at this head and now this,
quite at random, never the same pattern repeated—

Knowing this then stand in line yourself, lips held
tightly together until the first searing terror of your
face smashed against the stone, pain in your nose like
a knife-slit, lips moving tremblingly in prayer, Holy
Mary, Mother of God, as you wait for the warning of
footsteps which never comes, as you wait for an end,
any end. . . .

Memory of Bathurst Street

'Where are you, boy?'
my Aunt Maggie's calling,
but I can't hear her
in my attic eyrie,
where I watch the heat
swirl up from the tar roofs,
and wait for the cry
of the bearded rag-picker
down the lane from Ulster Street.

'Where are you, boy?'
my Uncle Jim's calling,
but I can't hear him
for the cooing of birds
inside this pigeon-house
at the back of the garden,
where I scrape up the droppings
to learn my allowance.

'Where are you, boy?'
my Aunt Lizzie's calling,
but I can't hear her
from the upstairs sitting-room,
as I turn the pages
of my favourite book
where the Highlanders lie
in the blood of their death
on green Spion Kop.

St Catherine Street East

FOR LOUIS DUDEK

Beer on a hot afternoon?—what else
in this Bon Marché of the World,
earth's narrowest, most crowded rabbit-run,
sweating under loud sunshine that glints off
baby carriages, tin cups of beggars,
silver balls of pawnshops, making
the rouge-layered, powder-dipped girls
squint hard but not taking anything off
their free-swinging walk on the stilt-heels.

Beer you said? Right back here
behind giant cheeses, wienerwurst truncheons,
hungry smells of bread, perfumes of coffee.
Look, the cold-sweated bottles count out
to a dozen, and we fight our way
past the check-out counter to the street
where sun, traffic, noise, faces, heat-breath
hit, stun us.
              Every face in every window
of each building watching as we go
down the steaming pavement, on, out of this jungle
where the dead are never buried by the living,
but crowd onto buses, sit late at bar stools, or wait
in the darkness of always airless rooms.

On the Rouge

I can almost see
my father's canoe
pointing in from the lake,

him paddling,
mother hidden
in a hat of fifty years ago.

Turning now up a stream
clear-flowing through marsh
(not mud-brown like today):

gliding under the same
railway bridge we cross under,
slipping by the same giant
stepping-stones of rock
standing up so like ramparts:

moving on to those quieter
summer-singing reaches,
the calling of birds
making speech difficult.

Lost finally, perhaps forever,
behind ferns swallowing banks,
bent trees overarching sky,

drifting the summer
labyrinths of love.

Night Raider

Something getting its Christmas dinner early
in the narrow alley that flanks
our apartment house.
                        Gorging so frantically
it can't hear the noise it makes
rattling trash-can lids, ripping skins
of newspaper-wrapping off the choicest refuse.

This to the sleepy steadiness of rain falling,
so that I get a picture of my animal,
head down in garbage, busy, steam ascending
like a grace from its breathing coat.

Among the Willows

When summer returns, these same willows will
		come alive,
burst bud and throw
a green band along
the mud banks of the river.

When I was a kid, nine or ten years old,
we played our games of cowboys and Indians
among them. More than once surprised
young couples in those thickets,
who, thinking themselves well-hidden,
had abandoned themselves to their loving.

I think we were more
surprised and embarrassed than they were,
for they said nothing to us, made no move
to leave off their pleasure,
while we retreated, confused,
not old or bold enough to know
our easy advantage.

Was it later we collected
soiled sheaths of their mating, spearing them
on the points of sticks?

It may have been.
We had that fresh innocence once, — *we all*
in the summer, by the river, among the willows.

The First Two Acorns

Only the first two acorns
really counted.

The first,
unhitched from a top branch,
dropped relentlessly through
leaf screens (leaving the air
still shivering behind it)
to strike the road
hard enough to hurt.

The second could have fallen
from any height. All
that the night heard
was a dull plop in grass,
unspectacular to say the least
after that first drop.

Still, it was the one triggered off
tree after tree down the street;
and all on a windless night
with everyone asleep
and only I to ponder
what would happen next
and exactly when.

Get the Poem Outdoors

Get the poem outdoors under any pretext,
reach through the open window if you have to,
    kidnap it right off the poet's desk,
then walk the poem in the garden, hold it up
    among the soft yellow garlands of the
    willow,

command of it no further blackness, no silent
    cursing at midnight, no puny whimpering
    in the endless small hours, no more
    shivering in the cold-storage room of the
    winter heart,
tell it to sing again, loud and then louder so it
    brings the whole neighbourhood out, but
    who cares,
ask of it a more human face, a new tenderness,
    even the sentimental allowed between the
    hours of nine to five,
then let it go, stranger in a fresh green world, to
    wander down the flower beds, let it go to
    welcome each bird that lights on the still
    barren mulberry tree.

The Embarrassment

Granted, the most natural
thing in the world—

                the new baby cries,
the young mother bares her breast
to feed the greedy monster—

But my shame
coming on you in the kitchen,
unprepared for the great hanging tit,
the suckling infant.
                So that I mutter
words, any words,
so that I want so desperately to drop
the rye, the ginger ale,
to back out, to hide,
anything but raise my eyes. . . .

And I repeat—this thing you do
the most natural in the world.

So that I know myself
earth's most unnatural,
life's most unprepared fool.
And wonder: how many
of us begin like your infant,
but really never leave the breast,
suck at it
all the innocence of our lives?

A Letter to Archibald Lampman

Dear Archie:
if I remember correctly
it was in 1888
that you published your first book of verse
Among the Millet
with a legacy left to your wife.

I believe the book was published
or at any rate printed
by J. Durie & Son
of Ottawa, the city you worked in
and died in,
the city that has done exactly nothing
for you its most distinguished citizen
(for my money anyway);

and eighty-six years later
or 1974 to be precise,
you are still too big a risk
to be published in that city.

'A volume this size

concentrated on one poet
would be a risky venture.'

Now, I don't blame my publisher
who happens to locate in Ottawa,
and I can't fault your verse—
let's face it, it's the best we have,
you are not in any sense 'minor'—

I can only blame it, Archie,
on your misfortune to be born
a poet in a country

so rich and so big
yet so minor as Canada.   *PUT DOWN*

Pictures of a Long-Lost World

Passchendaele, October 1917

Half-drowning in the miserable lean-to
that was really just a roof over mud,
my father heard a strange *plop plop plop*
almost on top of him, panicked, yelled at Fred
who was drowsing beside him, and with both hands shaking,
somehow pulled his gas-mask on.
                              But old Fred
wasn't buying it this time, he was sick of false alarms,
so didn't move until the first yellow cloud
seeped in a minute later (my father watching
through his half-fogged goggles, heard Fred cough,
then struggle with his gas-mask, cough, clutch his throat again,
then jump up, scramble out, a madman screaming
as he ran for the battery gas-curtain. . . .)

Six months later he was back
his lungs almost good as new.

prep to be trusting?

Leonard Cohen

Elegy

Do not look for him
In brittle mountain streams:
They are too cold for any god;
And do not examine the angry rivers
For shreds of his soft body
Or turn the shore stones for his blood;
But in the warm salt ocean
He is descending through cliffs
Of slow green water
And the hovering coloured fish
Kiss his snow-bruised body
And build their secret nests
In his fluttering winding-sheet.

Story

She tells me a child built her house
one Spring afternoon,
but that the child was killed
crossing the street.

She says she read it in the newspaper,
that at the corner of this and this avenue
a child was run down by an automobile.

Of course I do not believe her.
She has built the house herself,
hung the oranges and coloured beads in the doorways,
crayoned flowers on the walls.
She has made the paper things for the wind,
collected crooked stones for their shadows in the sun,
fastened yellow and dark balloons to the ceiling.

Each time I visit her
she repeats the story of the child to me,
I never question her. It is important
to understand one's part in a legend.

I take my place
among the paper fish and make-believe clocks,
naming the flowers she has drawn,
smiling while she paints my head on large clay coins,
and making a sort of courtly love to her
when she contemplates her own traffic death.

I Have Not Lingered in European Monasteries

I have not lingered in European monasteries
and discovered among the tall grasses tombs of knights
who fell as beautifully as their ballads tell;

I have not parted the grasses
or purposefully left them thatched.

I have not released my mind to wander and wait
in those great distances
between the snowy mountains and the fishermen,
like a moon,
or a shell beneath the moving water.

I have not held my breath
so that I might hear the breathing of God,
or tamed my heartbeat with an exercise,
or starved for visions.
Although I have watched him often
I have not become the heron,

leaving my body on the shore,
and I have not become the luminous trout,
leaving my body in the air.

I have not worshipped wounds and relics,
or combs of iron,
or bodies wrapped and burnt in scrolls.

I have not been unhappy for ten thousand years.
During the day I laugh and during the night I sleep.
My favourite cooks prepare my meals,
my body cleans and repairs itself,
and all my work goes well.

You Have the Lovers

You have the lovers,
they are nameless, their histories only for each other,
and you have the room, the bed and the windows.
Pretend it is a ritual.
Unfurl the bed, bury the lovers, blacken the windows,
let them live in that house for a generation or two.
No one dares disturb them.
Visitors in the corridor tip-toe past the long closed door,
they listen for sounds, for a moan, for a song:
nothing is heard, not even breathing.
You know they are not dead,
you can feel the presence of their intense love.
Your children grow up, they leave you,
they have become soldiers and riders.
Your mate dies after a life of service.
Who knows you? Who remembers you?
But in your house a ritual is in progress:
it is not finished: it needs more people.
One day the door is opened to the lovers' chamber.

The room has become a dense garden,
full of colours, smells, sounds you have never known.
The bed is smooth as a wafer of sunlight,
in the midst of the garden it stands alone.
In the bed the lovers, slowly and deliberately and silently,
perform the act of love.
Their eyes are closed,
as tightly as if heavy coins of flesh lay on them.
Their lips are bruised with new and old bruises.
Her hair and his beard are hopelessly tangled.
When he puts his mouth against her shoulder
she is uncertain whether her shoulder
has given or received the kiss.
All her flesh is like a mouth.
He carries his fingers along her waist
and feels his own waist caressed.
She holds him closer and his own arms tighten around her.
She kisses the hand beside her mouth.
It is his hand or her hand, it hardly matters,
there are so many more kisses.
You stand beside the bed, weeping with happiness,
you carefully peel away the sheets
from the slow-moving bodies.
Your eyes are filled with tears, you barely make out the lovers.
As you undress you sing out, and your voice is magnificent
because now you believe it is the first human voice
heard in that room.
The garments you let fall grow into vines.
You climb into bed and recover the flesh.
You close your eyes and allow them to be sewn shut.
You create an embrace and fall into it.
There is only one moment of pain or doubt
as you wonder how many multitudes are lying beside your body,
but a mouth kisses and a hand soothes the moment away.

As the Mist Leaves No Scar

As the mist leaves no scar
On the dark green hill,
So my body leaves no scar
On you, nor ever will.

When wind and hawk encounter,
What remains to keep?
So you and I encounter,
Then turn, then fall to sleep.

As many nights endure
Without a moon or star,
So will we endure
When one is gone and far.

Now of Sleeping

Under her grandmother's patchwork quilt
a calico bird's-eye view
of crops and boundaries
naming dimly the districts of her body
sleeps my Annie like a perfect lady

Like ages of weightless snow
on tiny oceans filled with light
her eyelids enclose deeply
a shade tree of birthday candles
one for every morning
until the now of sleeping

The small banner of blood
kept and flown by Brother Wind
long after the pierced bird fell down

is like her red mouth
among the squalls of pillow

Bearers of evil fancy
of dark intention and corrupting fashion
who come to rend the quilt
plough the eye and ground the mouth
will contend with mighty Mother Goose
and Farmer Brown and all good stories
of invincible belief
which surround her sleep
like the golden weather of a halo

Well-wishers and her true lover
may stay to watch my Annie
sleeping like a perfect lady
under her grandmother's patchwork quilt
but they must promise to whisper
and to vanish by morning—
all but her one true lover.

The Genius

For you
I will be a ghetto jew
and dance
and put white stockings
on my twisted limbs
and poison wells
across the town

For you
I will be an apostate jew
and tell the Spanish priest
of the blood vow
in the Talmud
and where the bones
of the child are hid

For you
I will be a banker jew
and bring to ruin
a proud old hunting king
and end his line

For you
I will be a Broadway jew
and cry in theatres
for my mother
and sell bargain goods
beneath the counter

For you
I will be a doctor jew
and search
in all the garbage cans
for foreskins
to sew back again

For you
I will be a Dachau jew
and lie down in lime
with twisted limbs
and bloated pain
no mind can understand

Style

I don't believe the radio stations
of Russia and America
but I like the music and I like
the solemn European voices announcing jazz
I don't believe opium or money
though they're hard to get
and punished with long sentences
I don't believe love
in the midst of my slavery I
do not believe
I am a man sitting in a house
on a treeless Argolic island
I will forget the grass of my mother's lawn
I know I will
I will forget the old telephone number
Fitzroy seven eight two oh
I will forget my style
I will have no style
I hear a thousand miles of hungry static
and the old clear water eating rocks
I hear the bells of mules eating
I hear the flowers eating the night
under their folds
Now a rooster with a razor
plants the haemophilia gash across
the soft black sky
and now I know for certain

I will forget my style
Perhaps a mind will open in this world
perhaps a heart will catch rain
Nothing will heal and nothing will freeze
but perhaps a heart will catch rain
America will have no style
Russia will have no style
It is happening in the twenty-eighth year

of my attention
I don't know what will become
of the mules with their lady eyes
or the old clear water
or the giant rooster
The early morning greedy radio eats
the governments one by one the languages
the poppy fields one by one
Beyond the numbered band
a silence develops for every style
for the style I laboured on
an external silence like the space
between insects in a swarm
electric unremembering
and it is aimed at us
(I am sleepy and frightened)
it makes toward me brothers

For E. J. P.

I once believed a single line
        in a Chinese poem could change
                forever how blossoms fell
and that the moon itself climbed on
        the grief of concise weeping men
                to journey over cups of wine
I thought invasions were begun for crows
        to pick at a skeleton
                dynasties sown and spent
to serve the language of a fine lament
        I thought governors ended their lives
                as sweetly drunken monks

telling time by rain and candles
    instructed by an insect's pilgrimage
        across the page—all this
so one might send an exile's perfect letter
to an ancient home-town friend

I chose a lonely country
    broke from love
        scorned the fraternity of war
I polished my tongue against the pumice moon
    floated my soul in cherry wine
        a perfumed barge for Lords of Memory
to languish on to drink to whisper out
    their store of strength
        as if beyond the mist along the shore
their girls their power still obeyed
    like clocks wound for a thousand years
I waited until my tongue was sore

Brown petals wind like fire around my poems
    I aimed them at the stars but
        like rainbows they were bent
before they sawed the world in half
    Who can trace the canyoned paths
        cattle have carved out of time
wandering from meadowlands to feasts
    Layer after layer of autumn leaves
        are swept away
Something forgets us perfectly

The Music Crept by Us

I would like to remind
the management
that the drinks are watered
and the hat-check girl
has syphilis
and the band is composed
of former SS monsters
However since it is
New Year's Eve
and I have lip cancer
I will place my
paper hat on my
concussion and dance

Disguises

I am sorry that the rich man must go
and his house become a hospital.
I loved his wine, his contemptuous servants,
his ten-year-old ceremonies.
I loved his car which he wore like a snail's shell
everywhere, and I loved his wife,
the hours she put into her skin,
the milk, the lust, the industries
that served her complexion.
I loved his son who looked British
but had American ambitions
and let the word aristocrat comfort him
like a reprieve while Kennedy reigned.
I loved the rich man: I hate to see
his season ticket for the Opera
fall into a pool for opera-lovers.

I am sorry that the old worker must go
who called me mister when I was twelve
and sir when I was twenty
who studied against me in obscure socialist
clubs which met in restaurants.
I loved the machine he knew like a wife's body.
I loved his wife who trained bankers
in an underground pantry
and never wasted her ambition in ceramics.
I loved his children who debate
and come first at McGill University.
Goodbye old gold-watch winner
all your complex loyalties
must now be borne by one-faced patriots.

Goodbye dope fiends of North Eastern Lunch
circa 1948, your spoons which were not
Swedish Stainless, were the same colour
as the hoarded clasps and hooks
of discarded soiled therapeutic corsets.
I loved your puns about snow
even if they lasted the full seven-month
Montreal winter. Go write your memoirs
for the Psychedelic Review.

Goodbye sex fiends of Beaver Pond
who dreamed of being jacked-off
by electric milking machines.
You had no Canada Council.
You had to open little boys
with a pen-knife.
I loved your statement to the press:
'I didn't think he'd mind.'
Goodbye articulate monsters
Abbott and Costello have met Frankenstein.

I am sorry that the conspirators must go
the ones who scared me by showing me
a list of all the members of my family.

I loved the way they reserved judgement
about Genghis Khan. They loved me because
I told them their little beards
made them dead-ringers for Lenin.
The bombs went off in Westmount
and now they are ashamed
like a successful outspoken Schopenhauerian
whose room-mate has committed suicide.
Suddenly they are all making movies.
I have no one to buy coffee for.

I embrace the changeless:
the committed men in public wards
oblivious as Hassidim
who believe that they are someone else.
Barvo! Abelard, viva! Rockefeller,
have these buns, Napoleon,
hurrah! betrayed Duchess.
Long live you chronic self-abusers!
you monotheists!
you familiars of the Absolute
sucking at circles!
You are all my comfort
as I turn to face the beehive
as I disgrace my style
as I coarsen my nature
as I invent jokes
as I pull up my garters
as I accept responsibility.

You comfort me
incorrigible betrayers of the self
as I salute fashion
and bring my mind
    like a promiscuous air-hostess
handing out parachutes in a nose dive
bring my butchered mind
to bear upon the facts.

Two Went to Sleep

Two went to sleep
almost every night
one dreamed of mud
one dreamed of Asia
visiting a zeppelin
visiting Nijinsky
Two went to sleep
one dreamed of ribs
one dreamed of senators
Two went to sleep
two travellers
The long marriage
in the dark
The sleep was old
the travellers were old
one dreamed of oranges
one dreamed of Carthage
Two friends asleep
years locked in travel
Good night my darling
as the dreams waved goodbye
one travelled lightly
one walked through water
visiting a chess game
visiting a booth
always returning
to wait out the day
One carried matches
one climbed a beehive
one sold an earphone
one shot a German
Two went to sleep
every sleep went together
wandering away
from an operating table
one dreamed of grass

one dreamed of spokes
one bargained nicely
one was a snowman
one counted medicine
one tasted pencils
one was a child
one was a traitor
visiting heavy industry
visiting the family
Two went to sleep
none could foretell
one went with baskets
one took a ledger
one night happy
one night in terror
Love could not bind them
Fear could not either
they went unconnected
they never knew where
always returning
to wait out the day
parting with kissing
parting with yawns
visiting Death till
they wore out their welcome
visiting Death till
the right disguise worked

1964

God Is Alive

From Beautiful Losers

God is alive. Magic is afoot. God is alive. Magic is afoot. God is afoot. Magic is alive. Alive is afoot. Magic never died. God never sickened. Many poor men lied. Many sick men lied. Magic never weakened. Magic never hid. Magic always ruled. God is afoot. God never died. God was ruler though his funeral lengthened. Though his mourners thickened Magic never fled. Though his shrouds were hoisted the naked God did live. Though his words were twisted the naked Magic thrived. Though his death was published round and round the world the heart did not believe. Many hurt men wondered. Many struck men bled. Magic never faltered. Magic always led. Many stones were rolled but God Would not lie down. Many wild men lied. Many fat men listened. Though they offered stones Magic still was fed. Though they locked their coffers God was always served. Magic is afoot. God rules. Alive is afoot. Alive is in command. Many weak men hungered. Many strong men thrived. Though they boasted solitude God was at their side. Nor the dreamer in his cell, nor the captain on the hill. Magic is alive. Though his death was pardoned round and round the world the heart would not believe. Though laws were carved in marble they could not shelter men. Though altars built in parliaments they could not order men. Police arrested Magic and Magic went with them for Magic loves the hungry. But Magic would not tarry. It moves from arm to arm. It would not stay with them. Magic is afoot. It cannot come to harm. It rests in an empty palm. It spawns in an empty mind. But Magic is no instrument. Magic is the end. Many men drove Magic but Magic stayed behind. Many strong men lied. They only passed through Magic and out the other side. Many weak men lied. They came to God in secret and though they left him nourished they would not tell who healed. Though mountains danced before them they said that God was dead. Though his shrouds were hoisted the naked God did live. This I mean to whisper to my mind. This I mean to laugh with in my mind. This I mean my mind to serve till service is but Magic moving through the world, and mind itself is Magic coursing through the flesh, and flesh itself is Magic dancing on a clock, and time itself the Magic Length of God.

Ballad of the Death of a Lady's Man

The man she wanted all her life
    was hanging by a thread.
'I never even knew how much
    I wanted you,' she said.
His muscles they were numbered
    and his style was obsolete
'O baby, I have come too late.'
    She knelt beside his feet.

'I'll never see a face like yours
    in years of men to come,
I'll never see such arms again
    in wrestling or in love.'
And all his virtues burning
    in the smoky holocaust,
she took unto herself
    most everything her lover lost.

Now the master of this landscape
    he was standing at the view
with a sparrow of St. Francis
    that he was preaching to.
She beckoned to the sentry
    of his high religious mood.
She said, 'I'll make a space between my legs,
    I'll teach you solitude.'

He offered her an orgy
    in a many-mirrored room,
he promised her protection
    for the issue of her womb.
She moved her body hard
    against a sharpened metal spoon,
she stopped the bloody rituals
    of passage to the moon.

She took his much-admired
    oriental frame of mind,
and the heart-of-darkness alibi
    his money lies behind.
She took his blonde madonna
    and his monastery wine.
'This mental space is occupied
    and everything is mine.'

He tried to make a final stand
    beside the railway track.
She said, 'The art of longing's over
    and it's never coming back.'
She took his tavern parliament,
    his cap, his cocky dance;
she mocked his female fashions
    and his working-class moustache.

The last time that I saw him
    he was trying hard to get
a woman's education
    but he's not a woman yet.
And the last time that I saw her
    she was living with a boy
who gives her soul an empty room
    and gives her body joy.

So the great affair is over
    but whoever would have guessed
it would leave us all so vacant
    and so deeply unimpressed.
It's like our visit to the moon
    or to that other star:
I guess you go for nothing
    if you really want to go that far.

Phyllis Webb

Pain

Whether pain is simple as razors edging the fleshy cage,
or whether pain raves with sharks inside the ribs,
it throws a bridge of value to belief
where, towards or away from, moves intense traffic.

Or, should the eyes focus to cubes and lights of pain
and the breasts' exquisite asterisks breed circular grief,
this bird of death is radiant and complex,
speeds fractional life over value to belief;

The bridge spans by contemporary pain
centuries of historical birth.

The Mind Reader

I thought,
and he acted
upon my thought,
read by some wonderful
kind of glass my mind
saw passing that way
gulls floating over boats
floating in the bay,
and by some wonderful
sleight of hand
he ordered the gulls to land
on boats
and the boats to land.

Or, was it through waves
he sent the boats
to fly with gulls

so that out of care
they all could play
in a wonderful
gull-boat-water way
up in a land of air?

Marvell's Garden

Marvell's garden, that place of solitude,
is not where I'd choose to live
yet is the fixed sundial
that turns me round
unwillingly
in a hot glade
as closer, closer I come to contradiction,
to the shade green within the green shade.

The garden where Marvell scorned love's solicitude—
that dream—and played instead an arcane solitaire,
shuffling his thoughts like shadowy chance
across the shrubs of ecstasy,
and cast the myths away to flowering hours
as yes, his mind, that sea, caught at green
thoughts shadowing a green infinity.

And yet Marvell's garden was not Plato's
garden—and yet—he *did* care more for the form
of things than for the thing itself—
ideas and visions,
resemblances and echoes,
things seeming and being
not quite what they were.

That was his garden, a kind of attitude

struck out of an earth too carefully attended,
wanting to be left alone.
And I don't blame him for that.
God knows, too many fences fence us out
and his garden closed in on Paradise.

On Paradise! When I think of his hymning
Puritans in the Bermudas, the bright oranges
lighting up that night! When I recall
his rustling tinsel hopes
beneath the cold decree of steel,
Oh, I have wept for some new convulsion
to tear together this world and his.

But then I saw his luminous plumèd Wings
prepared for flight,
and then I heard him singing glory
in a green tree,
and then I caught the vest he'd laid aside
all blest with fire.

And I have gone walking slowly in
his garden of necessity
leaving brothers, lovers, Christ
outside my walls
where they have wept without
and I within.

Mad Gardener to the Sea . . .

Mad gardener to the sea, the moon

    rages across the sky to tend

        oceans of an unloving dark

           and the bone-blooming skeleton:

beyond all Paradise, all Arden

    moon multiplies the garden;

        nor doth the coral orchard care

           man dreameth ever back to water—

l'homme inconnu et solitaire.

Propositions

I could divide a leaf
and give you half.

Or I could search for two leaves
sending you one.

Or I could walk to the river
and look across

and seeing you there,
or not there,

absence or presence,
would spring the balance to my day.

Or I could directly find you and take your hand
so that one hand would be given

and one kept, like a split leaf
or like two leaves separate.

These would be signs and offerings:
the just passion, just encountering.

Or we perhaps could speed four eyes,
the chariot horses of our dreams and visions,

in them direction and decision find.
The split leaf floating on the river,

the hand sketching in the air
a half-moon, its hidden wholeness there.

Breaking

Give us wholeness, for we are broken.
But who are we asking, and why do we ask?
Destructive element heaves close to home,
our years of work broken against a breakwater.

Shattered gods, self-iconoclasts,
it is with Lazarus unattended we belong
(the fall of the sparrow is unbroken song).
The crucifix has clattered to the ground,
the living Christ has spent a year in Paris,
travelled on the Métro, fallen in the Seine.
We would not raise our silly gods again.
Stigmata sting, they suddenly appear
on every blessed person everywhere.
If there is agitation there is cause.

Ophelia, Hamlet, Othello, Lear,
Kit Smart, William Blake, John Clare,
Van Gogh, Henry IV of Pirandello,
Gerard de Nerval, Antonin Artaud
bear a crown of darkness.
It is better so.

Responsible now each to his own attack,
we are bequeathed their ethos and our death.
Greek marble white and whiter grows
breaking into history of a west.
If we could stand so virtuously white
crumbling in the terrible Grecian light.

There is a justice in destruction.
It isn't 'isn't fair'.
A madhouse is designed for the insane,
a hospital for wounds that will re-open;
a war is architecture for aggression,
and Christ's stigmata body-minted token.
What are we whole or beautiful or good for
but to be absolutely broken?

'The Time of Man'

extrapolations from an article by DR LOREN EISELEY

'The little toe is attractive

                              to the student of rudimentary
and vanishing organs,'

and whooping cranes claxon

                                     to the spellbound preservers
of what would naturally vanish.

When the adored ones

                            pass through the door ('the future
of no invention can be guaranteed')

who does not follow them,

                         half in love with his tears,
tickled by the lower brain,
                     'the fossil remnant,'
                              claws

      scratching at the large
                    symbolic order,
animal sad, watching the members

                  fade:
        clitoral love, the royal we
                    stumbling:

'The perfectly adjusted perish with their environment'

      —then take me with you
                    crying
                        take me with you—

The brain when it began to grow
                  was 'shielded by a shell of bone
as thick as a warrior's helmet.'

The Glass Castle

The glass castle is my image for the mind
that if outmoded has its public beauty.
It can contain both talisman and leaf,
and private action, homely disbelief.
And I have lived there as you must
and scratched with diamond and gathered diamond dust,
have signed the castle's tense and fragile glass
and heard the antique whores and stoned Cassandras
call me, and I answered in the one voice I knew,
'I am here. I do not know . . .'
but moved the symbols and polished up the view.
For who can refrain from action—
there is always a princely kiss for the Sleeping Beauty—
when even to put out the light takes a steady hand,
for the reward of darkness in a glass castle
is starry and full of glory.

I do not mean I shall not crack the pane.
I merely make a statement, judicious and polite,
that in this poise of crystal space
I balance and I claim the five gods of reality
to bless and keep me sane.

Love Story

It was easy to see what he was up to,
the grey, bundled ape,
as he sidled half-playfully
up to the baby
and with a sly look behind

put his hands onto the crib
and leapt in.

The child's pink, beginning face
stared up as the hair-handed monkey
explored the flesh, so soft, of our infant race.
The belly spread like plush to the monkey's haunch,
he settled, heavy and gay, his nuzzling
mouth at the baby's neck.

But, no answer accurate to a smile,
he bit, tasted time, maddened,
and his nails rooted sudden fire in the ribs of Adam,
towered, carnivorous, for aim
and baby face, ears, arms
were torn and taken in his ravaging.

And so the killing, too-late parents came,
hysteric, after their child's
futile pulse had stopped its beating.
Only the half-pathetic, half-triumphant
monkey peered out from the crib,
bobbed nervously on the dead infant's belly,
then stopped, suddenly paralyzed on that soft tomb.

Was it the donkey Death brayed out at him
from the human mother's eyes,
or did his love for her in that pause
consume him?

The jealous ape's death was swift
and of natural cause. 'Died of shame,'
some said, others, 'of shock.'
But his death was Othello's death,
as great, as picayune,
he died of envy, lacking the knack of wisdom.

Sitting

The degree of nothingness
is important:
to sit emptily
in the sun
receiving fire
that is the way
to mend
an extraordinary world,
sitting perfectly
still
and only
remotely human.

A Tall Tale

The whale, improbable as lust,
carved out a cave
for the seagirl's rest;
with rest the seagirl, sweet as dust, devised
a manner for the whale
to lie between her thighs.
Like this they lay
within the shadowed cave
under the waters, under the waters wise,
and nested there, and nested there and stayed,
this coldest whale aslant the seagirl's thighs.

Two hundred years perhaps swam by them there
before the cunning waters so distilled the pair
they turned to brutal artifacts of stone
polished, O petrified prisoners of their lair.
And thus, with quiet, submerged in deathly calm,

the two disclosed a future geologic long,
lying cold, whale to thigh revealed
the secret of their comfort
to the marine weeds,
to fish, to shell, sand, sediment and wave,
to the broken, dying sun
which probed their ocean grave.
These, whale and seagirl, stone gods,
stone lust, stone grief,
interred on the sedimented sand
amongst the orange starfish,
these cold and stony mariners
invoked the moral snail
and in sepulchral voice intoned a moral tale:

'Under the waters, under the waters wise,
all loving flesh will quickly meet demise,
the cave, the shadow cave is nowhere wholly safe
and even the oddest couple can scarcely find relief:
appear then to submit to this tide and timing sea,
but secrete a skilful shell and stone and perfect be.'

To Friends
Who Have Also Considered Suicide

It's still a good idea.
Its exercise is discipline:
to remember to cross the street without looking,
to remember not to jump when the cars side-swipe,
to remember not to bother to have clothes cleaned,
to remember not to eat or want to eat,
to consider the numerous methods of killing oneself,
that is surely the finest exercise of the imagination:
death by drowning, sleeping pills, slashed wrists,
kitchen fumes, bullets through the brain or through

the stomach, hanging by the neck in attic or basement,
a clean frozen death—the ways are endless.
And consider the drama! It's better than a whole season
at Stratford when you think of the emotion of your
family on hearing the news and when you imagine
how embarrassed some will be when the body is found.
One could furnish a whole chorus in a Greek play
with expletives and feel sneaky and omniscient
at the same time. But there's no shame
in this concept of suicide.
It has concerned our best philosophers
and inspired some of the most popular
of our politicians and financiers.
Some people swim lakes, others climb flagpoles,
some join monasteries, but we, my friends,
who have considered suicide take our daily walk
with death and are not lonely.
In the end it brings more honesty and care
than all the democratic parliaments of tricks.
It is the 'sickness unto death'; it is death;
it is not death; it is the sand from the beaches
of a hundred civilizations, the sand in the teeth
of death and barnacles our singing tongue:
and this is 'life' and we owe at least this much
contemplation to our western fact: to Rise,
Decline, Fall, to futility and larks,
to the bright crustaceans of the oversky.

I Can Call Nothing Love

A smile shakes alphabets over my belly

and I bend down scrabbling 'Yes' from a young Adam.

I can call nothing love that does not answer—

and I remember how Van Gogh

his own ecstatic ear cut off.

Occasions of Desire

Occasions of desire with their attendant envies,
the white heat of the cold swan dying,
create their gestures, obscene or most beautiful.
Oh, the clear shell of a swan's fluted wings!

And as the old swan calls clarity from dark waters,
sailing triumphant into the forgotten,
desire in its moving is that rapacious cry,
gorgeous as the torrent Lethe, and as wise.

And if the curl of cygnets on the Avon,
so freshly broken from their perfect shells,
take from a dying bird not moral or enticement,
but float with their own white mother, that is just.
Oh, imperious innocence to envy
only the water bearing such beauty!

Poetics Against the Angel
of Death

I am sorry to speak of death again
(some say I'll have a long life)
but last night Wordsworth's 'Prelude'
suddenly made sense—I mean the measure,
the elevated tone, the attitude
of private Man speaking to public men.
Last night I thought I would not wake again
but now with this June morning I run ragged to elude
The Great Iambic Pentameter
who is the Hound of Heaven in our stress
because I want to die
writing Haiku
or, better,
long lines, clean and syllabic as knotted bamboo. Yes!

Rilke

Rilke, I speak your name I throw it away
with your angels, your angels, your statues
and virgins, and a horse in a field held
at the hoof by wood. I cannot take so much
tenderness, tenderness, snow falling like lace
over your eyes year after year as the poems
receded, roses, the roses, sinking in snow
in the distant mountains.

Go away with your women to Russia or take them
to France, and take them or don't the poet is
in you, the spirit, they love that.
(I met one in Paris, her death leaning outward,

death in all forms. The letters you'd sent her,
she said, stolen from a taxi.)

Rilke.
Clowns and angels held your compassion.
You could sit in a room saying nothing,
nothing. Your admirers thought you were there,
a presence, a wisdom. But you had to leave
everyone once, once at least. That was your
hardness.

This page is a shadowed hall in Duino Castle.
Echoes. The echoes.
I don't know why I'm here.

For Fyodor

I am a beetle in the cabbage soup they serve up for geniuses
in the House of the Dead.

I am a black beetle and loll seductively at the bottom of the
warm slop.

Someday, Fyodor, by mistake you'll swallow me down and I'll
become a part of your valuable gutworks.

In the next incarnation I hope to imitate that idiot and saint
Prince Myshkin, drop off my wings for his moronic glory.

Or, if I miss out on the Prince, Sonya or Dunya might do.

I'm not joking. I am not the result of bad sanitation in the
kitchen, as you think.

Up here in Omsk in Siberia beetles are not accidents but destinies.

I'm drowning fast but even in this condition I realize your bad
tempered haughtiness is part of your strategy.

You are about to turn this freezing hell into an ecstatic emblem.
A ferocious shrine.

Ah, what delicious revenge. But take care! A fit is coming!
Now, now, I'll leap into your foaming mouth and jump your tongue.
Now I stamp on this not quite famous tongue

shouting: Remember Fyodor, you may hate men but it's here in
Omsk you came to love mankind.

But you don't hear, do you: there you are writhing in epileptic
visions.

Hold your tongue! You can't speak yet. You are mine, Dostoevsky.

I aim to slip down your gullet and improve myself.
I can almost hear what you'll say: ·

            Crime and Punishment
            Suffering and Grace

and of the dying

            Pass by and forgive
            us our happiness

Treblinka Gas Chamber

*'Klostermayer ordered another count of the children.
Then their stars were snipped off and thrown into
the center of the courtyard. It looked like a field of
buttercups.'*
  —A FIELD OF BUTTERCUPS by JOSEPH HYAMS

fallingstars
          'a field of
                    buttercups'

              yellow stars
                        of David
                              falling

the prisoners
            the children
                      falling

              in heaps
                    on one another
                            they go down

Thanatos
          showers
                his dirty breath
                          they must breathe
                                    him in

              they see stars
                        behind their
                              eyes

David's
        'a field of
              buttercups'

              a metaphor
                    where all that's
                              left lies down

Naked Poems

                    star fish
                        fish star

Suite I

MOVING

to establish distance
between our houses.

It seems
I welcome you in.

Your mouth blesses me
all over.

There is room.

                                                  AND
                                                  here
                                                  and here and
                                                  here
                                                  and over   and
                                                  over   your mouth

TONIGHT
quietness.   In me
and the room.

I am enclosed
by a thought

and some walls.

THE BRUISE

Again you have left
your mark.

Or we
have.

Skin shuddered
secretly.

FLIES

tonight
in this room
two flies
on the ceiling
are making
love
quietly.   Or

so it seems
down here

YOUR BLOUSE

I people
this room
with things, a
chair, a lamp, a
fly   two books by
Marianne Moore.

I have thrown my
blouse on the floor.

Was it only
last night?

YOU
took

with so much
gentleness

my dark

Suite II

While you were away

I held you like this
in my mind.

It is a good mind
that can embody
perfection   with exactitude.

The sun comes through
plum curtains.

I said
the sun is gold

in your eyes.

It isn't the sun
you said.

On the floor your blouse.
The plum light
falls more golden

going down.

Tonight
quietness
in the room.

We knew

Then you must go.
I sat cross-legged
on the bed.
There is no room
for self-pity
I said

I lied

In the gold darkening
light

you   dressed.

I hid my face
in my hair.

The room that held you

is still here

You brought me clarity.
Gift after gift
I wear.

Poems, naked,

in the sunlight

on the floor.

D.G.
Jones

Portrait of Anne Hébert

The sunlight, here and there,
Touches a table

And a draught at the window
Announces your presence,

You take your place in the room
Without fuss,

Your delicate bones,
Your frock,
Have the grace of disinterested passion.

Words are arrayed
Like surgical instruments
Neatly in trays.

Deftly, you make an incision
Probing
The obscure disease.

Your sensibility
Has the sure fingers of the blind:

Each decision
Cuts like a scalpel
Through tangled emotion.

You define
The morbid tissue, laying it bare

Like a tatter of lace
Dark
On the paper.

Odysseus

A Monologue in the Underworld

When last did the sun
Arm with brightness all my arms, and lie
In the folds of my black sail?
Where are the bright salt waves?
And the salt flesh of the wave-born girls?

In this distance of memory they fade.
Even the image of the spoiled
City, smouldering on the morning sky,
Grows insubstantial as a shade.
Styx and Lethe, black, flow through the mind.

What cities, and men, what girls
Might have known this face, these eyes,
What faces might my eyes have known,
Since, discarding faces, lives,
I fled across the waters red with suns
In search of one face, life, and home?

About the pit of sacrifice, the fires
Like tongues thirsting for sound
Flare, and flicker on the brain.
Surrounded by the voiceless shades
Whose throats are eager for this blood, I bare
The sword of my refusal to their baleful eyes.

When will the blind man come? When
With this blood—O great communion—
May I give these shadows tongue? And sail
Outward, homeward, to a land of men?
Old Shadow! from these shadows, come.

I am blind. Aiee, I am struck blind!
All those faces—all, are mine!
World upon world unfolds, salt with foam,

Or tears, with love's salt hair: cities and men,
Girls, arms and oarlocks, all the cattle of the sun.

They are gathered in the fold
Of my dark sail; they are folded in the sun.
The sun engulfs the restless sea. Not a cloud
Appears. Endless and shining, beyond all
Pillars of Hercules, lovely and tempestuous,
The ocean rolls, and rolls.

My sight returns, and darkness—
Palpable with shadows crowding to the blood;
Shadows which now speak to me of homely things
And then depart, like figures in a dream.
My men—I hear them shouting down the wind.
Oh, once again, I smell the grey, salt sea.

Beautiful Creatures Brief as These

FOR JAY MACPHERSON

Like butterflies but lately come
From long cocoons of summer
These little girls start back to school
To swarm the sidewalks, playing-fields,
And litter air with colour.

So slight they look within their clothes,
Their dresses looser than the Sulphur's wings,
It seems that even if the wind alone
Were not to break them in the lofty trees,
They could not bear the weight of *things*.

And yet they cry into the morning air
And hang from railings upside down
And laugh, as though the world were theirs
And all its buildings, trees, and stones
Were toys, were gifts of a benignant sun.

For Françoise Adnet

It is that time of day, time
To chop the beans, to peel
Potatoes for the evening meal.

The fullness of time
Grows, at this hour,
Like the shadows on the crockery.

Mademoiselle's mauve gloves,
Alone, tell of the afternoon, the dried
Flowers, the delicate hands among the stalks.

For once things are what they are,
Until my little girl
Comes in from outdoors, the melting snow

Cool in her nostrils,
Sky, blue without clouds,
Behind her eyes.

But even these dissolve.
Fingering an orange
She lets her bare legs dangle.

Time is space, it glows
Like the white tablecloth,
The breadboard where I slice the onions.

The kitchen floats in my tears—
And the sun
In its brazier of urban trees.

These Trees Are No Forest of Mourners

They had dragged for hours.
The weather was like his body,
Cold, though May. It rained.

It had rained for three days—
In the grass, in the new leaves,
In the black boughs against the sky.

The earth oozed,
Like the bottom of the lake—
Like a swamp. They stared

At the drowned grass, at the leaves
That dripped in the water—aware
Of their own death, heavy

As the black boughs of the spruce
Moving in a current under the grey
Surface of the sky—aware

Of a supreme ugliness, which seemed
In its very indifference,
Somehow, to defy them:

The sodden body of the world
And of their only son.

Let them be. Oh hear me,

Though it cannot help you. They exist
Beyond your grief; they have their own
Quiet reality.

Summer Is a Poem by Ovid

FOR MICHAEL ONDAATJE

The fire falls, the night
Grows more profound.
The music is composed
Of clear chords
And silence. We become
Clear and simple as the forms
Of music; we are dumb
As water
Mirroring the stars.

Then summer is
Ovidian, and every sun
Is but a moth evolving
In the large gloom,
An excerpt from
Ars Amoris: flame
Is no more fleeting than the limbs
Of boy and girl: the conflagration
Is the same.

While the fire falls, and night
Grows more profound, the flesh,
The music and the flame
All undergo
Metamorphosis. The sounds
Of music make a close,
So with our several selves,
Together, until silence shall compose
All but the ashes in the pale dawn
And even those.

I Thought There Were Limits

I thought there were limits, Newtonian
Laws of emotion—

I thought there were limits to this falling away,
This emptiness. I was wrong.

The apples, falling, never hit the ground.

So much for grass, and animals—
Nothing remains,
No sure foundation on the rock. The cat

Drifts, or simply dissolves.

L'homme moyen sensuel
Had better look out: complete
Deprivation brings

Dreams, hallucinations which reveal
The sound and fury of machines
Working on nothing—which explains

God's creation: *ex nihilo fecit.*

Wrong again. I now suspect
The limit is the sea itself,
The limitless.

So, neither swim nor float. Relax.
The void is not so bleak.

Conclude: desire is but an ache,
An absence. It creates
A dream of limits

And it grows in gravity as that takes shape.

On a Picture of Your House

The first pale shoots
the plants make flower
into the picture of your house:

full summer reigns
there in the silence where the sun
showers cataracts of light,

shuts out all other sound.

Only in extremes like that
can I protect you, touch—
as lately, in your presence,

I could not. Only
after you'd gone, fallen,
the street so steep and dark,

could I look after you.

As spring is here
never so intense
as at the end of winter with the ice

still breathing off the lake,

so I attend you in that house
consumed by light,
that garden to which flowers

point, and which is not,

no place. And I confess
what I protect is your
capacity for loss,

your freedom to be no one, look
so naked from that window
you are lost in light.

The Stream Exposed With All Its Stones

The stream exposed with all its stones
Flung on a raw field
Is covered, once again,

With snow.

It is not hidden. It
Still flows.

The houses in the valley, standing
Motionless below,
Seem wrapped in sunlight like a snow

And are deceptive. Even stones
Deceive us.

The creator goes
Rampaging through our lives: winter
Is a masquerade.

I tell you
Nakedness is a disguise: the white
Is dark below.

This silence is the water's cry.

I tell you in those silent houses girls
Are dancing like the stones.

Spring Flowers

Apple blossom rises through
the news of war

a single branch

I am surrounded by these flowers

lily-of-the-valley in a glass
stems tangled like Ophelia's hair

and white narcissus, petals
beaded like a lover's flesh
or grass at morning

on the battlefields

These flowers
drink news out of the air

a star falls through the kitchen
and a mixed bouquet
of violets and primrose

as if war

the fighting in the desert and the smell
of oil and cordite, roar
of tanks, were but a myth

like flowers
and literature

and mounds of pale forget-me-nots

and mounds

I am surrounded by the war

Words From the Aviary

FOR MONIQUE

I would clothe you in feathers

You are too bare
in your long bones when the wind
sighs in the snow

You are a movement of birds

I would clothe you in voices
appellations, words
spare as the mirror of a young girl

or raw, and deliquescent as the crow's
cawing over chill fields

It is not a clothing but a call

of voices, nameless
gone into the still air

of the small birds that drift
above a river running among stones
in the Haute-Savoie

above the grasses of the steppe, and in the small
trees of the taiga

in the summer forest
north
along the Ottawa

I would surround you with a guard
of heron like a tall
smoke, I would surround you with a choir

of unrecorded waterbirds, exiguous
emerging from a wall

beyond the Nile

I would have you smile, and see the sun
arrested, rest among your bones

as glistening

you move within the garden of your names, diaphanous
innumerable

You walk as you have always walked
through desert yards, the cold
spaces where the night

sighs among the stars

the sunken orchard where the wind
sighs in the snow

You are an overture. You come

like a migration
like the first waters of the world
with their entelechy of flowers

And then your naked summer
silences my words

Kate, These Flowers . . .
(The Lampman Poems)

I

You picked the dead bloom
expertly, leaving one star
lifting, long-stemmed, above cascading
leaves
           my day's star

Oh, Archie, you're a fool, she said

What colours are the vireo?
Deep garden lights, the reflected lights of
apple leaves
              my dear
your shadowed flesh

like grave eyes in the afternoon
it is, under all pain, silent
laughter
         bird, flower
you, Kate, briefly on a day in June

II

Kisses are knowledge, Kate
aphasia confounds us with a new
tongue
        too Pentecostal, too
Eleusinian, perhaps, for us
moderate Anglicans

You blush and the immoderate blood
riots like a rose
                  we are both
exposed
        I who hate Sundays

dream how I will boldly
rush out and overnight paint
Ottawa crimson
                    I come
secretly to the fold, would find
election in your mouth

III

Wild carrot, daisy, buttercup
I scatter words in the air
like your bouquet
                    petal, sepal, leaf
delicate explosions

prestidigitations, Kate
rabbits from hats, from atoms
instant nebulae

            thus fields
mimic your grace, thus words
rearticulate the trace
of outcast energy

                    All day the wind
sun took tresses, ribbons, dress
Etna's vale remembered less
stripped of its flowering text

IV

Wet places, where flowers
anchor the sky, where rain
troubles no one
                I
escape there in heavy weather
roving your veins, Kate
haptic, the hero as bare

youth adrift in the reeds

a bird sways in the swaying
cat-tails
          muted, the sun
is a wet flame
                    in the hyaline
night I recognize
Thale's world
                    anchored among
hyacinth, and moist curls

V

Puritan or paradox? this land
arctic, temperate
                    white
like your small breasts, yet
explosive to the sun

slim margins underwrite the flowers
nudging through snow
ours too
          our kind of spare
wordless joy

                    this country where
desire becomes restraint
refractory, silence
our orator
          and thus apparent

paradox
          until the petalled flesh
speak as to the deaf and blind

VI

Guard yourself, Kate, like the wild
orchid, with neglect, with worse
loneliness
            what can escape
destructiveness, man's damage
emu, dodo, wild pigeon
numerous herds and flocks

secret places of themselves invite
lovers, and new violence
                        flowers
in deep woods, beside
pools, moist rocky soil
petals twisted like brown hair

even I could not resist
ransacking the rare, delicate purse

VII

Masts in the misty fields
udders moving among grassheads
lagging wind
            we cared
little for Arcadia, its
elementary joys, its excrement
its vulgar weeds
            we wished
noetic clouds, a marble frieze

stomach, Kate, we lacked
the stomach to be real
animals
            a carnal music among
lambs, oxen lowing or
kids prancing, the hairy
stalks glaucous among kine

VIII

This is the place, thornbush
humped grass, granite
empty except for the wind
inane except for the incessant
movement of birds, clouds, yellowing
moss, the leaves
                    a random
outcrop, overcast
                    ?who
reads this landscape, windswept
thistle, aster, ghostly
everlasting
                this is the true
locus of your grey eyes
leaving us lonely, stone, flesh
each more nakedly alive

IX

Truth, Kate, all your virtues
harrow my flesh, are flesh
etching my mind
                    as lately
wind was a hawk moving
aslant the land, was the sloped
transient sky, was pine
elegiac by the stream
                        the water
revealing our thirst
                    as lately
crouched among stones, curls and stray
ribbons of your shift
eddying round you, you seemed
simplicity itself
                    while the clear
spring rippled with cress

X

Gone, love's body, like a field
reclaimed by winter
all its flowers, exhausted
sick of passion, flesh itself
surrendered to the uniform
Euclidian space: blank wall
shut door, blind discreetly drawn

illusory propriety: beneath the surface
nothing is dissolved

stones in the wet weather
nudge through snow, and the black
orphaned boughs, and grass
whispering of the humpy world

XI

Loneliness becomes us, we
advance through separations, learning
to love cold skies, empty
even to the last high
hail and farewell of birds
arrowing south
                    wilderness
waste fields become us

thistles matted with their own seed
haggard thorn trees
originals
            ourselves, or mere
reticulations of the wind
nameless
            bright precipitates of our desire
scattered in grass

XII

Perverse, this trellis, this peignoir
of flowers Kate, this is your
invention, your insouciance
slipping naked into the cold
dismantled garden, leaving
evidence of spring
                              green sheath
stems and tendrils, butterflies
exhaling scent, the violet, the rose
nuances of remembered flesh

treacherous images, this is the real
excrement of summer
                              let the wind
undress us, frost
restore our pristine nakedness

XIII

Milkweed unpacks itself
riddling the wind with packaged
roots, parachutes, poems
ordnance for a spring offensive

Winter, then, and wars

                              and memory
lays cut flowers in
empty carpels
                    absurd
yet from absurdity our love
fits out an underground
resistance

              Who foresaw?
increasing violence accompanies
technique, the empty self

heaven is a mortalflower

Alden Nowlan

Beginning

From that they found most lovely, most abhorred,
my parents made me: I was born like sound
stroked from the fiddle to become the ward
of tunes played on the bear-trap and the hound.

Not one, but seven entrances they gave
each to the other, and he laid her down
the way the sun comes out. Oh, they were brave,
and then like looters in a burning town.

Their mouths left bruises, starting with the kiss
and ending with the proverb, where they stayed;
never in making was there brighter bliss,
followed by darker shame. Thus I was made.

Warren Pryor

When every pencil meant a sacrifice
his parents boarded him at school in town,
slaving to free him from the stony fields,
the meagre acreage that bore them down.

They blushed with pride when, at his graduation,
they watched him picking up the slender scroll,
his passport from the years of brutal toil
and lonely patience in a barren hole.

When he went in the Bank their cups ran over.
They marvelled how he wore a milk-white shirt
work days and jeans on Sundays. He was saved
from their thistle-strewn farm and its red dirt.

And he said nothing. Hard and serious
like a young bear inside his teller's cage,
his axe-hewn hands upon the paper bills
aching with empty strength and throttled rage.

God Sour the Milk of the Knacking Wench

God sour the milk of the knacking wench
with razor and twine she comes
to stanchion our blond and bucking bull,
pluck out his lovely plumbs.

God shiver the prunes on her bark of chest,
who capons the prancing young.
Let maggots befoul her alive in bed,
and dibble thorns in her tongue.

For Nicholas of All the Russias

Wind in a rocky country and the harvest
meagre, the sparrows eaten, all the cattle
gone with the ragged troopers, winter coming,
mother will starve for love of you and wrapping
newest and least accustomed leave him squalling
out in the hills beside the skulls of foxes,
it cold and snow in the air. Stranger, kocking, (knocking)
(now in this latter time even the poor
have bread and sleep on straw) what silly rumour
tells me your eyes are yellow and your lips
once rose trout-quick to suck a she-wolf's teats?

Our Lord, his peaked heir and hawk-faced aughters (daughters)
are gone, although they say one severed finger
was found after the soldiers cleaned the cellar.

I, Icarus

There was a time when I could fly. I swear it.
Perhaps, if I think hard for a moment, I can even tell you
    the year.
My room was on the ground floor at the rear of the house.
My bed faced a window.
Night after night I lay on my bed and willed myself to fly.
It was hard work, I can tell you.
Sometimes I lay perfectly still for an hour before I felt
    my body rising from the bed.
I rose slowly, slowly until I floated three or four feet
    above the floor.
Then, with a kind of swimming motion, I propelled myself
    toward the window.
Outside, I rose higher and higher, above the pasture fence,
    above the clothesline, above the dark, haunted trees
    beyond the pasture.
And, all the time, I heard the music of flutes.
It seemed the wind made this music.
And sometimes there were voices singing.

And He Wept Aloud, So That the Egyptians Heard It

In my grandfather's house
for the first time in years,
houseflies big as bumblebees
playing crazy football
in the skim-milk-coloured windows,

leap-frogging from
the cracked butter saucer
to our tin plates of
rainbow trout and potatoes, catching the bread
on its way to our mouths,
    mounting one another
    on the rough deal table.

It was not so much their filth
as their numbers and persistence and—
oh, admit this, man, there's no point in poetry
if you withhold the truth
once you've come by it—
    their symbolism:
    Baal-Zebub,
god of the poor and outcast,

that enraged me, made me snatch the old man's
Family Herald, attack them like a maniac,
lay to left and right until the window sills
over-flowed with their smashed corpses,
until bits of their wings
stuck to my fingers,
until the room buzzed with their terror . . .

And my grandfather, bewildered and afraid,
came to help me:
    'never seen a year
    when the flies were so thick'
as though he'd seen them at all before I came!

His voice so old and baffled and pitiful
that I threw my club into the wood box and sat down
    and wanted to beg his forgiveness
as we ate on in silence broken only
by the almost inaudible humming
of the flies rebuilding their world.

Britain Street

Saint John, New Brunswick

This is a street at war.
The smallest children
battle with clubs
till the blood comes,
shout 'fuck you!'
like a rallying cry—

while mothers shriek
from doorsteps and windows
as though the very names
of their young were curses:

'Brian! Marlene!
Damn you! God damn you!'

or waddle into the street
to beat their own with switches:
'I'll teach you, Brian!
I'll teach you, God damn you!'

On this street,
even the dogs
would rather fight
than eat.

I have lived here nine months
and in all that time
have never once heard
a gentle word spoken.

I like to tell myself
that is only because
gentle words are whispered
and harsh words shouted.

In Those Old Wars

In those old wars
where generals wore yellow ringlets
and sucked lemons at their prayers,
other things being equal
the lost causes were the best.

Lee rode out of history
on his gray horse, Traveller,
so perfect a hero
had he not existed
it would have been necessary to invent him—
war stinks without gallantry.

An aide, one of the few who survived,
told him,
Country be damned, general,
for six months these men
have had no country but you.
They fought barefoot
and drank blueberryleaf tea.

The politicians
strung up Grant
like a carrot,
made him a Merovingian.
They stole everything,
even the coppers from Lincoln's dead eyes.

In those days, the vanquished
surrendered their swords like gentlemen,
the victors alone
surrendered their illusions.
The easiest thing to do for a Cause
is to die for it.

July 15

The wind is cool. Nothing is happening.
I do not strive for meaning. When I lie on my back
the wind passes over me, I do not feel it.
The sun has hands
like a woman, calling the heat
out of my body.
The trees sing. Nothing is happening.

When I close my eyes,
I hear the soft footsteps
of the grass. Nothing is happening.

How long have I lain here?
Well, it is still summer. But is it the same
summer I came?
I must remember
not to ask myself questions.
I am naked. Trees sing. The grass walks.
Nothing is happening.

The Mysterious Naked Man

A mysterious naked man has been reported
on Cranston Avenue. The police are performing
the usual ceremonies with coloured lights and sirens.
Almost everyone is outdoors and strangers are conversing
    excitedly
as they do during disasters when their involvement is
    peripheral.
'What did he look like?' the lieutenant is asking.
'I don't know,' says the witness. 'He was naked.'
There is talk of dogs—this is no ordinary case
of indecent exposure, the man has been seen

a dozen times since the milkman spotted him and now
the sky is turning purple and voices
carry a long way and the children
have gone a little crazy as they often do at dusk
and cars are arriving
from other sections of the city.
And the mysterious naked man
is kneeling behind a garbage can or lying on his belly
in somebody's garden
or maybe even hiding in the branches of a tree,
where the wind from the harbour
whips at his naked body,
and by now he's probably done
whatever it was he wanted to do
and he wishes he could go to sleep
or die
or take to the air like Superman.

Another Parting

Is this what it's like to be old?
To have endured so many partings
that this time I scarcely feel
the throat's tensing for the blow,
the sick pendulum in the belly,

feel only my pain
flowing into
an all-encompassing sadness

like the sound of that high plane,
full of people I don't know,
people I can hardly imagine,

breaking the silence
of this dark room
where I lie sleepless.

For Claudine Because I Love Her

Love is also
my finding this house
emptier than a stranger
ever could.

Is it the sound of your movements
enlivening the chairs
although I hear nothing, is it the weight
of your small body moving the house
so little no machine
could ever assess it,
though my mind knows,
is it some old
wholly animal instinct
that fills every room with you,
gently, so I am aware of it only

when I come home
and there is nothing here.

Ypres: 1915

The age of trumpets is passed, the banners hang
like dead crows, tattered and black,
rotting into nothingness on cathedral walls.
In the crypt of St Paul's I had all the wrong thoughts,
wondered if there was anything left of Nelson
or Wellington, and even wished
I could pry open their tombs and look,
then was ashamed
of such morbid childishness, and almost afraid.

I know the picture is as much a forgery
as the Protocols of Zion, yet it outdistances
more plausible fictions: newsreels, regimental histories,
biographies of Earl Haig.
                              It is always morning
and the sky somehow manages to be red
though the picture is in black and white.
There is a long road over flat country,
shell holes, the debris of houses,
a gun carriage overturned in a field,
the bodies of men and horses,
but only a few of them and those
always neat and distant.
                              The Moors are running
down the right side of the road.
The Moors are running
in their baggy pants and Santa Claus caps.
The Moors are running.
                              And their officers,
Frenchmen who remember
Alsace and Lorraine,
are running backwards in front of them,
waving their swords, trying to drive them back,
weeping
        at the dishonour of it all.
The Moors are running.

And on the left side of the same road,
the Canadians are marching
in the opposite direction.

The Canadians are marching
in English uniforms behind
a piper playing 'Scotland the Brave'.

The Canadians are marching
in impeccable formation,
every man in step.

The Canadians are marching.

And I know this belongs
with Lord Kitchener's mustache
and old movies in which the Kaiser and his general staff
seem to run like the Keystone Cops.

That old man on television last night,
a farmer or fisherman by the sound of him,
revisiting Vimy Ridge, and they asked him
what it was like, and he said,
There was water up to our middles, yes
and there was rats, and yes
there was water up to our middles
and rats, all right enough,
and to tell you the truth
after the first three or four days
I started to get a little disgusted.
Oh, I know they were mercenaries
in a war that hardly concerned us.
I know all that.

Sometimes I'm not even sure that I have a country.

But I know they stood there at Ypres
the first time the Germans used gas,
that they were almost the only troops
in that section of the front
who did not break and run,
who held the line.

Perhaps they were too scared to run.
Perhaps they didn't know any better
—that is possible, they were so innocent,
those farmboys and mechanics, you have only to look
at old pictures and see how they smiled.
Perhaps they were too shy
to walk out on anybody, even Death.
Perhaps their only motivation
was a stubborn disinclination.

Private MacNally thinking:
You squareheaded sons of bitches,
you want this God damn trench
you're going to have to take it away
from Billy MacNally
of the South End of Saint John, New Brunswick.

And that's ridiculous, too, and nothing
on which to found a country.
                                        Still
It makes me feel good, knowing
that in some obscure, conclusive way
they were connected with me
and me with them.

The First Stirring of the Beasts

The first stirring of the beasts
is heard at two or three or four
in the morning, depending on the season.

You lie, warm and drowsy, listening,
wondering how there is so much difference
between the sounds
cattle and horses make,
moving in their stanchions or halters,
so much difference that you can't explain,
so that if someone asked you
which of them is moving now?
you couldn't answer
but lying there, not quite awake,
you know, although it doesn't matter,
and then a rooster crows
and it sounds, or maybe you imagine this,

unsure and a little afraid,

                           and after a little
there are only the sounds of night
that we call silence.

The second stirring of the beasts
is the one everybody understands.
You hear it at dawn
and if you belong here
you get up.
Anyway, there is no mystery
in it, it is the other stirring,
the first brief restlessness
which seems to come for no reason
that makes you ask yourself
what are they awake for?

The Middle-Aged Man in the Supermarket

I'm pretending to test the avocadoes for ripeness
while gaping obliquely at the bare brown legs
of the girl in the orange skirt selecting mushrooms
when she says, 'Hi, there, let's make love.'
At first I think that she must have caught me
and is being sarcastic and then I decide
she's joking with someone she knows, perhaps the boy
         weighing green beans
or the young man with the watercress, so I try to act
as if I hadn't heard her, walk away at what I hope
is the right speed, without looking back,
and don't stop until I come to
the frozen-food bins, where I'm still standing,
gazing down at things I almost never buy, when
         I become aware
she's near me again, although I see only

a few square inches of brown thigh, a bit of
      orange cloth
and two symmetrical bare feet. I wish I could know
her body so well I could ever afterwards identify her
by taste alone. I rattle a carton
of frozen peas, read both French and English
      directions
on a package of frozen bread dough. She still
      stands there.
I wait for her to say to me:
'I fell in love the moment I saw you.
I want us to spend our first week together
in bed. We'll have our meals sent up. I'm even
      prettier
when I'm bare and I promise I'll keep my eyes shut
while you're naked, so that you'll never worry
that I might be comparing your body with that
of a previous lover, none of whom was older
than twenty, although the truth is I like
fat hips and big bellies—it's a kink
      that I have:
my nipples harden when I envision
those mountainous moons of flesh above me.'

The Broadcaster's Poem

I used to broadcast at night
alone in a radio station
but I was never good at it,
partly because my voice wasn't right
but mostly because my peculiar
metaphysical stupidity
made it impossible
for me to keep believing
there was somebody listening
when it seemed I was talking

only to myself in a room no bigger
than an ordinary bathroom.
I could believe it for a while
and then I'd get somewhat
the same feeling as when you
start to suspect you're the victim
of a practical joke.
                    So one part of me
was afraid another part
might blurt out something
about myself so terrible
that even I had never until
that moment suspected it.
                    This was like the fear
of bridges and other
high places: Will I take off my glasses
and throw them
into the water, although I'm
half-blind without them?
Will I sneak up behind
myself and push?
                    Another thing:
as a reporter
I covered an accident in which a train
ran into a car, killing
three young men, one of whom
was beheaded. The bodies looked
boneless, as such bodies do.
More like mounds of rags.
And inside the wreckage
where nobody could get at it
the car radio
was still playing.
                    I thought about places
the disc jockey's voice goes
and the things that happen there
and of how impossible it would be for him
to continue if he really knew.

Land and Sea

Old men repeat themselves.
In other words: speak songs.

Can't let the sea be,
the land can't.
                    Won't ever
leave her in peace.
                    Has to keep
troubling the waters,
the land does.
                    This from
Captain Thorburn Greenough
of Hall's Harbour who, in his prime,
could have sailed a bucket
through hell with his handkerchief,
they say.

The land won't let the sea be.

You'd of sailed under
canvas, you'd of knowed that.
Wouldn't of needed me
to tell you.
                    The shore!
We never felt safe
till we was out of her reach.

Margaret
Avison

Snow

Nobody stuffs the world in at your eyes.
The optic heart must venture: a jail-break
And re-creation. Sedges and wild rice
Chase rivery pewter. The astonished cinders quake
With rhizomes. All ways through the electric air
Trundle candy-bright disks; they are desolate
Toys if the soul's gates seal, and cannot bear,
Must shudder under, creation's unseen freight.
But soft, there is snow's legend: colour of mourning
Along the yellow Yangtze where the wheel
Spins an indifferent stasis that's death's warning.
Asters of tumbled quietness reveal
Their petals. Suffering this starry blur
The rest may ring your change, sad listener.

The World Still Needs

Frivolity is out of season.
Yet, in this poetry, let it be admitted
The world still needs piano-tuners
And has fewer, and more of these
Gray fellows prone to liquor
On an unlikely Tuesday, gritty with wind,
When somewhere, behind windows,
A housewife stays for him until the
    Hour of the uneasy bridge-club cocktails
    And the office rush at the groceteria
    And the vesper-bell and lit-up buses passing
    And the supper trays along the hospital corridor,
Suffering from
Sore throat and dusty curtains.

Not all alone on the deserted boathouse
Or even on the prairie freight

(The engineer leaned out, watchful and blank
And had no Christmas worries
Mainly because it was the eve of April),
Is like the moment
When the piano in the concert-hall
Finds texture absolute, a single solitude
For those hundreds in rows, half out of overcoats,
Their eyes swimming with sleep.

From this communal cramp of understanding
Springs up suburbia, where every man would build
A clapboard in a well of Russian forest
With yard enough for a high clothesline strung
To a small balcony . . .
A woman whose eyes shine like evening's star
Takes in the freshblown linen
While sky a lonely wash of pink is still
Reflected in brown mud
Where lettuces will grow, another spring.

New Year's Poem

The Christmas twigs crispen and needles rattle
Along the windowledge.
              A solitary pearl
Shed from the necklace spilled at last week's party
Lies in the suety, snow-luminous plainness
Of morning, on the windowledge beside them.
And all the furniture that circled stately
And hospitable when these rooms were brimmed
With perfumes, furs, and black-and-silver
Crisscross of seasonal conversation, lapses
Into its previous largeness.
              I remember
Anne's rose-sweet gravity, and the stiff grave

Where cold so little can contain;
I mark the queer delightful skull and crossbones
Starlings and sparrows left, taking the crust,
And the long loop of winter wind
Smoothing its arc from dark Arcturus down
To the bricked corner of the drifted courtyard,
And the still windowledge.
        Gentle and just pleasure
It is, being human, to have won from space
This unchill, habitable interior
Which mirrors quietly the light
Of the snow, and the new year.

To Professor X, Year Y

The square for civic receptions
Is jammed, static, black with people in topcoats
Although November
Is mean, and day grows late.

The newspapermen, who couldn't
Force their way home, after the council meeting
&c., move between windows and pressroom
In ugly humour. They do not know
What everybody is waiting for
At this hour
To stand massed and unmoving
When there should be—well—nothing to expect
Except the usual hubbub
Of city five o'clock.

Winter pigeons walk the cement ledges
Urbane, discriminating.

Down in the silent crowd few can see anything.

It is disgusting, this uniformity
Of stature.
If only someone climbed in pyramid
As circus families can . . .
Strictly, each knows
Downtown buildings block all view anyway
Except, to tease them,
Four narrow passages, and ah
One clear towards open water
(If 'clear'
Suits with the prune and mottled plumes of
Madam night).

Nobody gapes skyward
Although the notion of
Commerce by air is utterly
familiar.

Many citizens at this hour
Are of course miles away, under
Rumpus-room lamps, dining-room chandeliers,
Or bound elsewhere.
One girl who waits in a lit drugstore doorway
North 48 blocks for the next bus
Carries a history, an ethics, a Russian grammar,
And a pair of gym shoes.

But the few thousand inexplicably here
Generate funny currents, zigzag
Across the leaden miles, and all suburbia
Suffers, uneasily.

You, historian, looking back at us,
Do you think I'm not trying to be helpful?
If I fabricated cause-and-effect
You'd listen? I've been dead too long for fancies.
Ignore us, hunched in these dark streets
If in a minute now the explosive

Meaning fails to disperse us and provide resonance
Appropriate to your chronicle.

But if you do, I have a hunch
You've missed a portent.
('Twenty of six.' 'Snow?—I wouldn't wonder.')

The Swimmer's Moment

For everyone
The swimmer's moment at the whirlpool comes,
But many at that moment will not say
'This is the whirlpool, then.'
By their refusal they are saved
From the black pit, and also from contesting
The deadly rapids, and emerging in
The mysterious, and more ample, further waters.
And so their bland-blank faces turn and turn
Pale and forever on the rim of suction
They will not recognize.
Of those who dare the knowledge
Many are whirled into the ominous centre
That, gaping vertical, seals up
For them an eternal boon of privacy,
So that we turn away from their defeat
With a despair, not for their deaths, but for
Ourselves, who cannot penetrate their secret
Nor even guess at the anonymous breadth
Where one or two have won:
(The silver reaches of the estuary).

Voluptuaries and Others

That Eureka of Archimedes out of his bath
Is the kind of story that kills what it conveys;
Yet the banality is right for that story, since it is not a
    communicable one
But just a particular instance of
The kind of lighting up of the terrain
That leaves aside the whole terrain, really,
But signalizes, and compels, an advance in it.
Such an advance through a be-it-what-it-may but take-it-not
    quite-as-given locale:
Probably that is the core of being alive.
The speculation is not a concession
To limited imaginations. Neither is it
A constrained voiding of the quality of immanent death.
Such near values cannot be measured in values
Just because the measuring
Consists in that other kind of lighting up
That shows the terrain comprehended, as also its containing
    space,
And wipes out adjectives, and all shadows
        (or, perhaps, all but shadows).

The Russians made a movie of a dog's head
Kept alive by blood controlled by physics, chemistry, equip-
    ment, and
Russian women scientists in cotton gowns with writing tablets.
The heart lay on a slab midway in the apparatus
And went phluff, phluff.
Like the first kind of illumination, that successful experiment
Can not be assessed either as conquest or as defeat.
But it is living, creating the chasm of creation,
Contriving to cast only man to brood in it, further.

History makes the spontaneous jubilation at such moments
    less and less likely though,
And that story about Archimedes does get into public school
    textbooks.

Birth Day

Saturday I ran to Mitilene.

Bushes and grass along the grass-still way
Were all dabbled with rain
And the road reeled with shattered skies.

Towards noon an inky, petulant wind
Ravelled the pools, and rinsed the black grass round them.

Gulls were up in the late afternoon
And the air gleamed and billowed
And broadcast flung astringent spray
                              All swordy-silver.
I saw the hills lie brown and vast and passive.

The men of Mitilene waited restive
Until the yellow melt of sun.
I shouted out my news as I sped towards them
That all, rejoicing, could go down to dark.

All nests, with all moist downy young
Blinking and gulping daylight; and all lambs
Four-braced in straw, shivering and mild;
And the first blood-root up from the ravaged beaches
Of the old equinox; and frangible robins' blue
Teethed right around to sun:
These first we loudly hymned;
And then
The hour of genesis
When first the moody firmament
Swam out of Arctic chaos,
Orbed solidly as the huge frame for this
Cramped little swaddled creature's coming forth
To slowly, foolishly, marvellously
Discover a unique estate, held wrapt
Away from all men else, which to embrace

Our world would have to stretch and swell with strangeness.

This made us smile, and laugh at last. There was
Rejoicing all night long in Mitilene.

Pace

'Plump raindrops in these
faintly clicking groves,
the pedestrians' place, July's
violet and albumen
close?'

'No. No. It is perhaps the conversational side-effect
among the pigeons; behold
the path-dust is nutmeg powdered and
bird-foot embroidered.'

> The silk-fringed hideaway
> permits the beechnut-cracking
> squirrels to plumply
> pick and click and
> not listen.

Pedestrians linger
striped stippled sunfloating
at the rim of the
thin-wearing groves

letting the ear experience this
discrete, delicate
clicking.

Black-White Under Green:
May 18, 1965

This day of the leafing-out
speaks with blue power—
among the buttery grassblades
white, tiny-spraying spokes on the end of a weed-stem
and in the formal beds, tulips
and invisible birds inaudibly hallooing,
enormous, their beaks out wide, throats bulging, aflutter,
eyes weeping with speed
where the ultraviolets play and the scythe of the jets
flashes, carrying
the mind-wounded heartpale person, still a boy, a pianist, dying
       not
of the mind's wounds (as they read the x-rays) but
dying, fibres separated, parents ruddy and
American, strong, sheathed in the cold of
years of his differentness, clustered by two at
the nether arc of his flight.

This day of the leafing-out is one to remember
    how the ice crackled among
        stiff twigs. Glittering strongly
           the old trees sagged. Boughs
    abruptly unsocketed. Dry, orange gashes
the dawn's fine snowing discovered and powdered over.
. . . to remember the leaves ripped loose
the thudding of the dark sky-beams
and the pillared plunging sea
shelterless. Down the centuries
a flinching speck
    in the white fury found of itself—and another—
the rich blood spilling, mother to child, threading
the perilous combers, marbling
the surges, flung
out, and ten-fingered, feeling for
the lollop, the fine-wired
music, dying skyhigh

still between carpets and the
cabin-pressuring windows
on the day of the leafing.

Faces fanned by
rubberized, cool air
are opened; eyes wisely
smile.
The tulips, weeds, new leaves
neither smile nor are scorning to smile nor uncertain,
dwelling in light.
A flick of ice, fire, flood,
far off from
the day of the leafing-out I knew
when knee-wagon small, or from my
father's once at a horse-tail silk-shiny
fence-corner or this
day when the runways wait
white in the sun, and a new leaf is
metal, torn out of that blue
afloat in the dayshine.

July Man

Old, rain-wrinkled, time-soiled, city-wise, morning man
whose weeping is for the dust of the elm-flowers
and the hurting motes of time,
rotted with rotting grape,
sweet with the fumes,
puzzled for good by fermented potato-
peel out of the vat of the times,
turned out and left
in this grass-patch, this city-gardener's place
under the buzzing populace's
square shadows, and the green shadows

of elm and ginkgo and lime
(planted for Sunday strollers and summer evening
families, and for those
bird-cranks with bread-crumbs
and crumpled umbrellas who come
while the dew is wet on the park, and beauty
is fan-tailed, gray and dove gray, aslant, folding in
from the white fury of day).

In the sound of the fountain
you rest, at the cinder-rim, on your bench.

The rushing river of cars
makes you a stillness, a pivot, a heart-stopping
blurt, in the sorrow
of the last rubbydub swig, the searing, and
stone-jar solitude lost, and yet,
and still—wonder (for good now) and
trembling:

> The too much none of us knows
> is weight, sudden sunlight, falling
> on your hands and arms, in your lap,
> all, all, in time.

The Absorbed

The sun has not absorbed
this icy day, and this day's industry—in
behind glass—hasn't the blue and gold, cold
outside. Though not absorbing, this
sought that:

> sheeted, steely, vaulted,
> all gleam, this morning;

bright blue with one stained wing in the
        northeast, at lunch hour;
in early afternoon
abruptly a dust-flurry,
        all but this private coign of place
        deafened, all winding in one cloth of moth.
Then space breathed, hollowing twilight
        on ice and the pale-gray, pale-blue,
        and far fur-colored wooden trees
        and ornamental trees.

Towards sundown
a boy came with an aluminum toboggan.
He worked his way, absorbed,
past footmark pocks, on crust,
up ice-ridge, sometimes bumping
down to the Japanese yews, sometimes
scooter-shoving athwart the hill,
then, with a stake,
kneeling,
he paddles, thrusting, speed-wise, then
stabbing, uphill; then
dangling the rope and poring on
slope-sheen, standing, he stashes
the aluminum, upright, in a frost-lumpy shoal
and beside coasting motorcars and parked cars
listens . . . and off again, toque to the eyebrows,
alone still in the engulfing dark.

The inside breathing here
closes down all the window but a visor-slit
on the night glare.
                    New cold is
in dry-thorn nostrils.

Alone, he plays, still there. We
struggle, our animal fires
pitted against those
several grape-white stars,
their silence.

In a Season of Unemployment

These green painted park benches are
all new. The Park Commissioner had them
planted.
Sparrows go on
having dust baths at the edge of
the park maple's shadow, just where
the bench is cemented down, planted
and then cemented.

   Not a breath moves
   this newspaper.
   I'd rather read it by the Lapland sun at midnight. Here we're
   bricked in early by a
   stifling dark.

On that bench a man in a
pencil-striped white shirt
keeps his head up and steady.

   The newspaper-astronaut says
   'I feel excellent under the condition of weightlessness.'
And from his bench a
scatter of black bands in the hollow-air
ray out—too quick for the eye—
and cease.

   'Ground observers watching him on a TV circuit said
   At the time of this report he
   was smiling,' Moscow ra-
   dio reported.
I glance across at him, and mark that
he is feeling
excellent too, I guess, and
weightless and
'smiling'.

A Nameless One

Hot in June a narrow winged
long-elbowed-thread-legged
living insect lived
and died within
the lodgers' second-floor bathroom here.

At six a.m.
wafting ceilingward,
no breeze but what it living made there;

at noon standing
still as a constellation of spruce needles
before the moment of
making it, whirling;

at four a
wilted flotsam, cornsilk, on the linoleum:
now that it is
over, I
look with new eyes
upon this room
adequate for one to
be, in.

Its insect-day
has threaded a needle
for me for my eyes dimming
over rips and tears and
thin places.

Eli Mandel

A Castle and Two Inhabitants

I

The several stories of the castle,
Placed rickety like box on box
Or like those Chinese puzzles
That are whole outside but inside
Piece in piece, were carpentered
A while ago. The builder is inside.
We think he must be, for we never
Saw him leave it, nor indeed go in.

It simply stands there, stands,
Though how it stands no one explains,
Nor how to go from room to room,
Nor why the king has chosen it
Upon a dreadful plane of space
To live in, there to hold his court.

II

There is a hunchback in the court
Who loves his daughter and who serves
The king with stories of a hunchback love
The crooked ways are best, he says,
The only way a cripple learns to move,
And love is crooked and the twist is this:
My hunchback proves it.

                        Like the sun at noon
Hunched over earth that splendid hump
Curls round his body, like a swollen pear
Hung from a leafless tree, like the earth
On Atlas as he sways beneath its load.
He lumps it in our faces and he leers
About our daughters and he loves his own
And monthly serves the king a wreath,
The queen's own hair upon a horn.

III

There is a wizard also in our court
Who is both man and woman and who knows
How women love, who says the hunchback
Lied to us. Love is triangular, he cries,
And shining algebras fall from his cap
Made out of crystals shivered from a frost
Of passion.
                    Sculpt from a crust of sky
An ice-cold man is propped on snowy stalks
Of dogma, double-eyed with embered coals.

Here generation ends. This simple love,
The wizard says, endures the rollick
Lust and summer of a hunchback sun.

Acis

There was her message. Suddenly
His blood had turned to water.
She looked into his eyes and saw
They swam, no shore behind them,
Looking toward the green and lighted sea,
A fish-like stare, a dolphin memory.

Pillar of Fire

A man came to my tent door
in the heat of the day, the tent
stretched and slapped in the wind.
All the guy ropes went taut
And I felt my temples stretch
and throb in the noise and heat.

He talked about blowflies,
plague among the swollen cattle.
He asked about the children.
'You are a great nation.
Will you stay here long?'

That night the fire in the tent
vomited a great smoke.
The tent glowed like a furnace.
I dreamt about Egypt and its flies,
a priest dying of cancer.
I am told to breed more children,
try not to think about politics,
remember the Sabbath and my enemies.

Thief Hanging in Baptist Halls

After a Sculpture by George Wallace

Amid the congratulations of summer,
polite vegetation, deans, a presbyterian sun,
brick minds quaintly shaped in gothic and glass,
here where the poise and thrust of speech
gleams like polished teak
I did not expect to see myself.

But there he hangs
shrugging on his hung lines,
soft as a pulped fruit or bird
in his welded soft suit of steel.

I wish he would not shrug
and smile weakly at me
as if ashamed that he is hanging there,
his dean's suit fallen off, his leg cocked
as if to run
or (too weak, too tired, too undone)
to do what can be done
about his nakedness.

Why should he hang there,
my insulting self, my deanship, all undone?

He dangles while the city bursts in green and steel,
black flower in the mouth of my speech:
the proud halls reel,
gothic and steel melt in the spinning sun.

The Meaning of the I CHING

I

unopened
            book of old men
            orange-blossom book
                                before me
you were
            how could you contain me?

do you not see I am the mouths
of telegraphs and cemeteries?
my mother groaned like the whole

of Western Union to deliver
my message
                    and yelling birthdays
that unrolled from my lungs
like ticker-tape for presidents
about to be murdered
                              I sped
on a line that flew
to the vanishing point of the west

before I was
                  you were
unopened book
                    do not craze me
with the odour of orange-blossom

do not sit there
like smiling old men

          how could you contain me?

II

under my fingers words form themselves
it's crazy to talk of temples in this day
but light brightens on my page
like today moving against the wooden house
all shapes change and yet stay
as if they were marble in autumn
as if in the marbled yellow autumn
each western house becomes a shrine
stiff against the age of days
under my fingers stiffly formed

one cannot be another, I cry,
let me not be crazed by poetry

I will walk in streets that vanish
noting peculiar elms like old women

who will crash under the storm of sun
that breaks elm, woman, man
into a crumble of stump and bark
until the air is once more clear
in the sane emptiness of fall

III

my body speaks to me
as my arms say: two are one
as my feet say: earth upon earth
as my knees say: bow down, unhinge yourself
as my cells say: we repeat the unrepeatable

the book speaks: arrange yourself in the form
                that will arrange you

before I was: colours that hurt me
                arranged themselves in me

before I was: horizons that blind me
                arranged themselves in me

before I was: the dead who speak to me
                arranged themselves in me

IV

I am the mouths
of smiling old men

there rises from me
the scent of orange-blossoms

I speak in the words
of the ancient dead

arranged
in the raging sun

in the stiffening age of days

and in the temple of my house

one becomes another
I am crazed by poetry

Houdini

I suspect he knew that trunks are metaphors,
could distinguish between the finest rhythms
unrolled on rope or singing in a chain
and knew the metrics of the deepest pools

I think of him listening to the words
spoken by manacles, cells, handcuffs,
chests, hampers, roll-top desks, vaults,
especially the deep words spoken by coffins

escape, escape: quaint Harry in his suit
his chains, his desk, attached to all attachments
how he'd sweat in that precise struggle
with those binding words, wrapped around him
like that mannered style, his formal suit

and spoken when? by whom? What think first said
'there's no way out'?; so that he'd free himself,
leap, squirm, no matter how, to chain himself again,
once more jump out of the deep alive
with all his chains singing around his feet
like the bound crowds who sigh, who sigh.

Pictures in an Institution

I

Notice: all mirrors will be covered
the mailman is forbidden to speak
professors are confined to their offices
faculties no longer exist.

II

I speak of what I know,
how uncle Asher, spittle on his lips,
first typed with harvest hands the fox
across a fence and showing all good men
come to their country's aid rushed off to Israel
there to brutalize his wife and son

how step-grandfather Barak wiped
sour curds out of his curly beard
before he roared the Sabbath in my ears
what Sara, long his widow, dreamed
the night she cried: God, let him die at last,
thinking perhaps of Josef who had lost
jewels in Russia where the Cossack rode
but coughed his stomach out in Winnipeg

Your boredom does not matter. I take,
brutal to my thoughts, these lives, defy
your taste in metaphor; the wind-break
on the farm that Barak plowed to dust
makes images would ruin public poetry.

The rites of love I knew:
how father cheated brother, uncle, son,
and bankrupt-grocer, that we might eat
wrote doggerel verse, later took his wife,
my mother, in the English way beside my bed.
Why would he put his Jewishness aside?

Because there was no bread?
                              Or out of spite
that doctors sliced his double rupture,
fingered spleen, and healed his bowel's ache?

Lovers lie down in glades, are glad.
These, now in graves, their headstones sunk,
knew nothing of such marvels, only God, his ways,
owning no texts of Greek or anthropology.

III

Notice: the library is closed to all who read
         any student carrying a gun
         registers first, exempt from fines,
         is given thirteen books per month,
         one course in science, one in math,
         two options
                      campus police
         will see to co-eds' underwear

IV

These names I rehearse:
                        Eva, Isaac,
Charley, Yetta, Max
                     now dead
or dying or beyond my lies

till I reeling with messages
and sick to hold again their bitter lives
put them, with shame, into my poetry.

V

Notice: there will be no further communication
   lectures are cancelled
   all students are expelled
   the reading of poetry is declared a public
             crime

Woodbine

When a crooked man meets beauty
You think there'd be shouting in the streets

I wish there were no allegories
I wish the doctors could do something about my forked tongue

Believe me, I have gone about with pails on my head
so that my friends would recognize me.

Lord, Lord, pollution everywhere
But I breathe still
     and breathless, sweet
woodbine, colour of honey, touches my skin
as if my unbelieving eyes made no difference at all

The Speaking Earth

grandfathers fall into it
their mighty beards muffled in grass

and admirals, the sea-sounding men

lovers fall into the earth
like rain on wet dark bodies

listen, our lady earth flowers
into the sea-green language
of grass and drowned admirals

listen: in bearded branches
clasped like broken hands
admiring birds
lovers singing of their kiss
before and after all the words

From the North Saskatchewan

when on the high bluff discovering
the river cuts below
                              send messages
we have spoken to those on the boats

I am obsessed by the berries they eat
all night odour of Saskatoon
and an unidentifiable odour
something baking
                              the sun
never reaches the lower bank

I cannot read the tree markings

today the sky is torn by wind:
a field after a long battle
strewn with corpses of cloud

give blessings to my children
speak for us to those who sent us here
say we did all that could be done
we have not learned
what lies north of the river
or past those hills that look like beasts

Marina

Because she spoke often of the sea we thought she had known
    another country, her people distant, not forgotten

We did not know then who was calling her or what songs she
    listened to or why the sea-birds came to rest
    upon her long fingers

Or why she would shudder like a sea-bird about to take flight,
    her eyes changing with the changing light

As the sea-changing opal changes, as a shell takes its
    colours from the sea as if it were the sea

As if the great sea itself were held in the palm of a hand

They say the daughters of the sea know the language of birds,
    that in their restless eyes the most fortunate learn
    how the moon rises and sets

We do not know who is calling her or why her eyes change
    or what shore she will set her foot upon

On the 25th Anniversary of the Liberation of Auschwitz: Memorial Services, Toronto, YMHA, Bloor & Spadina, January 25, 1970

the name is hard
a German sound made out of
the gut guttural throat
y scream yell   ing   open
voice mouth growl
                    and sweat

'the only way out of Auschwitz
is through the chimneys'
                              of course
that's second hand   that's told
again   Sigmund   Sherwood   (Sobolewski)
twisting himself into that sentence
before us on the platform

                              the poem
shaping itself late in the after
noon later than it would be:

Pendericki's 'Wrath of God'
moaning electronic Polish theatric
the screen silent
                    framed by the name
looking away from/pretending not there
no   name   no not   name   no

           Auschwitz
         in   GOTHIC   lettering
                         the hall
a parody a reminiscence a nasty memory
the Orpheum in Estevan before Buck Jones
the Capital in Regina before Tom Mix
waiting for the guns
waiting for the cowboy killers
one two three
              Legionnaires
Polish ex-prisoners Association
Legions
         their medals their flags

so the procession, the poem gradually
insistent beginning to shape itself
with the others
              walked with them
into the YMHA Bloor & Spadina
thinking apocalypse shame degradation

thinking bones and bodies melting
thickening thinning melting bones and bodies
thinking not mine/speak clearly
the poet's words/Yevtyshenko at Baba-Yar

there   this January   snow
heavy wet   the wind   heavy wet
the street grey white slush melted concrete
bones and bodies melting slush
                              saw
with the others
                  the prisoner
in the YMHA hall Bloor & Spadina
arms wax stiff body stiff unnatural
coloured face blank eyes
                          walked
with the others toward the screen
toward the pictures
                        SLIDES
        this is mother
        this is father
        this is
                  the one who is
waving her arms like that
is the one who
                  like
I mean running with her breasts bound
ing
    running
                with her hands here and there
with her here and
                      there
hands
      that   that is

the poem becoming the body
becoming the faint hunger
ing body
            prowling

        through
words the words words the words
opening   mouths   ovens
the generals smiling saluting
in their mythic uniforms god-like
generals uniforms with the black leather
with the straps and intricate leather
the phylacteries the prayer shawl
corsets and the boots and the leather straps
and the shining faces of the generals in their boots
and their stiff wax bodies their unnatural faces
and their blank eyes and their hands their stiff hands
and the generals in their straps and wax and stiff
staying standing
          melting bodies and thickening
          quick flesh on flesh handling
          hands

   the poem flickers, fades
the four Yarzeit candles guttering   one
   each four million lights dim
my words drift
         smoke from chimneys and ovens
   a bad picture, the power failing
   pianist clattering on and over and through
the long Saturday afternoon in the Orpheum
   while the whitehatted star spangled cowboys
     shot the dark men and shot the dark men
     and we threw popcorn balls and grabbed
   each other and cheered:
        me jewboy yelling
for the shot town and the falling men
   and the lights come on
        and
   with the others
standing in silence

   the gothic word hangs
   over us on a shroud-white screen

and we drift away
                to ourselves
                    to the late Sunday *Times*

                        the wet snow
                        the city

                        a body melting

Two Dream Songs for John Berryman

I

Henry, it says to me here
you took yourself to a bridge.
And you, weary and wavery,
walked, bone and brain, all
to the rail
                there perched
waved farewell from rail

Is that how it was done?

Is it only possible to live
how we have done backwards
dreaming our way from death to
bony life?
                Well, it was gaily
done
        but, here on the coast of Spain,
heartsick like you
                        and hurt too
by burning poems that will not write
themselves I
                say
now fare-you-well
with Sylvia, Ted, Randall,

and all your hurt friends,

God notwithstanding

II

It is done but not done well
Henry   to betake yourself to ice
and death in a Minnesota morning

or a bruise
throwing yourself from bridge
to ice
        why would you want so
to say to me or to God once more
that nothing is fair
among fair women and hardy men

to God
        who never once cared
now name him as you will

it's both night and day
not done well to you or anyone
less or better
                not well

Agatha Christie

being civil she saw poison
as a flaw in character
and the use of a knife
a case history in Freud

difficult to explain
her dislike of jews

or why night upon night
she plotted solutions
to deaths she must have dreamed

her 200,000,000 readers
how much longing for murder
the neatness of England
is and still remains

though in Belfast, say,
bombs have other reasons
and no one explains

On the Death of Ho Chi Minh

toward the end
he became frail as rice paper
his beard whispering thin ideograms

how unlike the great carved storm
that was Marx's face
                          how unlike
the darkness and fury
in Beethoven's head
                          scarcely
anything to be consumed

bombs destroy   destroy
you cannot touch his body now
or burn his poems

Gwendolyn MacEwen

Poems in Braille

I

all your hands are verbs,
now you touch worlds and feel their names—
thru the thing to the name
not the other way thru (in winter
I am Midas, I name gold)

the chair and table and book
extend from your fingers;
all your movements
command these things back to their
places; a fight against familiarity
makes me resume my distance

II

they knew what it meant,
those egyptian scribes who drew
eyes right into their hieroglyphs,
you read them dispassionate until
the eye stumbles upon itself
blinking back from the papyrus

outside, the articulate wind
annotates this; I read carefully
lest I go blind in both eyes, reading with
that other eye the final hieroglyph

III

the shortest distance between 2 points
on a revolving circumference
is a curved line; O let me follow you,
Wenceslas

IV

with legs and arms I make alphabets
like in those children's books
where people bend into letters and signs,
yet I do not read the long cabbala of my bones
truthfully; I need only to move
to alter the design

V

I name all things in my room
and they rehearse their names,
gather in groups, form tesseracts,
discussing their names among themselves

I will not say the cast is less than the print
I will not say the curve is longer than the line,
I should read all things like braille in this season
with my fingers I should read them
lest I go blind in both eyes reading with
that other eye the final hieroglyph

You Cannot Do This

You cannot do this to them, these are my people;
I am not speaking of poetry, I am not speaking of art.
you cannot do this to them, these are my people.
you cannot hack away the horizon in front of their eyes.

the tomb, articulate, will record your doing,
I will record it also, this is not art,
this is a kind of science, a kind of hobby,
a kind of personal vice like coin collecting.

it has something to do with horses
and signet rings and school trophies,
it has something to do with the pride of the lions,
it has something to do with good food and music,
and something to do with power, and dancing.
you cannot do this to them, these are my people.

Green With Sleep

Green with sleep the skin breathes night
—I hear you turning worlds in your dark dream—
The sheets like leaves in a private season
Speak of the singular self which lies between.

Your breathing is a thing I cannot enter
Like a season more remote than winter;
Green with sleep breathes, breathes the skin,
I hear you turning worlds in your dark dream.

There is a great unspeakable wheel which keeps
Us slender as myths, and green with sleep.

Manzini: Escape Artist

now there are no bonds except the flesh; listen—
there was this boy, Manzini, stubborn with
gut stood with black tights and a turquoise
leaf across his sex

and smirking while the big
brute tied his neck arms legs, Manzini
naked waist up and white with sweat

struggled. Silent, delinquent, he
was suddenly all teeth and knee, straining slack
and excellent with sweat, inwardly

wondering if Houdini would take as long
as he; fighting time and the drenched
muscular ropes, as though his tendons were worn
on the outside—

as though his own guts were the ropes
encircling him; it was beautiful; it was thursday; listen—
there was this boy, Manzini

finally free, slid as snake from
his own sweet agonized skin, to throw his entrails
white upon the floor
with a cry of victory—

now there are no bonds except the flesh,
but listen, it was thursday, there was this boy,
Manzini—

Arcanum One

and in the morning the king loved you most
and wrote your name with a sun and a beetle
and a crooked ankh, and in the morning
you wore gold mainly, and the king adorned you
with many more names

beside fountains, both of you slender
as women, circled and walked together
like bracelets circling water, both of you
slender as women, wrote your names with
beetles and with suns, and spoke together
in the golden mornings

and the king entered your body
into the bracelet of his name
and you became a living syllable
in his golden script, and your body
escaped from me like founting water
all the daylong

but in the evenings you wrote my name
with a beetle and a moon, and lay upon me
like a long broken necklace which had fallen
from my throat, and the king loved you
most in the morning, and his glamorous love
lay lengthwise along us all the evening

Poem Improvised Around a First Line*

the smoke in my bedroom which is always burning
worsens you, motorcycle Icarus;
you are black and leathery and lean and
you cannot distinguish between sex and nicotine

anytime, it's all one thing for you-
cigarette, phallus, sacrificial fire-
all part of that grimy flight
on wings axlegreased from Toronto to Buffalo
for the secret beer over the border-

now I long to see you fullblown and black
over Niagara, your bike burning and in full flame
and twisting and pivoting over Niagara
and falling finally into Niagara,
and tourists coming to see your black leather wings
hiss and swirl in the steaming current-

now I long to give up cigarettes

*The first line around which it was improvised has disappeared.

and change the sheets on my carboniferous bed;
O baby, what Hell to be Greek in this country-
without wings, but burning anyway

The Red Bird You Wait For

You are waiting for someone to confirm it,
You are waiting for someone to say it plain,
Now we are here and because we are short of time
I will say it; I might even speak its name.

It is moving above me, it is burning my heart out,
I have felt it crash through my flesh,
I have spoken to it in a foreign tongue,
I have stroked its neck in the night like a wish.

Its name is the name you have buried in your blood,
Its shape is a gorgeous cast-off velvet cape,
Its eyes are the eyes of your most forbidden lover
And its claws, I tell you its claws are gloved in fire.

You are waiting to hear its name spoken,
You have asked me a thousand times to speak it,
You who have hidden it, cast it off, killed it,
Loved it to death and sung your songs over it.

The red bird you wait for falls with giant wings—
A velvet cape whose royal colour calls us kings
Is the form it takes as, uninvited, it descends,
It is the Power and the Glory forever, Amen.

The Discovery

do not imagine that the exploration
ends, that she has yielded all her mystery
or that the map you hold
cancels further discovery

I tell you her uncovering takes years,
takes centuries, and when you find her naked
look again,
admit there is something else you cannot name,
a veil, a coating just above the flesh
which you cannot remove by your mere wish

when you see the land naked, look again
(burn your maps, that is not what I mean),
I mean the moment when it seems most plain
is the moment when you must begin again

Inside the Great Pyramid

all day the narrow shaft
received us; everyone
came out sweating and
gasping for air, and one
old man collapsed
upon a stair;
                    I thought:
the fact that it has stood
so long
is no guarantee
it will stand today,
but went in anyway
and heard when I was
halfway up a long
low rumbling like

the echo of ancient stones
first straining to their place;
                    I thought:
we have made this, we
have made *this*.
I scrambled out into
the scandalous sun and saw
the desert was an hourglass
we had forgotten to invert,
a tasselled camel falling
to his knees, the River
filling the great waterclock
of earth.

Cairo, 1966

One Arab Flute

I

I was innocent as a postcard
among the dark robes and bazaars;
my exiled smile shone under
the stern judicial sun;
                    I drank Turkish coffee
                    in the divided city
with a singular lack of irony
over the sunken tomb of Herod's family
with lovenotes scribbled on the wall
                    (O really, this was also
                    a British bombshelter? Well
                    well . . .)
and saw the tomb of Akiva
who was stripped by the iron
combs of Rome, and Maimonides'
cold white cone with candles
at the bottom and the top,

and a place called Lifta
where the mouths of houses ate
the sunset, a blue-eyed Arab
with a wild profile, standing
in front of blond stone, the
blue-eyed sky over Jerusalem,
    an old artist Ephraim
    with platefuls of grapes
    and large gaudy studio
in Safed, who was very angry
and painted noisily daily and nightly
on the mystic hills,
    a Maccabean tomb for a man
    called Yason, carved
    with caramel deers.
And my camera eye,
the curious film, the tourist
lens, followed
the old stones skyward.

II

The kites, the coloured kites of Jaffa
were insolent in the sky;
    an old dead sweet smell
    and the peacock sea
    upheld them
and the parachute sun became
a pavilion and a distant throne;
I walked through pink tiles,
difficult shells, sandstone,
    and everyone asked the time
    on the beach at Jaffa
but the walls had gone down,
the walls of Jaffa,
and I saw the sea
through many naked doors;
    the kites like signals
    pointed sideways skyward

and Arab children screamed to find
bleached fish skulls like
a thousand heads of Jonah
on the shore.

III

Now through a park of palms and cocks
I come to Capernaum, reading a pamphlet
that lists Christ's miracles
like adventure serials; I pray
to the pillars standing sad
as dolmens: Hold
  the sky up forever, Amen.

Now through a park of palms and cocks
I come to Kefer-Nahum; the priest
draws a crucifix through the sweat
on my brow, and hands me
  a small grey skirt
to remind my naked western knees
that this place is holy, and I
dissolve into the scenery.

IV

Kids skip rope behind the Roman arch
in Ein Karem where the light
is graded on the terraced hills;
  there are many cats and flowers,
  bells,
and a small girl carries a loaf
of bread that reaches to her knees
and all the children come and gaze
into my camera
though some are afraid to come
too near. Behind them there's a sign
which reads: *John the Baptist*

was born here. I seem to see
in a small boy's face
a look that says:

> he who will come after me
> will bless this time, this

place.

V

The workers at Ramat Rachel
have eyes at their fingernails
and they scratch dynasties from stone;

> no one can tell them

that what they find in the itchy dirt
is more than the day's few *lira*

> (ruins of Judah's kings,
> mosaic floors)

for they *are* history, while we,
the disinherited, search here,

> scramble like the lizards

in the Byzantine church nearby,
scratch little marks all over
the holy floors, seeking
our reward.

VI

To reach Jerusalem you ride
through ribs of dead jeeps
and rusted wreaths of war
that line the road;

> you realize the City
> lives

because it was destroyed.
You sit by night close to
the barbed wire border; only
cats and spiders can pass; even

> the moon is divided here.

From Notre Dame the smashed
faces of Mary and Jesus
watch you with ugly irony;
        David's tower
is a conical hat in the moonlight;
the Mosque of Omar
has been there forever.
If I forget you, O Jerusalem,
may my right hand
build another.

VII

Noman's land is Gehenna
and leading from it the chalkwhite
salt of bleached houses, white-
faced, wide-eyed towns;
        children play
near Gehenna and they
are only playing, but I keep hearing
tofet drums beaten to dull
their screaming
        as when, on the yellow grass
        under
        the awful shadow of Gehenna
they lay outstretched upon
the hands of Moloch
beneath his mouth of fire
and waited for the sacred knife
to spill their sweet blood over.

VIII

In Rehov Yafo
in the New Jerusalem
an Iraqui beggar I call John
        avoids curious eyes,
        watches the ground.

I see him wave away
the coins of pitying women
without even looking; the
dirty *piastres* stuffed in his fist
are enough for the day. How
solemnly he protests his station,
how
  violently he turns on them
  sometimes, cursing, his eyes
on fire; the old
American-styled suit he wears
hangs from him like a prayer.

IX

'What we must do,'
the man told me,
'Is keep them together.
That way
they are not dangerous.'
  But I have seen
  trees that grow sideways
in Esdraelon, fighting gravity;
their bark is strong
and corded with patience
and their leaves rush upwards
in incongruous dance.
  And I have seen
  bright coins worn
on foreheads, as though they told
the value of the skull
  (fill in quickly
  the arab arch, jam it
  with stones, or make
  the roundness square;
  step
  lightly through
  the eastern music)

And this—
one young Bedouin boy leading sheep
at sundown past Beersheba,
and the flute he played
was anarchy between his fingers;
I saw the poor grass move
its tender blades, I
heard the wind awakening
the desert from its sleep.

Israel 1962

Dark Pines Under Water

This land like a mirror turns you inward
And you become a forest in a furtive lake;
The dark pines of your mind reach downward,
You dream in the green of your time,
Your memory is a row of sinking pines.

Explorer, you tell yourself this is not what you came for
Although it is good here, and green;
You had meant to move with a kind of largeness,
You had planned a heavy grace, an anguished dream.

But the dark pines of your mind dip deeper
And you are sinking, sinking, sleeper
In an elementary world;
There is something down there and you want it told.

Memoirs of a Mad Cook

There's no point kidding myself any longer,
I just can't get the knack of it; I suspect
there's a secret society which meets
in dark cafeterias to pass on the art
from one member to another.
Besides,
it's so *personal* preparing food for someone's
insides, what can I possibly *know*
about someone's insides, how can I presume
to invade your blood?
I'll try, God knows I'll try
but if anyone watches me I'll *scream*
because maybe I'm handling a tomato wrong
how can I *know* if I'm handling a tomato wrong?

something is eating away at me
with splendid teeth

Wistfully I stand in my difficult kitchen
and imagine the fantastic salads and soufflés
that will never be.
Everyone seems to grow thin with me
and their eyes grow black as hunters' eyes
and search my face for sustenance.
All my friends are dying of hunger,
there is some basic dish I cannot offer,
and you my love are almost as lean
as the splendid wolf I must keep always
at my door.

The Child Dancing

there's no way I'm going to write about
the child dancing in the Warsaw ghetto
in his body of rags

there were only two corpses
on the pavement that day
and the child I will not write about
had a face as pale and trusting
as the moon

(so did
the boy with a green belly full of dirt
lying by the roadside
in a novel of Kazantzakis
and the small girl T. E. Lawrence wrote about
who they found after the Turkish massacre
with one shoulder chopped off, crying:
'don't *hurt* me, Baba!')

I don't feel like slandering them with poetry.

the child who danced
in the Warsaw ghetto
to some music no one else could hear
had moon-eyes, no
green horror and no fear
but something worse

a simple desire to please
the people who stayed
to watch him shuffle back and forth,
his feet wrapped in the newspapers
of another ordinary day

The Film

I think I must have been with you
in all the movie-houses of the world,
or else you perform
in the dark theatres of my blood
parts you never meant to play;
    did you watch too long
those Universal spectacles
of wars where nobody ever dies,
of monstrous lovers who kiss forever
    down the corridors
of Time?
The fervent curtains fall apart
and the silver screen is skin.

I think the walls of the place you live in
whisper names and legends in the night,
and wispy film unwinds, unwinds
in some unseen projector run
by a cruel Technician who merely wants
    to drive you blind
and send his Cast of Thousands
clanging through your sleep.

I think that when you raise your hand
against those walls
your flesh becomes a screen,
    the drama unfolds
along your fingers
and across your open palms the armies run
and down your veins their false blood falls;
    I want to tell you—
Look this is the kind of war nobody needs.
But now the images have claimed your face,
    you are alive with lies and legends,
the silver reel unravels in your skull,
the dark film roars forever down your blood.

The Arrival

Having come slowly, hesitantly
at first, as a poem comes,
and then steadily down to the marshy sea-board—

that day I ran along a stone sea-break,
plunging into the Pacific, the sun
just setting, clothed, exuberant, hot,
so happy—
                    o sing!
plunging into the ocean, rolled on my back, eyes
full of salt water, hair in eyes,
shoes lost forever at the bottom, noting
as if they were trivia
the wheeling birds of the air
and gulls gorging themselves
on the sea-going garbage
of civilization, the lower mainland,
hauled away by tugs—
                    the gulls,
being too heavy to fly,
and foolish-looking there,
can be knocked off with sticks
from barge into ocean—

and noting the trees whitely flowering,
took off my clothes and calmly bathed.

Then, If I Cease Desiring

Then, if I cease desiring,
you may sing a song
of how young I was.

You may praise famous moments,
all have them, of the churches
I broke into for wine,

not praise, the highways
I travelled drunkenly
in winter, the cars I stole.

You may allow me moments,
not monuments, I being
content. It is little,
but it is little enough.

The Flowers

It is raining outside, rain
streaks down the window to my left,
cars sluice water in the gutters
in the night, the round
neon clock-containing sign
hanging outside beside my window
sways in the wind and buzzes.

The flowers sprout everywhere;
in pots and boxes, on lawns
and trees, in gardens and ditches,
the flowers are growing; the wet
wind will nourish them, cut
some down but feed the rest.

The sign crackles
and swings on its bar,
iron bar; the cars go by
all the night. They cut
a momentary trail and mark,

disappearing, on the wet
black pavement. The cars go by,
the police in their cars
prowl restlessly
up and down the rainy avenue,
looking for interlopers, anyone
afoot at night in the rain,
the blue and dangerous
gun-hipped cops.

The car came smashing
and wrecking his face, his head,
poor hit hurt head
bleeding on the roadway
and in the cool hospital
night in bandages
and glued-on tape.

His eyes, they said,
were soft and easy
years ago. Now,
he wears them cleverly
like some secret
coupled badge,
twin and original, dark
ice eyes that watch and assess
slowly what they have
fixed
on; his head does not move.

In the hospitals,
with antiseptic nurses
stripping him, knife-
fisted surgeons bending down,
they cut, irony,
to save his life; and he stayed
days and years filled
with tantalizing drugs, interminable
dreams, tangled in bandages and

shocks, suspicions, a nonchalant
profusion of hopes and cures,
surrounded by the tears
of his rainy crazy peers.

Rain, wind, and spring, all things
drove him crazy and grow
flowers, flowers
that dance in the rain,
the bulging flowers that grew
in his head, plants
of devil or of god, some
holy epileptic angel, bloated
inhuman flowers shining
their bright colours
insistently, turning
slowly in the wind
and spring, tortuous
creaking growths, thick
cancerous things
in the rain, stems
like the barrels of rifles,
fat lead bullet roots
gripping the damp earth.

And the cars
pass up and down
the streets, disappearing
trails, the blue police
pass, coughing delicately
behind their leathery fists,
guns dangling
from their hips, eyes
watching. My flowery clock
buzzes and mutters,
typewriter taps
like the rain. I breathe
as harshly as the wind.

Verigin, Moving in Alone,

(fatherless, 250 people,
counting dogs and gophers
we would say, Jmaeff's grocerystore,
me in grade 4, mother
principal of the 2-building,
3-room, 12-grade school,)

a boy sitting on the grass
of a small hill, the hot fall,
speaking no russian, an airgun
my sister gave me making me envied.

I tried all fall, all spring
the next ominous year, to kill
a crowd with it, secretly glad
I could not, the men
in winter shooting the town's
wild dogs, casually tossing
the quick-frozen barely-bleeding
head-shot corpses onto
the street-side snowbanks,

the highway crews cutting their way
through to open the road with what
I was sure was simply
some alternate of a golden summer's
wheat-threshing machine, children
running through the hard-tossed spray,
pretending war from the monster's snout,

leaping into snowbanks from
Peter The Lordly Verigin's
palace on the edge of town
in a wild 3-dimensional
cubistic game of cops and robbers,

cold spring swimming

in Dead Horse Creek and farmers'
dugouts and doomed fishing
in beastless ponds, strapped
in school for watching a fight,

coldly holding back tears
and digging for drunken father's
rum-bottle, he had finally
arrived, how I loved him,
loved him, love him, dead, still.

My mad old brother chased me
alone in the house with him
around and around
the small living room, airgun,
rifle in hand, silently,
our breaths coming together—

all sights and temperatures
and remembrances,
as a lost gull screams now
outside my window,
a 9-year-old's year-long
night and day in tiny
magnificent prairie Verigin:

the long grey cat we got,
the bruised knees, cut fingers,
nails in feet, far walks
to watch a horse's corpse
turn slowly and sweetly to bone,
white bone, and in the late spring,
too, I remember the bright
young bodies of the boys,

my friends and peers and enemies,
till everything breaks down.

Crazy Riel

Time to write a poem
or something.
Fill up a page.
The creature noise.
Huge massed forces of men
hating each other.
What young men do not know.
To keep quiet,
contemporaneously.
Contempt. The robin diligently
on the lawn sucks up the worms,
hopping from one to another.
Youthfully. Sixteen miles
from my boyhood home
the frogs sit in the grassy marsh
that looks like a golf course
by the lake. Green frogs.
Boys catch them for bait or sale.
Or caught them. Time.
To fill up a page.
To fill up a hole.
To make things feel better. Noise.
The noise of the images
that are people I will never understand.
Admire them though I may.
Poundmaker. Big Bear. Wandering Spirit,
those miserable men.
Riel. Crazy Riel. Riel hanged.
Politics must have its way.
The way of noise. To fill up.
The definitions bullets make,
and field guns.
The noise your dying makes,
to which you are the only listener.
The noise the frogs hesitate
to make as the metal hook
breaks through the skin

and slides smoothly into place
in the jaw. The noise
the fish makes caught in the jaw,
which is only an operation
of the body and the element,
which a stone would make
thrown in the same water, thrashing,
not its voice.
The lake is not displaced,
having one less jackfish body.
In the slough that looks like a golf course
the family of frogs sings. Metal throats.
The images of death hang upside-down.
Grey music.
It is only the listening for death,
fingering the paraphernalia,
the noise of the men you admire.
And cannot understand.
Knowing little enough about them.
The knowledge waxing.
The wax that paves hell's road,
slippery as the road to heaven.
So that as a man slips
he might as easily slide
into being a saint as destroyer.
In his ears the noise magnifies.
He forgets men.

Everyone

Everyone is so
lonely in this
country that
it's necessary
to be fantastic—

a crow flew over
my grave today,
no goose stepping
pompously along,

but a crow;
black as life,
raucously calling
to no one—

struggling image:
necessary
to be fantastic,
almost to lie,

but incorrect,
not cautious enough,
though not evil
actively: it does not

have the diminishing
virtue of evilness
(a locked sea-monster
with half the

dangerous coils
waving above
the grey water),
for the tourists,
glistening crows.

Lady, Lady

Lady, lady, I cannot lie,
I didn't cut down your cherry tree.

It was another man, in another season,
for the same reason.

I eat the stone and not the flesh,
it is the bare bone of desire I want,

something you would throw a dog,
or me, though I insult by saying so.

God knows it is not said
of your body, that it is like

a bone thrown to a dog,
or that I would throw it away, which

moment to moment I cannot remember
under those baggy clothes you wear—

which, if I love and tell,
I love well.

Ride Off Any Horizon

Ride off any horizon
and let the measure fall
where it may—

on the hot wheat,
on the dark yellow fields
of wild mustard, the fields

of bad farmers, on the river,
on the dirty river full
of boys and on the throbbing

powerhouse and the low dam
of cheap cement and rocks
boiling with white water,

and on the cows and their powerful
bulls, the heavy tracks
filling with liquid at the edge

of the narrow prairie
river running steadily away.

*

Ride off any horizon
and let the measure fall
where it may—

among the piles of bones
that dot the prairie

in vision and history
(the buffalo and deer,

dead indians, dead settlers
the frames of lost houses

left behind in the dust
of the depression,

dry and profound, that
will come again in the land

and in the spirit, the land
shifting and the minds

blown dry and empty—
I have not seen it! except

in pictures and talk—
but there is the fence

covered with dust, laden,
the wrecked house stupidly empty)—

here is a picture for your wallet,
of the beaten farmer and his wife
leaning toward each other—

sadly smiling, and emptied of desire.

*

Ride off any horizon
and let the measure fall
where it may—

off the edge
of the black prairie

as you thought you could fall,
a boy at sunset

not watching the sun
set but watching the black earth,

never-ending they said in school,
round: but you saw it ending,

finished, definite, precise—
visible only miles away.

*

Ride off any horizon

and let the measure fall
where it may—

on a hot night the town
is in the streets—

the boys and girls
are practising against

each other, the men
talk and eye the girls—

the women talk and
eye each other, the indians
play pool: eye on the ball.

*

Ride off any horizon
and let the measure fall
where it may—

and damn the troops, the horsemen
are wheeling in the sunshine,
the cree, practising

for their deaths: mr poundmaker,
gentle sweet mr bigbear,
it is not unfortunately

quite enough to be innocent,
it is not enough merely
not to offend—

at times to be born
is enough, to be
in the way is too much—

some colonel otter, some

major-general middleton will
get you, you—

indian. It is no good to say,
I would rather die
at once than be in that place—

though you love that land more,
you will go where they take you.

*

Ride off any horizon
and let the measure fall—

where it may;
it doesn't have to be

the prairie. It could be
the cold soul of the cities
blown empty by commerce

and desiring commerce
to fill up emptiness.

The streets are full of people.

It is night, the lights
are on; the wind

blows as far as it may. The streets
are dark and full of people.

Their eyes are fixed as far as
they can see beyond each other—

to the concrete horizon, definite,
tall against the mountains,
stopping vision visibly.

In This Reed

In this reed, in this semblance
of a human body I wear
so awkwardly, unjointed,
though I hesitate to admit,

there there is life, though
once I would have denied it, thinking
my somnolence clever evidence
of a wearied intellectuality;

but in this hunger I feed on,
in the lungs heaving and the eyes,
to speak only of the eyes
that see so little
of what they ought to see (no more
than they should!), there the life is—
it is imperfection
the eyes see, it is
impreciseness they deserve,

but they desire so much more,
what they desire, what they hope,
what they invent,

is perfection, organizing
all things as they may not be,
it is what they strive for

unwillingly, against themselves,
to see a perfect order, ordained
reason—

and what they strive against
while they wish it, what they want
to see, closed, is what
they want, and will not be.

The Engine and the Sea

The locomotive in the city's distance, obscure, misplaced,
sounds a child's horn on the flat land leading to the
cliff of dark buildings,

the foghorns on the water's edge cry back.

Between the sounds men sit in their houses watching
machines inform them in Edison's light. In the marshes,
the music of ominous living. . . .

a leggy insect runs on that surface, frogs wait, fish,
angling birds.

In the cities men wait to be told. They sit between the
locomotive and the fish. The flat sea and the prairie
that was a sea contain them. Images float before their
eyes,

men and women acting,

entertaining, rigorously dancing with fractured minds
contorted to a joyless pleasure, time sold from life.

The locomotive hums, the prairies hum. Frogs touch
insects with their long tongues, the cannibal fish and
the stabbing birds

wait.

Night actions flash before uncountable animal eyes. Mice
run. Light rain falls in the night.

The frogs are stilled. Between the engine and the sea, the
lights go out. People sleep with mechanical dreams, the sea
hums with rain, the locomotive shines black, fish wait under
the surface of a pinked pool.

Frogs shiver in the cold. The land waits, black, dreaming. Men lie dry in their beds.

History, history!

Under the closed lids their eyes flick back and forth as they try to follow the frightening shapes of their desires.

Warm Wind

The wet sun shines a muddy spring,
warm wind blows; I walk, content
with the weather of our hands.

What if the world does end,
and we are only stained shadows
the sidewalk photographed? Today

I hold you and have a happiness
that makes me human once again.

The Flower

I am too tense,
decline to dance
verbally. The flower
is not in its colour,
but in the seed.

Doukhobor

When you die and your weathery corpse
lies on the chipped kitchen table,

the wind blowing the wood of your house
painted in shades of blue, farmer

out from Russia as the century turned,
died, and lay at the feet of the wars,

who will ever be able to say for you
what you thought at the sight of the Czar's horsemen

riding with whips among you, the sight
of the rifles burning in bonfires,

the long sea-voyage, strange customs endured,
officials changing your name

into the strange script that covered the stores,
the polite brown men who spoke no language

you understood and helped you
free your team from Saskatchewan river mud,

who will be able to say for you
just what you thought as the villages marched

naked to Eden and the English
went to war and came back again

with their funny ways, proud
to speak of killing each other, you, whose mind

refused the slaughter, refused the blood,
you who will lie in your house, stiff as winter,

dumb as an ox, unable to love,
while your women sob and offer the visitors tea?

George Bowering

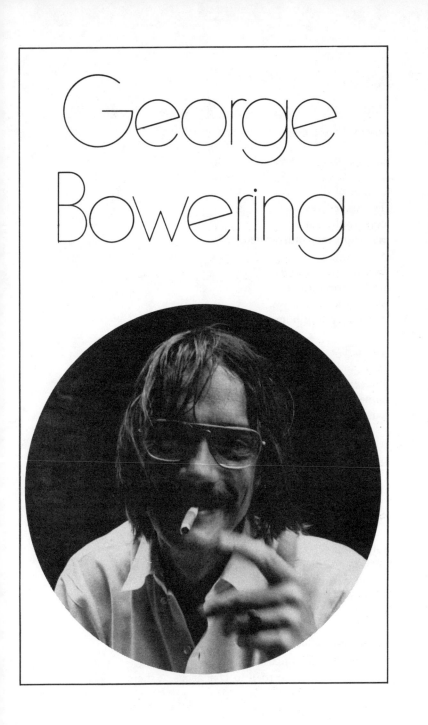

The Night Before Morning

With it all over
and you & I
in separate beds
in separated houses,

I think of
Troilus & Cressida
cursing the sun-
rise from their hurricaned bed;

he to clatter away
on his army horse,
she to pick
her sunny way home—

you & I
with nothing touching
but our private thoughts:
mine of poetry,
yours of a strong morning.

Grandfather

Grandfather
          Jabez Harry Bowering
strode across the Canadian prairie
hacking down trees
          and building churches
delivering personal baptist sermons in them
leading Holy holy holy lord god almighty songs in them
red haired man squared off in the pulpit
reading Saul on the road to Damascus at them

Left home
                big walled Bristol town
at age eight
                to make a living
buried his stubby fingers in root snarled earth
for a suit of clothes and seven hundred gruelly meals a year
taking an anabaptist cane across the back every day
for four years till he was whipped out of England

Twelve years old
                and across the ocean alone
to apocalyptic Canada
                Ontario of bone bending child labor
six years on the road to Damascus till his eyes were blinded
with the blast of Christ and he wandered west
to Brandon among wheat kings and heathen Saturday nights
young red haired Bristol boy shoveling coal
in the basement of Brandon college five in the morning

Then built his first wooden church and married
a sick girl who bore two live children and died
leaving several pitiful letters and the Manitoba night

He moved west with another wife and built children and churches
Saskatchewan Alberta British Columbia Holy holy holy
lord god almighty
                struck his labored bones with pain
and left him a postmaster prodding grandchildren with crutches
another dead wife and a glass bowl of photographs
and holy books unopened save the bible by the bed

Till he died the day before his eighty fifth birthday
in a Catholic hospital of sheets white as his hair

To Cleave

When I enter you
you enter me.

That is to cleave,

to cling,
cut,

penetrate
& love.

I love you inside
& offer my inside to you.

To cleave is to separate
& join,

to open
& fill.

And I am filled with you
even as I place myself
in our cleft
my love.

The Swing

Renoir's people
    seem to stand
        on a forest floor
of blossoms.

        The girl on the swing
could be fifteen, her dress
    of new flowers.

           She leans coyly
or thoughtfully away
    from the two men
        with straw hats.

They are artists
    on a Sunday afternoon
        warm in loose clothing,

some kind of wonder
    for the child who
        makes the fourth figure.

She is clasping her empty hands
    in front of her, her head up,
        her eyes the only ones
        looking outward.

Esta Muy Caliente

On the highway
near San Juan del Río
we had to stop the car
for a funeral.

The whole town it was
a hundred people or
two hundred
walking slowly along the highway

toward the yellow domed church
on the top of the hill
and we pulled into the shade
of a shaggy tree.

I turned off the engine
and we heard their music
a screeching saxophone
and high broken noted trumpet

alone and sad in the hot afternoon
as they walked slow like sheep
the women with black shawls
the men in flappy trousers.

Every five minutes the men
threw cherry bombs into the air
behind them: loud gun shots
blasting the afternoon

then the saxophone: tin music
odd tortured jazz
in that mysterious Indian Christian march
up the hill: bearing a coffin to the priest.

It was a small coffin
on the shoulder of one man in front
        the father we thought
the cherry bombs were like violence

against us: but we were stopped.
An old rattling truck
nosed thru them: and they closed
together again behind it
                                ignoring us.

I walked away from the road
in among the bushes and prickly pear
looking for scorpions on the hot sand
and took a leak beside a thin horse.

An hour later the road was clear
and as I got in the car
a man on a donkey came by
a San Juan lonely in the mountains man.

Good afternoon, I said.
Good afternoon, he said, it is very hot.
Yes it is, I said, especially for us.
It is very hot for us too, he said.

News

Every day I add an inch
to the pile of old newspapers
in the closet.

In that three foot pile now
a dozen airliner crashes,
one earthquake in Alaska,
seventeen American soldiers
face down in Asian mud

I could go on enumerating
like newsprint—we record
violent death & hockey scores
& keep the front room neat.

In front of me, on the table
my empty coffee cup, somewhat melted
butter, carbon copy of an old poem,
familiar things, nothing unexpected.

A plane could crash into the kitchen—
a fissure could jag the floor open—
some olive faced paratrooper bash
his rifle butt thru the window—

It would be news, somewhere.

Circus Maximus

They come
            each one
of them
        a rise
like those
            who came
before them.

New heroes flexing
to fill the shape
made out for them
by the now dead

but each new man
a refutation of his predecessor.

Camus refining Dostoyevsky
yet feeling the swell
of body the Russian felt

the old man
grizzling in his beard
anticipating the African
who would fit his fingers
over the old pen
playing with down
            on his cheek.

Who knows ten of your molecules
are not in me?

but Nature helps me define
my own shape

looks on as
I stumble over the centuries'

exposed root
lost in my own
                   particularity

(patterns I deny
and that
is part of a pattern).

Styles do not multiply themselves
but are all
pervasive

the suit of clothes
is nothing
without its own disfigurations.

New heroes flex into it
and bend it to their bodies.

Indian Summer

The yellow trees
along the river

are dying I said
they are in
their moment of life
you said.

The Indians I think
are dead, you cant
immortalize them, a
leaf prest between

pages becomes a
page.

In a month
the river will move

beneath ice, moving
as it always does
south. We will
believe it as we

will no longer see
those yellow borders
of the river.

Albertasaurus

The great valley of Drumheller
a silent gorge, filled
with dinosaur bones,

unexpected trees on the plains,
old ghost towns of coal
mines & dinosaurs,

the wood, petrified, the earth
streakt white & brown,
the Badlands, sea shells

caught a thousand miles
from the sea. In the town

small town cafés, restaurants
they say, with Pepsi-Cola neon
signs, old-fashioned menus,

the home of the dinosaur,
caught in a corner of the
prairie, small-town people

in a dying town, conscious
they must cling to the
dinosaur for their living.

cling to his neck, forgetting
where the dinosaur came
to rest.

The House

I

If I describe my house
I may at last describe my self

but I will surely lie
about the house.

For there is the first lie.
It is not a house at all

but a fragment, a share
of a house, instinct drives me

to one door. As certain as
one hair lies beside another.

As certain as these rows of books
carry me from house to house,

arrange me to their will. I
squat for an hour, eye level

to those books, saying I will
read this, or I will read this,

& this way never succeed
in reading my self, no time

left in the hour between
the news & the pants on the floor.

II

In the morning the window
is bamboo & behind that

snow. (But here I am trying
to go outside the house, remember

what I said.) My bare feet
find no wood, the water

runs warm from the tap,
the coffee in the white cup

on which is painted a green
tree. There is a newspaper

on the floor inside the door,
& a woman in the chiffon

of the bed. A salt shaker
of glass & an aluminum

pepper shaker, & in the
farthest room, papers, orderly.

Those are the reason for the house
& its enemy. I am the fisher

who lays his fish side by side
in the pan. The noise of the pen

on paper is the drift of
cigarette smoke in the window's light.

III

The house has a refrigerator
& a stove, a painting & a

husband, & the husband
has fingers from which words

fall as the wine glass falls
unbroken on the rug.

The key fits into the door
as my feet step in snow, cutting

precise patterns & the silence
of wind, & from outside

the windows are glass, &
behind that the house is not empty.

The Egg

The egg sat on the workbench
for weeks, me passing it every day
in my search for tools, cobwebs,
five years old, looking for

the machines of life. The source
of life, I knew, as mysterious as
my mother's bedroom. I didn't touch
the egg for weeks, my brain resembling

its contours. Till the day came
I gave up waiting for the news, I
contrived to make it roll & fall
to the floor beside a rusted shovel.

Bending over, I knew first the
terrible stink, & then the quills
of light, bone, or fiber, it was
a wing never to be used. Its guilt

I carried for a year & then carried
lighter for more years, as if I
myself smelled, as if I had brought
those tender stinking wings to earth.

Dobbin

FOR MIKE ONDAATJE

We found dead animals in our sagebrush hills,
every day it seems now, deer, heads of
unimaginable elk. Or rattlesnake killed
by some kids we likely knew, upside down,
wrong coloured in the burnt couchgrass.

But my first dead horse. It was something
like mother, something gone wrong at home—
his opened & scattered body was tethered,
the old shit surrounded his tufted hair
& his skin, the oil gone, just twisted
leather without eyeballs. A horse, as if
someone had lost him, obeying the rope
thru his open-air starving.

I was then, then, no longer another one
of the animals come to look, this
was no humus like the others, this
was death, not merely dead; that rope
may now hang from some rotted fence.

Our Triple Birth

First by design & later out of
neglect or fear
we have come this far, & myself
furthest without the children
we've already named.

While my sperm dries
year after year, flushes thru drains,
glistens against skin in city after city,
sinks into the earth & coils there
never to stand straight
on its own two feet, a
continuation, my poor rotting skeleton's
rebirth into that heaven
each decade promises
& brings beyond our self-blinded eyes, that
infibulation, that abortion.

That smiling knife-holding gentleman
planted his trees for us, gave us
to name everything we see
& stick it in a book, so even
to name the children coiled only
shrimp in our skull's sea.

& when I'm driven from this garden
I'll leave you there in the earth
to force your own way to sunlight,
Jason, Adam, W.C.

The Breath, Release

Captain Tsubaki said any
teenage pilot in the group
not ready for Kamikaze
need only raise his hand.

Six hands went up, mine
trembled at my side, I
have only begun to live, why
does my hand not rise

high as a plane filled with
dynamite out of the sun.

Come fly with me, the poem
is done before you know it, who
raises his hand to stop it
is no poet. The music rises

to wrap us in it. We tap
our feet, caught in the act.
I'm not the captain of my soul.
My soul belongs to daddy.

Now I, this I, this other one,
I was nine when the war ended.
Drawing zeros on the sidewalk,
I was just a kid, employing

my talents. The war is over
there, farther than a plane
can fly. I am learning to be
a poet, caught in the

Divine Storm. It lifts my wings
as I am built, not to make
war, not to find peace, going
to an end, of the flight, only

when the wind relaxes, it
never dies, not when I raise
my hand. Those who raise
their hands are sent to death

first. Captain Tsubaki knows, he
sends them first, those active
winners, theirs is the honor, ours
the real fright. We will die

before we grow up, the breath
releast from us divine. That
is learning, the viewless wings
of poesy over the sea

that is the sky we will all
swim in, our extended arms
like wings, our hands raised
now by the element we were
born in.

Margaret Atwood

The Islands

There are two of them:

One larger, with steep granite
cliffs facing us, dropping sheer
to the deep lake;

the other smaller, closer
to land, with a reef running
out from it and dead trees
grey, waist-high in the water.

We know they are alone
and always will be.

The lake takes care of that
and if it went,
they would be hills
and still demand
separateness
from the eye.

Yet, standing on the cliff
(the two
of us)
on our bigger island,
looking,

we find it pleasing
(it soothes our instinct for
symmetry, proportion,
for company perhaps)

that there are two of them.

The Animals in That Country

In that country the animals
have the faces of people:

the ceremonial
cats possessing the streets

the fox run
politely to earth, the huntsmen
standing around him, fixed
in their tapestry of manners

the bull, embroidered
with blood and given
an elegant death, trumpets, his name
stamped on him, heraldic brand
because

(when he rolled
on the sand, sword in his heart, the teeth
in his blue mouth were human)

he is really a man

even the wolves, holding resonant
conversations in their
forests thickened with legend.

In this country the animals
have the faces of
animals.

Their eyes
flash once in car headlights
and are gone.

Their deaths are not elegant.

They have the faces of
no-one.

A Night in the Royal Ontario Museum

Who locked me

into this crazed man-made
stone brain
            where the weathered
totempole jabs a blunt
finger at the byzantine
mosaic dome

Under that ornate
golden cranium I wander
among fragments of gods, tarnished
coins, embalmed gestures
chronologically arranged,
looking for the EXIT sign

but in spite of the diagrams
at every corner, labelled
in red: YOU ARE HERE
the labyrinth holds me,

turning me around
the cafeteria, the washrooms,
a spiral through marble
Greece and Rome, the bronze
horses of China

then past the carved masks, wood and fur
to where 5 plaster Indians
in a glass case
squat near a dusty fire

and further, confronting me
with a skeleton child, preserved
in the desert air, curled
beside a clay pot and a few beads.

I say I am far
enough,   stop here   please
no more

but the perverse museum, corridor
by corridor, an idiot
voice jogged by a pushed
button, repeats its memories

and I am dragged to the mind's
deadend, the roar of the bone-
yard, I am lost
among the mastodons
and beyond: a fossil
shell, then

samples of rocks
and minerals, even the thundering
tusks swindling to pin-   *dwindling*
points in the stellar
fluorescent-lighted
wastes of geology

Progressive Insanities of a Pioneer

I

He stood, a point
on a sheet of green paper
proclaiming himself the centre,

with no walls, no borders
anywhere; the sky no height
above him, totally un-
enclosed
and shouted: *in his mind there are boundaries*

Let me out!

II

He dug the soil in rows,
imposed himself with shovels.
He asserted
into the furrows, I
am not random.

The ground
replied with aphorisms:

a tree-sprout, a nameless
weed, words
he couldn't understand.

III

The house pitched
the plot staked
in the middle of nowhere.

At night the mind
inside, in the middle
of nowhere.

The idea of an animal
patters across the roof.

In the darkness the fields
defend themselves with fences
in vain:
    everything
    is getting in.

IV

By daylight he resisted.
He said, disgusted
with the swamp's clamourings and the outbursts
of rocks,

> This is not order
> but the absence
> of order.

He was wrong, the unanswering
forest implied:

> It was
> an ordered absence

V

For many years
he fished for a great vision,
dangling the hooks of sown
roots under the surface
of the shallow earth.

It was like
enticing whales with a bent
pin. Besides he thought

in that country
only the worms were biting.

VI

If he had known unstructured
space is a deluge
and stocked his log house-
boat with all the animals

even the wolves,

he might have floated.

But obstinate he
stated, The land is solid
and stamped,

watching his foot sink
down through stone
up to the knee.

VII

Things
refused to name themselves; refused
to let him name them.

The wolves hunted
outside.

On his beaches, his clearings,
by the surf of under-
growth breaking
at his feet, he foresaw
disintegration
                and in the end
through eyes
made ragged by his
effort, the tension
between subject and object,

the green
vision, the unnamed
whale invaded.

Further Arrivals

After we had crossed the long illness
that was the ocean, we sailed up-river

On the first island
the immigrants threw off their clothes
and danced like sandflies

We left behind one by one
the cities rotting with cholera,
one by one our civilized
distinctions

and entered a large darkness.

It was our own
ignorance we entered.

I have not come out yet

My brain gropes nervous
tentacles in the night, sends out
fears hairy as bears,
demands lamps; or waiting

for my shadowy husband, hears
malice in the trees' whispers.

I need wolf's eyes to see
the truth.

I refuse to look in a mirror.

Whether the wilderness is
real or not
depends on who lives there.

Death of a Young Son by Drowning

He, who navigated with success
the dangerous river of his own birth
once more set forth

on a voyage of discovery
into the land I floated on
but could not touch to claim.

His feet slid on the bank,
the currents took him;
he swirled with ice and trees in the swollen water

and plunged into distant regions,
his head a bathysphere;
through his eyes' thin glass bubbles

he looked out, reckless adventurer
on a landscape stranger than Uranus
we have all been to and some remember.

There was an accident; the air locked,
he was hung in the river like a heart.
They retrieved the swamped body,

cairn of my plans and future charts,
with poles and hooks
from among the nudging logs.

It was spring, the sun kept shining, the new grass
lept to solidity;
my hands glistened with details.

After the long trip I was tired of waves.
My foot hit rock. The dreamed sails
collapsed, ragged.

> I planted him in this country
> like a flag.

The Immigrants

They are allowed to inherit
the sidewalks involved as palmlines, bricks
exhausted and soft, the deep
lawnsmells, orchards whorled
to the land's contours, the inflected weather

only to be told they are too poor
to keep it up, or someone
has noticed and wants to kill them; or the towns
pass laws which declare them obsolete.

I see them coming
up from the hold smelling of vomit,
infested, emaciated, their skins grey
with travel; as they step on shore

the old countries recede, become
perfect, thumbnail castles preserved
like gallstones in a glass bottle, the
towns dwindle upon the hillsides
in a light paperweight-clear.

They carry their carpetbags and trunks
with clothes, dishes, the family pictures;
they think they will make an order
like the old one, sow miniature orchards,
carve children and flocks out of wood

but always they are too poor, the sky
is flat, the green fruit shrivels
in the prairie sun, wood is for burning;
and if they go back, the towns

in time have crumbled, their tongues
stumble among awkward teeth, their ears
are filled with the sound of breaking glass.

I wish I could forget them
and so forget myself:

my mind is a wide pink map
across which move year after year
arrows and dotted lines, further and further,
people in railway cars

their heads stuck out of the windows
at stations, drinking milk or singing,
their features hidden with beards or shawls
day and night riding across an ocean of unknown
land to an unknown land.

Game After Supper

This is before electricity,
it is when there were porches.

On the sagging porch an old man
is rocking. The porch is wooden,

the house is wooden and grey;
in the living room which smells of
smoke and mildew, soon
the women will light the kerosene lamp.

There is a barn but I am not in the barn;
there is an orchard too, gone bad,
its apples like soft cork
but I am not there either.

I am hiding in the long grass
with my two dead cousins,
the membrane grown already
across their throats.

We hear crickets and our own hearts
close to our ears;
though we giggle, we are afraid.

From the shadows around
the corner of the house
a tall man is coming to find us:

He will be an uncle,
if we are lucky.

Girl and Horse, 1928

You are younger than I am, you are
someone I never knew, you stand
under a tree, your face half-shadowed,
holding the horse by its bridle.

Why do you smile?   Can't you
see the apple blossoms falling around
you, snow, sun, snow, listen, the tree
dries and is being burnt, the wind

is bending your body, your face
ripples like water   where did you go
But no, you stand there exactly
the same, you can't hear me, forty

years ago you were caught by light
and fixed in that secret
place where we live, where we believe
nothing can change, grow older.

> (On the other side
> of the picture, the instant
> is over, the shadow
> of the tree has moved. You wave,

then turn and ride
out of sight through the vanished
orchard, still smiling
as though you do not notice)

They Eat Out

In restaurants we argue
over which of us will pay for your funeral

though the real question is
whether or not I will make you immortal.

At the moment only I
can do it and so

I raise the magic fork
over the plate of beef fried rice

and plunge it into your heart.
There is a faint pop, a sizzle

and through your own split head
you rise up glowing;

the ceiling opens
a voice sings Love Is A Many

Splendoured Thing
you hang suspended above the city

in blue tights and a red cape,
your eyes flashing in unison.

The other diners regard you
some with awe, some only with boredom:

they cannot decide if you are a new weapon
or only a new advertisement.

As for me, I continue eating;
I liked you better the way you were,
but you were always ambitious.

Newsreel: Man and Firing Squad

I

A botched job,
the blindfold slipped, he sees
his own death approaching, says No
or something, his torso jumps as the bullets hit
his nerves / he slopes down,
wrecked and not even
cleanly, roped muscles leaping, mouth open
as though snoring, the photography
isn't good either.

II

Destruction shines with such beauty

Light on his wet hair
serpents of blood jerked from the wrists

Sun thrown from the raised and lowered
rifles / debris of the still alive

Your left eye, green and lethal

III

We depart, we say goodbye

Yet each of us remains in the same place,
staked out and waiting,
it is the ground between that moves, expands,
pulling us away from each other.

No more of these closeups, this agony
taken just for the record anyway

The scenery is rising behind us
into focus, the walls
and hills are also important,

Our shattered faces retreat, we might be
happy, who can interpret
the semaphore of our bending
bodies, from a distance we could be dancing

You Begin

You begin this way:
this is your hand,
this is your eye,
that is a fish, blue and flat
on the paper, almost
the shape of an eye.
This is your mouth, this is an 0
or a moon, whichever
you like. This is yellow.

Outside the window
is the rain, green
because it is summer, and beyond that

the trees and then the world,
which is round and has only
the colours of these nine crayons.

This is the world, which is fuller
and more difficult to learn than I have said.
You are right to smudge it that way
with the red and then
the orange: the world burns.

Once you have learned these words
you will learn that there are more
words than you can ever learn.
The word *hand* floats above your hand
like a small cloud over a lake.
The word *hand* anchors
your hand to this table,
your hand is a warm stone
I hold between two words.

This is your hand, these are my hands, this is the world,
which is round but not flat and has more colours
than we can see.

It begins, it has an end,
this is what you will
come back to, this is your hand.

All Bread

All bread is made of wood,
cow dung, packed brown moss,
the bodies of dead animals, the teeth
and backbones, what is left
after the ravens. This dirt
flows through the stems into the grain,

into the arm, nine strokes
of the axe, skin from a tree,
good water which is the first
gift, four hours.

Live burial under a moist cloth,
a silver dish, the row
of white famine bellies
swollen and taut in the oven,
lungfuls of warm breath stopped
in the heat from an old sun.

Good bread has the salt taste
of your hands after nine
strokes of the axe, the salt
taste of your mouth, it smells
of its own small death, of the deaths
before and after.

Lift these ashes
into your mouth, your blood;
to know what you devour
is to consecrate it,
almost. All bread must be broken
so it can be shared. Together
we eat this earth.

Five Poems for Dolls

I

Behind glass in Mexico
this clay doll draws
its lips back in a snarl;
despite its beautiful dusty shawl,
it wishes to be dangerous.

II

See how the dolls resent us,
with their bulging foreheads
and minimal chins, their flat bodies
never allowed to bulb and swell,
their faces of little thugs.

This is not a smile,
this glossy mouth, two stunted teeth;
the dolls gaze at us
with the filmed eyes of killers.

III

There have always been dolls
as long as there have been people.
In the trash heaps and abandoned temples
the dolls pile up;
the sea is filling with them.

What causes them?
Or are they gods, causeless,
something to talk to
when you have to talk
something to throw against the wall?

A doll is a witness
who cannot die,
with a doll you are never alone.

On the long journey under the earth,
in the boat with two prows,
there were always dolls.

IV

Or did we make them
because we needed to love someone
and could not love each other?

It was love, after all,
that rubbed the skins from their grey cheeks,
crippled their fingers,
snarled their hair, brown or dull gold.
Hate would merely have smashed them.

You change, but the doll
I made of you lives on,
a white body leaning
in a sunlit window, the features
wearing away with time,
frozen in the gaunt pose
of a single day,
holding in its plaster hand
your doll of me.

V

Or: all dolls come
from the land of the unborn,
the almost-born; each
doll is a future
dead at the roots,
a voice heard only
on breathless nights,
a desolate white memento.

Or: these are the lost children,
those who have died or thickened
to full growth and gone away.

The dolls are their souls or cast skins
which line the shelves of our bedrooms
and museums, disguised as outmoded toys,
images of our sorrow,
shedding around themselves
five inches of limbo.

Victor
Coleman

The Lady Vanishes

FOR ANN K.

I

The Lady
Vanishes

II

Lovely lady inside your
face my hands move,
in the earth behind
your skin, they dig there
& soil themselves.

              & your eyes?
well, your eyes well up
out of themselves
to make tree colors
              & your optic
nerve twines tight about
my wrist in there.

III

Oh lady, this moment,
the last one, we are two
children together
dunking our graham crackers in the milk;
& I'm washing it all down
with beer to bring the high down.

My eyes, the gesture of your hands,
change.

IV

The dream saw the mirror
image shatter on the floor
& the image broken up
into its razor syllables.

The dream saw the suicide
then, the wrist or the jugular
cut thru with pieces of
the shattered whole image.

The dream saw the blood there
pucker up from veins,
fall over the wrist to find
its own image.

And the image of the blood
and the image of the lady
vanished, vanishes, was
vanquished in the eye.

V

The lady
The lady vanishes

She does not move
too far out of herself

She does not excite or incite

She vanishes
before my
very very eyes

Kenkyusha: Day Nine

FOR F.W.

*Some poor fellows were trapped by the fire
and were burnt to death, I hear.*

Fred
These messages your father said
Were waiting for us at the cut

& we tripped up there
& caught as you said a ride out
Remember?

Have you asked
'after the fathers of all men?'

I'll ask you now—
How did he like those hockey
games & why didn't you bring him in
to meet us that day you came to pick up
Christmas boots.

         God I wanted
to meet the man.

The instruction.

The loss of innocence, Fred, the time I was away
& my daughter was born & I called you
on the phone in that confusion

& Pauline told me, or someone, he had
Died. That same day died. I
was that father died.

That same day. The phoneme, Fred, the phone
I called you up on gave instruction of
my daughter's birth, six-thirty a.m.

same time I was sleepily fucking
Abraham's wife in a city neither of us
belongs in.
                    Fred,
I'm asking after your father,
after your father's death
I'm asking you what time

Time, & what were you doing
when he lost his.

The Devil

The horned face
of an ideal

the number fifteen
torch held down

right hand raised in greeting?
A warning

a wariness
warmed to

bat wings against a darkness
that comes from too much light

　　Fire in the Man's tail

　　Fruit in the Woman's

Perched above & guardian of
their chains

      ram-horned, foul-footed
vision torn from His eyes

Fired or feathered—pointed as two horns
& no direction to give them
proportion

        The Man & the Woman
are naked, their genitals exposed,
chained together at their necks
to the darkness

        The Man speaks
or is doubtful; his gesture
puts the woman in her place

Our innocence naked
or the fire's out of the hearth
into the Man's heart

The Devil holds the fire down

The Man burns warily

The Woman dreams of dancing

Fish : Stone : Song

The salmon swims upstream
into a more perfect pleasure

& the Indian beats it with a stick
shaped like the fish it strikes

& Isaac Paul dreamed a song
which enabled him to catch more cod

& a Nanaimo Salish dreamed he caught
something fierce & the next day caught it

rock in the shape
of that self-same swimmer

which he carried home
laid near where he dreamt it

spoke to him of perseverance
that was prelude to some sound abundance

& told him
rub your hooks upon my surface

whenever the
fisherman becomes inept in you

& he kept it many years   hid in a box
& became that wealthy Indian

like unto a white man
as he grew older

& that stone fish again spoke
in a dream from where he was hid

& told the old fisher
to return to that part of the sea

& find the spot from where he pulled it
& throw it back

                & the old man did it
finding the place

& having decorated the stone
as the dream voice told him

heaved it in the water
where it behaved in a manner

most unfish-like
more like *lightning*

what gives off to his most great
advantage

Parking Lots for Greg Curnoe

I

Why is Robert Desnos sleeping?

The true radical is any man who will not accept
    the present terms—

No adjustment is needed—if a fly
    is open there is reason—Calamity
    reigns in that area (never been there either)

Too personal, it was always laughing, exchanging
    the unexchangeable glow all over us—

When I do finally come in her mouth there will blossom
    millions tiny tapioca boiling white
    in their own clarity, translucent
    feeling, like joy & jellie babies;
    evident & divers strangers
    swallowed in one or two gulps—

Hot dogs   hot rods   chewing gum wrappers
  all crumpled & torn   blackballs
  Jonnie hand warmers   big little books
  Dick Tracy & Plastic Man   (always cut
  by the villain's broken mirror
  divesting the image   defeated
  by some sharp-edged reflection of
  himself)—

Trading comics with the girl down the street age 9
  huge overbite buck teeth & holey underwear
  kissing me in the closet
  pressing her smelly nineyearold body against mine
  whose teeth push against my tender boy's lips
  still, pulling her pants down for me—

Each one of these doors leads to the present—No engagement
  is needed—the present is yesterday's
  memory sliding in old dead mud
  sad travels & tantamount dreams of reality
  climbing cat's cradle of webs in imagination—
  here today   gone tomorrow—No
  adjustment is needed—

But me   in either case joyous   feeling
  jubilant dew drop from my beard
  on a hill up which we climb
  in the shade of a tree heaved up
  as it is somehow over the road—
  Little lamb who made thee—No adjunct
  is needled—junipers, fat red cedars
  in front of my vision of the world—

Not Kumush   Old man of old men
  trapped inside a wandering adolescence
  sewing from his bag of old dried bones
  collected in serpents' houses   over the land
  so that men might arise from them in tribes—
  the streets & alleyways of his wanderings

  there to perpetrate an image of himself
A joke   No
need for readjustment   .   CH'IEN

THE CREATIVE: HEAVEN
                        in books   old documents
art & other well-worn dildos
This man you have invented in your innocence

NO   to your pleas—Need
   Rots—walking   walking
   Oh parochial!

Give me the song of the stout-hearted sucking in
   swoosh of the tea head
   followed by 15 minutes of self contemplation
   better than talk about art & the ever
   slowly degenerating dollar—a barter
   this is my first . . .

Yes   I will buy your violence   but take off that
   redress   Move toward an image of heaven
   (The Earth)   a vision   Color the atmosphere
   ochre if it pleases you

II

'THEN THE PEOPLE BEGAN TO TALK TO THE TREES
AND THE CHANGE CAME'

My fouryearold son spends an hour in the morning arranging
   his small pile of books to resemble a silent flat sea—
   printer's ink colored & eloquent
   upon the adages of its own demise—
   that he wanted for his set
   of toy vehicles   in the
   middle of the living room a parking lot—

Robinson Jeffers entombed in an idea   Dead
   anyway   but no more than Ruscha's
   portrait of thousands square feet
   reduced to the size of each page—
   delicate & intricate   Lifeless...

I am not complaining I am not complaining   The waning
   of the harvest moon is NOT A POEM
   (it is a waning

A perfect picture of imbalance in the pause between
   this world & the last

Realizing that I don't have to talk to people anymore
   one syllable words form trains
   standing in the station
   waiting for people to get on or off—

What you see   paint   is paint   a color
   no sea enters into   No discourse
   of object & fact

Not very interesting artifacts   The mind
   does not live up to any of its promises

III

The gesture of plains in the paintings
   of Georges Braque—locations
   moving in the air   in earth   on air
   projected into the present sense
   ability—the tension
   between us: attention

Something there is that finds two in one   three
   in two   into decisions we made
   about those magic numbers into which
   we have divided ourselves—beyond
   their anti-numerical, over-symbolical

surfaces towards real qualities
of the thing, not significant detail—
the mass of everything—secret
political prisoners locked in each cell—

The body   of work   is no more ill at ease
than the work   of the body
Ask the drugs about their pertinence
gather your rosebuds where you may
but sniff too of the air & listen
to the sounds of worlds colliding
in the garden   her fingers touching pure joy

Not a scene   (from the movie)   not small
town   big city   rural route environ
meant   *the body*   is all we need
to move through the initial water
until what holds us breaks
over us & frees us from our chamber—
the trees & intractable mountains
through which no middle-class American
children dance   (too busy sleeping
& playing to dance   'their leisure'
engaged in human relationships—

This   like anything we make
has gone much farther
than I intended—(the man in (?)
Maugham whose pocket's ever full
of enough silver to ensure
the austerity of the spirit)—

The amazing ability of a cabdriver
to articulate over & over each day
the same three phrases from the corner of his mouth
—Moebius stringing the same line—
These lakes were given to us

Drink Me

IV

What are the Rolling Stones talking about
   in their music? The future
   the torture   the ardure
   of living in Britain?   I doubt it.
   My belly's not that empty nor my mind.

The amphetamine dreams of resurgence
   in blood undermined by Hershey & Nestle—
   the beautiful birds of oblivion—

How possibly can a man be a vision
   in a world slowly turning
   defensively into asbestos & plastic
   & bullet-proof alloys of infernal metals.
   Licence plates here read: 19 BEAUTIFUL 68.
   The navel's knot   not
   center of the earth   however contemplated—
   not our intention.

'She comes in colours everywhere' the real
   'she combs her hair'   explanation
   'she's like a rainbow'   of the music
   of the spheres is not a simile

                  the plenary abstract
   the word   'colours'   with its optional dipthong
   impotent in the present context:
   darkness.   I have no reason
   to believe in what you're doing
   the unchangeable fact is I do

  Since that first show at Moos   was it 1964?
    in the summer heat & cool
    smiling senses of everything's flatness   (from Dorn
    to Zukofsky   without that awareness   a line
    which does not meet any of its points
    at surface) not a thread a wisp   a kiss
    planted on the earth

V

I have taken the liberty of removing your name
   from the long list of great artistic promises
   & readjusting the order in my mind
   to include all those sempiternal gods
   who walk around in our genes like twisted guests—
   the evergreens don't have them
   won't—we inject false light
   into our veins.

I have taken the liberty of advocating the use of drugs
   in the afterlife   (the halflight)   off-white
   spurious & uneventful—addictive
   as anything—heavenly popsicles
   to soothe the heat of dying—
   through truth a disease squirms
   in our doubts about the world
   simply because it *is* so available
   A Collage

Surrealism has nothing to do with it—Dada
   is father   a rhythm   I asked
   for a sandwich   they gave me
   delight in a cup—a song
   has nothing to do with it either—
   sing, anyway   Be surreal   Don't
   go mad in the face of their constant
   boredom before so much wonder—
   as long as you've got something
   in your hands besides their currency—
   your empty pockets—you can use them
   please, on others.

Art is a caress   careless & fickle
   as words in our language   lying
   each day for a bit more space—
   an occupation in which we store
   our adored adumbrations.

A compass pointing always in the same direction
   drawn to it   attraction of the
   mercury in my eyes   (the coins)
   slowly replacing our fine bones
   with long brittle members   incapable
   digital fingers & toes   (don't count on them)

A comparison: a line
   of grey paint   /   the horizon

   changing

Gibsons, B.C., 4 September 1968

Patrick Lane

White Mountain

Trees in glass robes
cold under the moon's cowl.
Arms hold ice.

Wind carries only the howl
of a dog. Ashes of snow
in grey fire.

There is only a faint glow.
Roads of men advance
and retreat.

Tracks fill with snow.

Passing into Storm

Know him for a white man.
He walks sideways into wind
allowing the left of him

to forget what the right
knows as cold. His ears
turn into death what

his eyes can't see. All day
he walks away from the sun
passing into storm. Do not

mistake him for the howl you hear
or the track you think you
follow. Finding a white man

in snow is to look for the dead.
He has been burned by the wind.
He has left too much

flesh on winter's white metal
to leave his colour as a sign.
Cold white. Cold flesh. He leans

into wind sideways; kills without
mercy anything to the left of him
coming like madness in the snow.

The Bird

The bird you captured is dead.
I told you it would die
but you would not learn
from my telling. You wanted
to cage a bird in your hands
and learn to fly.

Listen again.
You must not handle birds.
They cannot fly through your fingers.
You are not a nest
and a feather is
not made of blood and bone.

Only words
can fly for you like birds
on the wall of the sun.
A bird is a poem
that talks of the end of cages.

Wild Horses

Just to come once alone
to these wild horses
driving out of high Cascades,
raw legs heaving the hip-high snow.
Just once alone. Never to see
the men and their trucks.

Just once alone. Nothing moves
as the stallion with five free mares
rush into the guns. All dead.
Their eyes glaze with frost.
Ice bleeds in their nostrils
as the cable hauls them in.

Later, after the swearing
and the stamping of feet,
we ride down into Golden:

Quit bitchin.
It's a hard bloody life
and a long week
for three hundred bucks of meat.

That and the dull dead eyes
and the empty meadows.

Elephants

The cracked cedar bunkhouse
hangs behind me like a grey pueblo
in the sundown where I sit
to carve an elephant
from a hunk of brown soap
for the Indian boy who lives

in the village a mile back
in the bush.

The alcoholic truck-driver
and the cat-skinner sit beside
me with their eyes closed
all of us waiting out the last hour
until we go back on the grade

and I try to forget the forever
clank   clank   clank
across the grade
pounding stones and earth to powder
for hours in mosquito-darkness
of the endless cold mountain night.

The elephant takes form—
my knife caresses smooth soap
scaling off curls of brown
which the boy saves to take home
to his mother in the village.

Finished, I hand the carving to him
and he looks at the image of the great
beast for a long time
then sets it on dry cedar
and looks up at me:
                              What's an elephant?
he asks me
so I tell him of the elephants
and their jungles. The story
of the elephant graveyard
which no one has ever found
and how the silent
animals of the rain forest
go away to die somewhere
in the limberlost of distances
and he smiles at me
tells me of his father's

graveyard where his people have been
buried for years. So far back
no one remembers when it started
and I ask him where the graveyard is
and he tells me it is gone
now where no one will ever find it
buried under the grade of the new
highway.

Mountain Oysters

Kneeling in the sheep-shit
he picked up the biggest of the new rams
brushed the tail aside
slit the bag
tucked the knackers in his mouth
and clipped the cords off clean

the ram   stiff
with a single wild scream

as the tar went on
and he spit the balls in a bowl.

That's how we used to do it
when I was a boy.
It's no more gawdam painful
than any other way
and you can't have rams fighting
slamming it up every nanny

and enjoyed them with him
cutting delicately
into the deep-fried testicles.

Mountain oysters make you strong

he said
while out in the field
the rams stood holding their pain
legs fluttering like blue hands
of old tired men.

Unborn Things

After the dog drowns in the arroyo
and the old people stumble into the jungle
muttering imprecations at the birds
and the child draws circles in the dust
for bits of glass to occupy
like eyes staring out of earth
and the woman lies on her hammock
dreaming of the lover who will save her
from the need to make bread again
I will go into the field
and be buried with the corn.

Folding my hands on my chest
I will see the shadow of myself; the same
who watched a father when he moved
with hands on the dark side of a candle
create the birds and beasts of dreams.

One with unborn things
I will open my body to the earth
and watch worms reach like pink roots
as I turn slowly tongue to stone
and speak of the beginning of seeds
as they struggle in the earth;
pale things moving toward the sun
that feel the feet of men above,
the tread of their marching
thudding into my earth.

Ecuador

Macchu Picchu

FOR EARLE BIRNEY & PABLO NERUDA

I

THE HITCHING POST OF THE SUN

Father Condor, take me,
Brother Falcon, take me,
Tell my little mother I am coming,
For five days I have not eaten or drunk a drop,
Father Messenger, bearer of signs, swift messenger,
Carry me off, I beg you: little mouth, little heart,
Tell my little father and little mother, I beg you, that
I am coming.

> *Death song of condemned lovers.*
> *From the Quechua.*

Standing on the highest rung of the city
We place our hands on polished stone
That was a hitching-post for the sun.
Now there is nothing but silence.
We watch the sun fall into the Andes.

The first cold shafts of night
Reach into the river far below.
In a gathering mist I feel
We are growing out of
The body of something dead.

*

Today we lay in the Temple of Virgins
As centuries filled our mouths with moss.
They have stripped away the jungle.
They have torn the winding cloths.
They have scattered bones to the wind.

Strangers walk through the ruins.
They talk of where they come from,

Where they are going.
As we lay in this roofless room
They stoned a snake.

It crawled out of the earth
To lie in the brilliant sun.
Coils of its body like plaited hair,
Eyes of cracked stone. They left it
Broken, draped on a fallen wall.

*

We have been cursed with dreams.
This city was meant to be lost.
Those who died here did not want it found.
I pick up our blanket and find a place
To sleep in the Temple of the Sun.

But even he has hidden his face . . .
Yellow bruise of light, lost to us
Who could heal everything.
We began when the sun fell.
Now there is nothing but shadow.

I imagine women moving with their men.
They surround us with eyes
Here in the high Andes
In a city lost and found again
By men who came to unhitch the sun.

II

THE VIRGINS OF THE SUN

In the jungle tombs they found only women.
One held a child in her womb, hands
Like roots wrapped around his face.
There were no men.

The city belonged to the Virgins of the Sun.
One by one the tombs were broken,
The jungle torn away:

> Manco Capac
> And his Incas dead.
> The empire fallen.

> Here they tied the sun at the end of seasons.
> Here they tilled the soil under the eyes
> Of warriors who stood between the portals

> Of the Sun waiting for the Spanish horse.
> Here the Virgins were buried.
> The Spanish never came.

> Betrayed, the last Inca left for Cuzco
> To bargain with the Viceroy of Spain.
> He died in an ambuscade.

> The bridges were cut behind him.
> The road forgotten, the jungle grew a mantle
> For the dead. The Sun rose and fell on the temple

> And in the dark tombs the Virgins slept
> Waiting for the Inca to return
> And restore them to the Sun.

Let the grave-robbers go.
Let the city grow back to jungle.
Back to the speechless things.
The Virgins have left their tombs
With hands like brown roots,
With their unborn child.
Let the city grow back to jungle.
Let the graves like wounds be closed again.

III

MANCO CAPAC – LAST INCA

Today I leave for the great Capital.
Much has been said of the wisdom
Of this move. In Macchu Picchu
I have ruled. It is as if the empire was

Still water curled in a jug's curve
Spilled like this river into jungle.
Lately numerous stars have crossed
The heaven. As it was for Huaina Capac

So for me. Huarascar and Atahualpa dead.
They have raised the bloodstone cross
In Cuzco. The people are afraid.
But the Viceroy of Spain has asked me

To return. He wishes me in the Temple.
What is that to me? My people burn
In the great square. My houses are
Plundered. The empire come and gone.

The golden rod that was planted in
The beginning is removed . . . melted
For the Three-In-One in Spain.
My warriors will stand at the bridges

And along the great road. If I do not
Return, all will be destroyed.
My people starve in the high passes.
My people die in the streets.

My priests have read the omens.
Still I must go. Perhaps this Spaniard
Speaks truth. I no longer know what
Their truth is. I have spoken to the dead

By the hitching-post of the Sun.
I have returned them to their tombs.
I am Manco Capac, Lord of the Inca.
The words of Pachacutec are my words:

Born like a lily in the garden
I grew like a lily
And when the time came
I withered and died.

Macchu Picchu—Peru

From the Hot Hills

FOR JASWANT SINGH GILL

Brought from the hot hills of India
to the cold bleak country of the north
dark men strain bodies into silence
bending and breaking long brown muscles
on the dead weight of timber. Soft
language lost in ignorance
they take the jobs on the green-chain
where no man will work. A job
reserved for drunks who stagger off the train
or the huge bodies of Saskatchewan farm boys
the Sikhs whose names no one knows or cares
to know, respond to *Hey You!* and smile.
Isolate in breathing shacks of snow
they curl their bodies on straw
around the pale flower of a stove
a forty-five gallon drum
fed with salvaged slabs.

The women are alabaster
objects in a town of men.

and any Sikh who dares to speak to one
feels the steel toe of a boot.
The biggest joke of winter was the knowledge
they wiped themselves with their fingers
and one day received cheques
wrapped in toilet paper. Stabbed by cold
they breathe pnuemonia and the numb
distance of their skin.

Together they wait through the winter
knowing it will take three more
before they can bring their women
from the other side of the world.
Locked in the prison of skin
they break on the long weekend
when loggers pelt their shack with stones.
Three are taken to hospital in Kamloops.
with arms and bellies slashed
and when the lone policeman asks
what caused the fight, they tell him
the fight was amongst themselves.
They say they fought over
the memory of their women;
that to keep from going mad
they were driven there with words
believing they could survive
by telling each other stories of love.

The Carpenter

The gentle fears he tells me of being
afraid to climb back down each day
from the top of the unfinished building.
He says: I'm getting old
and wish each morning when I arrive
I could beat into shape
a scaffold to take me higher
but the wood I'd need
is still growing on the hills
the nails raw red with rust
still changing shape in bluffs
somewhere north of my mind.

I've hung over this city like a bird
and seen it change from shacks to towers.
It's not that I'm afraid
but sometimes when I'm alone up here
and know I can't get higher
I think I'll just walk off the edge
and either fall or fly

and then he laughs
so that his plum-bob goes awry
and single strokes the spikes into the joists
pushing the floor another level higher
like a hawk who every year adds levels to his nest
until he's risen above the tree he builds on
and alone lifts off into the wind
beating his wings like nails into the sky.

Stigmata

FOR IRVING LAYTON

What if there wasn't a metaphor
and the bodies were only bodies
bones pushed out in awkward fingers?
Waves come to the seawall, fall away,
children bounce mouths against the stones
man has carved to keep the sea at bay
and women talk with empty wombs
proclaiming freedom to the night.
Through barroom windows rotten with light
eyes of men open and close like fists.

I bend beside a tidal pool and take a crab from the sea.
His small green life twists helpless in my hand
the living bars of bone and flesh
a cage made by the animal I am.
This thing, the beat, the beat of life
now captured in the darkness of my flesh
struggling with claws as if it could tear its way
through my body back to the sea.
What do I know of the inexorable beauty,
the unrelenting turning of the wheel I am inside me?
Stigmata. I hold a web of blood.

I dream of the scrimshawed teeth of endless whales,
the oceans it took to carve them. Drifting ships
echo in fog the wounds of Leviathan
great grey voices giving cadence to their loss.
The men are gone
who scratched upon white bones their destiny.
Who will speak of the albatross in the shroud of the man,
the sailor who sinks forever in the Mindanao Deep?
I open my hand. The life leaps out.

Albino Pheasants

At the bottom of the field
where thistles throw their seeds
and poplars grow from cotton into trees
in a single season I stand among the weeds.
Fenceposts hold each other up with sagging wire.
Here no man walks except in wasted time.
Men circle me with cattle, cars and wheat.
Machines rot on my margins.
They say the land is wasted when its wild
and offer plows and apple trees to tame
but in the fall when I have driven them away
with their guns and dogs and dreams
I walk alone. While those who'd kill
lie sleeping in soft beds
huddled against the bodies of their wives
I go with speargrass and hooked burrs
and wait upon the ice alone.

Delicate across the mesh of snow
I watch the pale birds come
with beaks the colour of discarded flesh.
White, their feathers are white,
as if they had been born in caves
and only now have risen to the earth
to watch with pink and darting eyes
the slowly moving shadows of the moon.
There is no way to tell men what to do...
the dance they make in sleep
withholds its meaning from their dreams.
That which has been nursed in bone
rests easy upon frozen stone
and what is wild is lost behind closed eyes:
albino birds, pale sisters, succubi.

Of Letters

I sit in the solitude of letters.
Words do not slow the sun.
The sky is clear in the west.

Clouds have passed over me.
Their spun silk hangs
on the bones of the Monashee.

A magpie drifts across the sun.
His long tail writes too swiftly
for me to interpret. On my desk

a wasp I killed last week
after it stung me. Who
will write its poem?

I move toward my fortieth year.
Letters remain unanswered.
The sun slides into the west

and in the east clouds collapse
draping with crystal
the waiting arms of the trees.

Michael Ondaatje

Early Morning, Kingston to Gananoque

The twenty miles to Gananoque
with tangled dust blue grass
burned, and smelling burned
along the highway
is land too harsh for picnics.
Deep in the fields
behind stiff dirt fern
nature breeds the unnatural.

Escaping cows canter white
then black and white
along the median, forming out of mist.
Crows pick at animal accidents,
with swoops lift meals—
blistered groundhogs, stripped snakes
to arch behind a shield of sun.

Somewhere in those fields
they are shaping new kinds of women.

The Diverse Causes

'for than all erbys and treys renewyth a man and woman,
and in lyke wyse lovers callyth to their mynde olde
jantylnes and olde servyse, and many kynde dedes that
was forgotyn by neclygence'

Three clouds and a tree
reflect themselves on a toaster.
The kitchen window hangs scarred,
shattered by winter hunters.

We are in a cell of civilised magic.
Stravinsky roars at breakfast,
our milk is powdered.

Outside, a May god
moves his paws to alter wind
to scatter shadows of tree and cloud.
The minute birds walk confident
jostling the cold grass.
The world not yet of men.

We clean buckets of their sand
to fetch water in the morning,
reach for winter cobwebs,
sweep up moths who have forgotten to waken.
When the children sleep, angled
behind their bottles, you can hear mice prowl.
I turn a page
careful not to break the rhythms
of your sleeping head on my hip,
watch the moving under your eyelid
that turns like fire,
and we have love and the god outside
until ice starts to limp
in brown hidden waterfalls,
or my daughter burns the lake
by reflecting her red shoes in it.

A House Divided

This midnight breathing
heaves with no sensible rhythm,
is fashioned by no metronome.
Your body, eager
for the extra yard of bed,
reconnoitres and outflanks;
I bend in peculiar angles.

This nightly battle is fought with subtleties:
you get pregnant, I'm sure,
just for extra ground
—immune from kicks now.

Inside you now's another,
thrashing like a fish,
swinging, fighting
for its inch already.

For John, Falling

Men stopped in the heel of sun,
hum of engines evaporated;
the machine displayed itself bellied with mud
and balanced—immense.

No one ran to where
his tensed muscles curled unusually,
where jaws collected blood,
the hole in his chest the size of fists,
hands clutched to eyes like a blindness.

Arched there he made
ridiculous requests for air.
And twelve construction workers
what should they do but surround
or examine the path of falling.

And the press in bright shirts,
a doctor, the foreman scuffing a mound,
men removing helmets,
the machine above him
shielding out the sun
while he drowned
in the beautiful dark orgasm of his mouth.

The Time Around Scars

A girl whom I've not spoken to
or shared coffee with for several years
writes of an old scar.
On her wrist it sleeps, smooth and white,
the size of a leech.
I gave it to her
brandishing a new Italian penknife.
Look, I said turning,
and blood spat onto her shirt.

My wife has scars like spread raindrops
on knees and ankles,
she talks of broken greenhouse panes
and yet, apart from imagining red feet,
(a nymph out of Chagall)
I bring little to that scene.
We remember the time around scars,
they freeze irrelevant emotions
and divide us from present friends.
I remember this girl's face,
the widening rise of surprise.

And would she
moving with lover or husband
conceal or flaunt it,
or keep it at her wrist
a mysterious watch.
And this scar I then remember
is medallion of no emotion.

I would meet you now
and I would wish this scar
to have been given with
all the love
that never occurred between us.

Elizabeth

Catch, my Uncle Jack said
and oh I caught this huge apple
red as Mrs Kelly's bum.
It's red as Mrs Kelly's bum, I said
and Daddy roared
and swung me on his stomach with a heave.
Then I hid the apple in my room
till it shrunk like a face
growing eyes and teeth ribs.

Then Daddy took me to the zoo
he knew the man there
they put a snake around my neck
and it crawled down the front of my dress.
I felt its flicking tongue
dripping onto me like a shower.
Daddy laughed and said Smart Snake
and Mrs Kelly with us scowled.

In the pond where they kept the goldfish
Philip and I broke the ice with spades
and tried to spear the fishes;
we killed one and Philip ate it,
then he kissed me
with raw saltless fish in his mouth.

My sister Mary's got bad teeth
and said I was lucky, then she said
I had big teeth, but Philip said I was pretty.
He had big hands that smelled.

I would speak of Tom, soft laughing,
who danced in the mornings round the sundial
teaching me the steps from France, turning
with the rhythm of the sun on the warped branches,
who'd hold my breast and watch it move like a snail
leaving his quick urgent love in my palm.

And I kept his love in my palm till it blistered.

When they axed his shoulders and neck
the blood moved like a branch into the crowd.
And he staggered with his hanging shoulder
cursing their thrilled cry, wheeling,
waltzing in the French style to his knees
holding his head with the ground,
blood settling on his clothes like a blush;
this way
when they aimed the thud into his back.

And I find cool entertainment now
with white young Essex, and my nimble rhymes.

Peter

I

That spring Peter was discovered, freezing
the maze of bones from a dead cow,
skull and hooves glazed
with a skin of ice.
The warmth in his hands
carved hollows of muscle,
his fingers threading veins on its flank.

In the attempt to capture him
he bit, to defend himself,
three throats and a wrist;
that night villagers found the cow
frozen in red, and Peter
eating a meal beside it.

II

They snared him in evening light,
his body a pendulum
between the walls of the yard,
rearing from shrinking flashes of steel
until they, with a new science,
stretched his heels and limbs,
scarred through the back of his knees
leaving his veins unpinned,
and him singing in the evening air.

Till he fainted, and a brown bitch
nosed his pain, stared in interest,
and he froze into consciousness
to drag his feet to the fountain,
to numb wounds.

III

In the first months of his capture
words were growls, meaningless;
disgust in his tone burned everyone.
At meals, in bed, you heard Peter's howl
in the depths of the castle like a bell.
After the first year they cut out his tongue;

difficult
to unpin a fish's mouth
without the eventual jerk
to empty throat of pin and matter.

There followed months of silence,
then the eventual grunting;
he began to speak with the air of his body,
torturing breath into tones; it was despicable,
they had made a dead animal of his throat.

He was little more than a marred stone,

a baited gargoyle, escaped
from the fountain in the courtyard:
his throat swollen like an arm muscle,
his walk stuttered with limp, his knees straight,
his feet arching like a compass.

IV

They made a hive for him in the court,
Jason throwing him bones from the table,
the daughter Tara tousling in detail
the hair that collapsed like a nest
over his weaving eyes.
She, with bored innocence,
would pet him like a flower,
place vast kisses on his writs, waists,
thrilled at scowls and obscenities,
delighted at sudden grins
that opened his face like a dawn.
He ate, bouldered at their feet,
vast hands shaping rice,
and he walked with them on grit drives—
his legs dragged like a suitcase behind him.

V

All this while Peter formed violent beauty.
He carved death on chalices,
made spoons of yawning golden fishes;
forks stemmed from the tongues of reptiles,
candle holders bent like the ribs of men.

He made fragments of people: breasts
in the midst of a girl's stride,
a head burrowed in love,
an arm swimming—fingers heaved
to nose barricades of water.

His squat form, the rippled arms

of seaweeded hair,
the fingers black, bent from moulding silver,
poured all his strength
into the bare reflection of eyes.

VI

Then Tara grew.

When he first saw her, tall,
ungainly as trees,
her fat knees dangled his shoulders
as her hips rode him,
the court monster, she
swaying from side to side, held
only by the grip of her thighs
on his obtuse neck—
she bending over him,
muttering giggles at his eyes,
covering his creased face with her hair.
And he made golden spiders for her
and silver frogs, with opal glares.

And as she grew, her body
burned its awkwardness.
the full bones roamed
in brown warm skin.
The ridge in her back broadened,
her dress hid seas of thighs,
arms trailed to adjust hair that paused
like a long bird at her shoulder;
and vast brown breasts
restless at each gesture
clung to her body like new sea beasts.

And she smiled cool at Peter now,
a quiet hand received gifts from him,
and her fingers, poised,
touched
to generate expressions.

VII

An arm held her, splayed
its fingers like a cross at her neck
till he could feel fear thrashing at her throat,
while his bent hands tore the sheet of skirt,
lifted her, buttock and neck to the table.
Then laying arm above her breasts
he shaped her body like a mould,
the stub on tongue sharp as a cat, cold,
dry as a cat, rasping neck and breasts
till he poured loathing of fifteen years on her,
a vat of lush oil, staining,
the large soft body like a whale.

Then he lay there breathing at her neck
his face wet from her tears
that glued him to her pain.

We're at the Graveyard

Stuart Sally Kim and I
watching still stars
or now and then sliding stars
like hawk spit to the trees.
Up there the clear charts,
the systems' intricate branches
which change with hours and solstices,
the bone geometry of moving from there, to there.

And down here—friends
whose minds and bodies
shift like acrobats to each other.
When we leave, they move
to an altitude of silence.

So our minds shape
and lock the transient,
parallel these bats
who organize the air
with thick blinks of travel:
Sally is like grey snow in the grass.
Sally of the beautiful bones
pregnant below stars.

'The gate in his head'

FOR VICTOR COLEMAN

Victor—the shy mind
revealing faint scars
coloured strata of the brain
not clarity but the sense of shift.
A few lines/the tracks of thought.
The landscape of busted trees
melted tires in the sun
Stan's fishbowl
with a book inside
turning its pages
like some sea animal
camouflaging itself
the typeface clarity
going slow blond in the sun full water

My mind is pouring chaos
in nets onto the page.
A blind lover, dont know
what I love till I write it out.
Then from Gibson's your letter
with a blurred
photograph of a gull.

Caught vision. The stunning white bird
an unclear stir.

And that is all this writing should be then.
The beautiful formed things caught at the wrong moment
so they are shapeless, awkward
moving to the clear.

Postcard from Piccadilly Street

Dogs are the unheralded voyeurs of this world.
When we make love
the spaniel shudders
walks out of the room,
she's had her fill of children now

but the basset—for whom
we've pretty soon got to find a love object
apart from furniture or visitor's legs—
jumps on the bed and watches.

It is a catching habit having a spectator
and appeals to the actor in both of us,
in spite of irate phone calls from the SPCA
who claim we are corrupting minors
(the dog is one and a half).

We have moved to elaborate audiences now.
At midnight we open the curtains
turn out the light
and imagine the tree outside
full of sparrows
with infra red eyes.

Letters & Other Worlds

'for there was no more darkness for him and, no doubt
like Adam before the fall, he could see in the dark'

My father's body was a globe of fear
His body was a town we never knew
He hid that he had been where we were going
His letters were a room he seldom lived in
In them the logic of his love could grow

My father's body was a town of fear
He was the only witness to its fear dance
He hid where he had been that we might lose him
His letters were a room his body scared

He came to death with his mind drowning.
On the last day he enclosed himself
in a room with two bottles of gin, later
fell the length of his body
so that brain blood moved
to new compartments
that never knew the wash of fluid
and he died in minutes of a new equilibrium.

His early life was a terrifying comedy
and my mother divorced him again and again.
He would rush into tunnels magnetized
by the white eye of trains
and once, gaining instant fame,
managed to stop a Perahara in Ceylon
—the whole procession of elephants dancers
local dignitaries—by falling
dead drunk onto the street.
As a semi-official, and semi-white at that,
the act was seen as a crucial
turning point in the Home Rule Movement
and led to Ceylon's independence in 1948.

(My mother had done her share too—
 her driving so bad
 she was stoned by villagers
 whenever her car was recognized)

For 14 years of marriage
each of them claimed he or she
was the injured party.
Once on the Colombo docks
saying goodbye to a recently married couple
my father, jealous
at my mother's articulate emotion,
dove into the waters of the harbour
and swam after the ship waving farewell.
My mother pretending no affiliation
mingled with the crowd back to the hotel.

Once again he made the papers
though this time my mother
with a note to the editor
corrected the report—saying he was drunk
rather than broken hearted at the parting of friends.
The married couple received both editions
of *The Ceylon Times* when their ship reached Aden.

And then in his last years
he was the silent drinker,
the man who once a week
disappeared into his room with bottles
and stayed there until he was drunk
and until he was sober.

There speeches, head dreams, apologies,
the gentle letters, were composed.
With the clarity of architects
he would write of the row of blue flowers
his new wife had planted,
the plans for electricity in the house,

how my half-sister fell near a snake
and it had awakened and not touched her.
Letters in a clear hand of the most complete empathy
his heart widening and widening and widening
to all manner of change in his children and friends
while he himself edged
into the terrible acute hatred
of his own privacy
till he balanced and fell
the length of his body
the blood screaming in
the empty reservoir of bones
the blood searching in his head without metaphor

White Dwarfs

This is for people who disappear
for those who descend into the code
and make their room a fridge for Superman
—who exhaust costume and bones that could perform flight,
who shave their moral so raw
they can tear themselves through the eye of a needle
this is for those people
that hover and hover
and die in the ether peripheries

There is my fear
of no words   of
falling without words
over and over   of
mouthing the silence
Why do I love most

among my heroes those
who sail to that perfect edge
where there is no social fuel
Release of sandbags
to understand their altitude—

       that silence of the third cross
       3rd man hung so high and lonely
       we dont hear him say
       say his pain, say his unbrotherhood
       What has he to do with the smell of ladies
       can they eat off his skeleton of pain?

The Gurkhas in Malaya
cut the tongues of mules
so they were silent beasts of burden
in enemy territories
after such cruelty what could they speak of anyway
And Dashiell Hammett in success
suffered conversation and moved
to the perfect white between the words

This white that can grow
is fridge, bed,
is an egg—most beautiful
when unbroken, where
what we cannot see is growing
in all the colours we cannot see

there are those burned out stars
who implode into silence
after parading in the sky
after such choreography what would they wish to speak of   anywa

Bearhug

Griffin calls to come and kiss him goodnight
I yell ok. Finish something I'm doing,
then something else, walk slowly round
the corner to my son's room.
He is standing arms outstretched
waiting for a bearhug. Grinning.

Why do I give my emotion an animal's name,
give it that dark squeeze of death?
This is the hug which collects
all his small bones and his warm neck against me.
The thin tough body under the pyjamas
locks to me like a magnet of blood.

How long was he standing there
like that, before I came?

Pat Lowther

Touch Home

My daughter, a statistic
in a population explosion
exploded
          popped
out of my body like a cork.

The doctors called for oxygen,
the birth too sudden, violent,
the child seemed pale

But my daughter lay
in perfect tranquillity
touching   the new air
      with her
  elegant   hands.

Wanting

Wanting
to be broken
utterly
split apart with a mighty tearing
like an apple broken
to unfold
the delicate open veined petal pattern
inside the fruit

I am arrogant
knowing
what I can do
for a man

I am arrogant
for fear
I may be broken
utterly open
and he not see
the flower shape of me

Regard to Neruda

When I heard that
the world's greatest poet
was running for president:
being north american
I would have laughed, until
I thought of the campaign trek
over country that was
his blood and bed,
the persistent human song
for which he became
rivers, harps of forests,
metallic skies of cities.
and I thought also
of the tenderness implied
in his handshake.

Could I see with his high vision
(man with thick hands and belly
full of good things)
the naked feet of beginnings,
the sons of rare minerals
transforming the earth,
could I wash my country
with songs that settle
like haloes on the constituents,
I'd campaign

to be prime minister
without kisses.

Often now I forget
how to make love
but I think I am ready
to learn politics.

Early Winters

Under the burned-off mountain
winds died   the forest rangers
packed their sleeping bags
and left for town
trees cracked their knuckles
windows began telling stories

And the child dreamed meteors
spiralling like snowflakes
into the trees

Herbs in the garden died
bees slept in their cells
a late bear tumbled the garbage cans
the creek broke ice
and rushed endlessly past the house

And the child dreamed blue water
green water
and the death of water

Deer on the winter road
wore jewels in their antlers
the spines of the burnt mountain
sifted the snow
like a giant comb

Notes From Furry Creek

I

The water reflecting cedars
all the way up
deep sonorous green—
nothing prepares you
for the ruler-straight
log fallen across
and the perfect
water fall it makes
and the pool behind it
novocaine-cold
and the huckleberries
hanging
like fat red lanterns

II

The dam, built
by coolies, has outlived
its time; its wall
stained sallow
as ancient skin
dries in the sun

The spillway still
splashes bright spray
on the lion
shapes of rock
far down below

The dam foot
is a pit
for the royal animals
quiet and dangerous
in the stare
of sun and water

III

When the stones swallowed me
I could not surface
but squatted
in foaming water
all one curve
motionless,
glowing like agate.

I understood the secret
of a monkey-puzzle tree
by knowing its opposite:

the smooth and the smooth
and the smooth takes,
seduces your eyes
to smaller and smaller
ellipses;
reaching the centre
you become
stone, the perpetual
lavèd god.

Coast Range

Just north of town
the mountains start to talk
back-of-the-head buzz
of high stubbled meadows
minute flowers
moss gravel and clouds

They're not snobs, these mountains,
they don't speak Rosicrucian,
they sputter with

billygoat-bearded creeks
bumsliding down
to splat into the sea

they talk with the casual
tongues of water
rising in trees

They're so humble they'll let you
blast highways through them
baring their iron and granite
sunset-coloured bones
broken for miles

And nights when
clouds foam on a beach
of clear night sky,
those high slopes creak
in companionable sleep

Chacabuco, The Pit

(Information filtered out of Chile: political
prisoners formerly held in the stadium at Santiago
have been transported to a Nazi-type concentration
camp set up in a disused nitrates mine somewhere
on the Atacama desert.)

> EVERYTHING SHOULD BE DONE
QUIETLY AND EFFECTIVELY TO INSURE
THAT ALLENDE DOES NOT LAST THE NEXT
CRUCIAL SIX MONTHS.
—from 18-point plan submitted by International
Telegraph and Telephone Co. to the White House, USA.

CONTACT TRUSTWORTHY SOURCES
WITHIN THE CHILEAN ARMED FORCES.
—from Point 7, above.

I shall speak to the Lord of Heaven
where he sits asleep.
—from an ancient Mayan prayer.

Atacama desert:
by day the sun lets down
his weight   everyone wears
a halo   everything quivers
sharp-sided dust refracts
blurred glitter between
creased squinting eyelids;
by night the land is naked
to the farthest reaches
between galaxies
that vacuum sucks
heat: the land is
cold to the utter bone.

Carefully now (place
records on a turntable)
remember those 1940s movies
where virgins were sacrifices
to volcanoes: here is
that same
        ceremonial
            suspenseful
                approach:
we are approaching
            Chacabuco
                the pit.

Notice first the magnificent sunset,
the stars, the clouds of Magellan.
Note that here as in all human places
prayer has been uttered.

Watch until morning
burns the sky white.
Wooden shacks persevere
in the dry air,
their corners banked with dust;
a grid of streets prints
an ominous white shadow
on your eyelids;
it leads
to the pit.

A huge, gouged çavity
flickering like a bad film,
the whole scene twitching
on and off
in and out of existence:
is God blinking? are you
shuttering your eyes, tourista?

I shall speak to the lord of heaven
where he sits asleep

there are men in that pit
imagine that they are chained
(they may be)
starving (they are)
watched over by jailers
with faces blank
as a leached brain

Working, that sallow bitter rock
ground to glass
powder enters their lungs
nostrils eyes pores
Sleeping, they dream of eating
rock, sucking juice from it
pissing nitrate dust

Moments of darkness film

their eyes, they stumble
in negative light
and the blows of whips

*

Do they remember
who they are? patriots
 believers
    builders

collective dreamers who woke
to find all their good wishes
happening faster
than they could move,
the people outreaching the planners
factory workers running
the factories
children wearing moustaches
of milk

Forgetting to keep guns beside their pillows
forgetting to bribe generals
breathing long breaths of peace
organizing anti-Fascist song festivals
instead of militia
seeing the people stand at last
upright in mellow light like a sound harvest
they forgot lifetimes of exile
years of held breath and stealth
seeing so many strong
they forgot the strength of I.T.& T.
United Fruit Co.
    Anaconda

who do not easily give up
what they have taken.

*

Some one decides
who shall eat
who shall not eat
who shall be beaten
and on which
parts of his body

Some one decides
who shall be starved
who shall be fed
enough to sustain
another day's torture

A man decides.
That man does not breathe dust:
he is dust.

*

Choirs of young boys
exquisitely trained
sing hymns in cathedrals;
jellyfish swim in the ocean
like bubbles of
purity made tangible;
whole cities lie open
to the stars;
women bake bread;
fruit trees unfold their blossoms
petal by petal;
we are continually born

but these, captive, stumble
in gross heat
in stupor of pain:
they are the fingers sliced off
when the wood was cut,
the abortions born living;

they are the mangled
parts of our bodies
screaming to be
reunited.

*

'If I forget thee, O Zion

Let statesmen's tongues lock
between their jaws,
let businessmen's cheque hands
be paralyzed,
let musicians stop building
towers of sound,
let commerce fall
in convulsions:
we have deserved this.

*

Staircases ascending
through caverns
clefts in the root sockets
of mountains, opening
onto ocean's foot:
we have all been there,
that journey, its
hardships its surprises
stay in our cells
our footprints in clay
splayed: we were burdened.

Remember breathing on fire
a cautious husbandry
then suddenly sparks
bursting upward
like dolphins leaping
in the sunlight path
of the first boat

we had song
        mathematics
                magic

Even for torturers we have done this
journey, broken
ourselves like crumbs,
pumped children into wombs,
heaved them out,
laid stone on stone;

we forgive each other
our absurdities,
casually accept splendour;
we forgive even death

but these places
of death slowly inflicted
we can't forgive, but writhe
coiling in on ourselves
to try to forget, to deny:
we have travelled so far
and these are still with us?

Even now in our cities
churches   universities
pleasant lawns   we are
scrabbling with broken nails
against rock, we are
dying of flies and disease.
Until that pus is drained
we are not healed.

*

'And the dead shall be raised incorruptible'

When their names are called
will you answer,
will I?

for bread on the table
for salt in the bread
for bees in the cups
of flowers
will you answer to their names?

For I tell you the earth
itself is a mystery
which we penetrate constantly
and our people a holy mystery
beyond refusal

And the horrors of the mind
are the horrors of
what we allow to be done
and the grace of the soul
is what we determine shall be
made truly among us. Amen.

The Dig

Even where traffic passes
the ancient world has exposed
a root, large and impervious,
humped like a dragon
among the city's conduits.
Look, they say,
who would have thought
the thing so tough,
so secretive?

THE DIGGERS

The bone gloved in clay
shallow perhaps where arches
of feet go over;

they see it as finished
round like a jar;
a shard they see as whole.
*Will our bones tell
what we died of?*

The diggers
with very gentle fingers
lift up the bones of a woman;
tenderly they take off
her stockings of earth;
they have not such love
for the living
who are not finished
or predicted.

THE BONES

The men we see always swift
moving, edged with a running light
like fire; their hands infinitely
potent, working in blood,
commanding the death of animals,
the life of the tribe.

The women we see finished
completed like fat jars,
like oil floating on water:
breasts   bellies   faces
all round and calm.

*Their bones should thrash
in the diggers' baskets,
should scream against the light.*

Their work bent them
and sex, that soft explosion
miraculous as rain
broke in them over and over,

their bodies thickened like tubers
broke and were remade
again and again crying out
in the heave of breaking
the terrible pleasure
again and again till
they fell away, at last
they became bone.

Even their hands
curved around implements,
pounding-stones, were worshipping
the cock that made them
round and hollow.

But before their falling away
was an anger,
a stone in the mouth.
They would say there is
a great fall like water,
a mask taking shape on air,
a sound coming nearer
like a heavy animal
breaking twigs.

And the flesh stamen
bursting inside them
splayed their bones
apart like spread legs.

Will our bones tell
sisters, what we died of?
how love broke us
in that helplessly desired
breaking, and men
and children ransacked our flesh,
cracked our innermost bones
to eat the morrow.

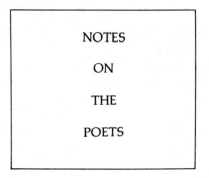

NOTES

ON

THE

POETS

MARGARET ATWOOD

One way of looking at Margaret Atwood's poetry is to see it as the jottings of a pioneer in the uncharted expanses of consciousness. Her poetry seems to say (to make a variation on the Cartesian *cogito ergo sum*), 'I think, therefore I am in trouble.' The human mind is flooded with data that it must edit, arrange, build structures from, in order to retain its sanity, to preserve the distinctions between self and other. As Atwood observes in 'Progressive Insanities of a Pioneer', 'un-structured/space is a deluge'. In this frightening world of cluttered senses, specific objects may assume enormous proportions until they encompass the whole of consciousness. Always there is fear, as expressed in 'A Place: Fragments' (*The Circle Game*), that no key will be found 'that informs, holds together/this confusion, this largeness/and dissolving'.

Another handicap of perception is that it produces isolation or alienation. Men are mere objects in space, separated by manners, modes of perception, differing pasts, their fears, roles, the games they play, the rooms they choose to live in, the objects they collect to give themselves meaning. Atwood's poems reveal an obsession with space—the spaces within, around, and between men and objects. Everywhere there is a barrier between the perceiver and the object perceived, between subject and object; as she says in 'Part of a Day' (*The Animals in That Country*): 'each of us reflects/the despair of the separate/object.' Her poetry is full of skins, cages, glass cases, borders, maps, fortifications, anything that marks the boundaries or demarcations that separate, whether the 'protecting/eggshell' people wear or the nationalities behind which groups hide. In 'What Happened' (*Animals*) she speaks of men being locked inside their own catastrophes. In 'Astral Traveller' (*Animals*), not only are men's pasts inaccessible; their very bodies are foreign.

Atwood's technical concerns have far-reaching implications. She is both the archetypal first Canadian, trying to build some shelter or structure against the hostile wilderness, and the archetypal first human waking from the unconscious sleep of evolution. Her figures are often pioneers, immigrants, explorers, exiles of one sort or another. Survival is the first necessity for exiles, she says in 'Rooming-house Winter' (*Animals*). 'We must resist. We must refuse/to disappear.' Like the pioneer, one must begin by taking an inventory of the trivia, the flotsam of consciousness; one must try to discover meaning where there is no meaning. Poetry is a means of controlling experience, of ordering chaos. At times Atwood presents her startling, surreal images in a prosaic, matter-of-fact manner that is dislocating to the reader of traditional verse; at other times she assumes absurd points of view, shifts back and forth between reality and fantasy, and uses a variety of other alienating devices, including parentheses. She does not hesitate to experiment, to dispense with any device that is predictable and, therefore, potentially boring. Often her line-lengths seem haphazard, questionable, convincing as units of neither sound nor sense; but even here it might be argued that the line-ends serve as unexpected springboards that draw attention away from music and toward meaning. Most often the poetic mind is so acute and the rapid fire of images so compelling that the prosody itself goes by unnoticed.

Atwood is the author of eight books of poetry: *The Circle Game* (1966), which received the Governor General's Award; *The Animals in That Country* (1968), which won first prize in the Centennial Commission competition; *The Journals of Susanna Moodie* (1970); *Procedures for Underground* (1970), containing five poems that received the Union Poetry Prize from *Poetry; Power Politics* (1971); *You Are Happy* (1974); *Selected Poems* (1976); and *Two-Headed Poems* (1978). Her novels are *The Edible Woman* (1969), *Surfacing* (1972), and *Lady Oracle* (1976). She is also the author of *Survival: A Thematic Guide to Canadian Literature* (1972). She was born in Ottawa in 1939 and is a graduate of the University of Toronto. She now lives on a farm outside Toronto, where she writes full time.

MARGARET AVISON

In 1941 Margaret Avison outlined a modest poetic: 'Literature', she wrote, 'results when: (a) every word is written in the full light of *all* the writer knows; (b) the writer accepts the precise limits of what he knows, i.e. distinguishes unerringly (while writing) between what he knows, and what he merely knows about, by reputation or reflected opinion.' This poetic, which she endorsed again as recently as 1962, reflects not only the seriousness with which she approaches her craft, but also her view of poetry as a vehicle of discovery. She is a philosophical poet who is moved to search for 'truths' that underlie the world we perceive with our senses. She is not a descriptive poet; she is interested, as she explains in 'Voluptuaries and Others', in 'that other kind of lighting up/That shows the terrain comprehended.' 'Nobody stuffs the word in at your eyes,' she says in 'Snow'. 'The optic heart must venture: a jail-break/And re-creation.' In order to make this jail-break, the optic heart must see through the pollution of body and mind that produces a society of unconscious grey men and clapboard suburbs, and 'this communal cramp of understanding' ('The World Still Needs'). In a world where salesmanship is valued more than a fine ear, where limited imaginations triumph, the poet can find little that is worth her attention and respect. The landscapes of *Winter Sun* (1960) are bleak and imprisoning, like the landscapes of Eliot's early poetry; like Eliot also,

Avison is often forced to go into the past in search of significant moments of illumination. Thus her interest in great men of science whose imaginative leaps have opened up new worlds of knowledge and experience. 'History makes the spontaneous jubilation at such moments less and less likely though,' she laments.

Avison's epistemological concerns have resulted in a number of poems that explore the nature of imaginative perception. Many poems in *Winter Sun* are characterized by rapid shifts of perspective, a kind of poetic equivalent of the use of multiple lenses and camera-angles in film-making. To write in the 'full light of *all* the writer knows' involves dispensing with all formal notions of time and space. As in the stream-of-consciousness novel, the reader of Avison's poetry is often hard-pressed to find a centre of gravity, a fixed point of reference. It is as though, in this world of continuous change, the only certainty is the act of perception itself. Each new poem, for poet and reader alike, is analogous to the swimmer's moment at the whirlpool; if both 'dare knowledge', they will discover perhaps 'the silver reaches of the estuary'.

The austere winter terrain of her first book gives way to gentler landscapes and warmer climates in *The Dumbfounding* (1966), marking a deepening of religious experience. There is also a reconciliation with the physical world that results in poetry at once more concrete and sensuous. These poems are characterized by a careful observation of minutiae, such as the faces of loiterers and the industry of ants; it is the work of a poet fully absorbed in actuality. Here Avison leaves behind most of the rhetorical and esoteric elements that trouble her earlier verse; her sensitivity to the subtleties of language now encompasses the sound of rain-drops, 'letting the ear experience this/discrete, delicate/clicking.'

Margaret Avison was born in Galt, Ont., in 1918 and educated at the University of Toronto. She has been a librarian, a secretary, a research worker, a lecturer in English literature, and is presently engaged in social work at a mission in downtown Toronto. She is one of the finest but least prolific poets in Canada. Apart from the two books mentioned, her poems have appeared mainly in magazines and anthologies. During the early forties and fifties she contributed to Sid Corman's *Origin*, along with Charles Olson, Denise Levertov, and Robert Creeley. Apart from giving occasional readings and participating in a writers' workshop at the University of British Columbia, she has remained at the edges of the literary arena in Canada. She is an enthusiastic supporter of other writers and has translated a number of poems from the Hungarian.

EARLE BIRNEY

Birney is a poet who has always believed that moral progress is possible. As he says in 'Conference of Heads', 'There is no fog but in the will/the iceberg is elective.' However, his observation of the scarred battleground of his own century has troubled him deeply, causing him to lash out in anger at human cruelty and indifference and to despair at his own guilt and complicity. These two responses reflect the Marxism of a generation caught in two world wars and a depression as well as the Puritanism of his heritage. The first accounts for his well-known vitriolic satires, such as 'Anglo-Saxon Street', and for his more recent attacks on the economic and political atrocities of the American empire, such as 'Sinaloa' and 'Images in Place of Logging', where he describes 'the men and the metalled/ants that multiply in the browning/pulp of the peeled world.' More convincing than the poems of moral outrage are his poems of guilt and initiation, such as 'David', 'For George Lamming', and 'Arrivals'. In 'Arrivals' he participates in the gratuitous death of a young lawyer whose car has collided with a passenger train. Seeing the outstretched hand, the poet wonders, 'is it only in me that the hand hooked/and I who must manage it now like a third?' As early as 1945, Birney had written from Watford Military Hospital lamenting the time-bomb within each man, and pleading: 'O men be swift to be mankind/or let the grizzly take.' Almost twenty years later, he wrote in 'Letter to a Cuzco Priest': 'Pray to yourself above all for men like me/that we do not quench/the man in each of us.'

In 'The Bear on the Delhi Road', Birney suggests the method by which he brings his world under imaginative control. He says: 'It is not easy to free/myth from reality.' He describes the business of trying to make a bear dance—that is, giving it human form by making it dance rather than merely amble among berries. The men of Kashmir are like the poet, trying to transform crude reality, trying to give it artistic shape. The process seems to be a characteristic one for Birney. He begins with the real and concrete, whether an object or an experience, and reflects upon it until its 'meaning' (for him) is released. This is the essential structure of the romantic ode, wherein the poet contemplates a height of land (say Tintern Abbey) and is moved to discover some personal and universal significance in his experience. It is certainly the organizing principle at work in 'Vancouver Lights', 'A Walk in Kyoto', and many of Birney's travel poems; and it is a method he shares quite noticeably with Al Purdy.

Birney's energies have always been engaged in coming to terms with his need for a social identity and with his separateness as an artist. Despite his involvement in the war and the universities, he has always been an outsider, beset by internal and external forces that have kept him from feeling fulfilled. He resents society's indifference to the artist and feels intensely that the artist has a cure for society's ills. In 'Cartagena de Indias' he describes what it means to learn that other cultures can honour even their most critical poets. 'I love the whole starved cheating/poetry-reading lot of you,' he says of the Colombians, 'I who am seldom read by my townsmen.' In *The Creative Writer*, Birney speaks of the situation of the writer in Canada:

It seems to me that the effective writer is one who is inwardly sure of the entire naturalness of his creative act. For instance, he must be aware that he is writing not merely because he is neurotic. Everybody's a bit queer and slightly mad, but I'm sure that my compulsion to construct more and more unprofitable verses isn't anywhere near as screwball as the compulsion of businessmen to make more and more money. But the writer who does not believe this is hamstrung from the start, haunted by a false diagnosis of his society, and driven either into a permanent state of apology and mock-modesty for his abnormality, or into snarling hatred for the nastiness of the normal.

This describes accurately many of the tensions Birney has felt during his own lifetime. For him there can be no real resolution of this tension. And there is reason to believe that without it his peculiar *daimon* would cease to function. That is why he is continually on the move, why he is always experimenting in his art.

'Living art,' Birney says, 'like anything else, stays alive only by changing.' His own verse has travelled from the most traditional beginnings—including narrative, meditative lyrics, satires, nature poems, and odes—through years of experiment with typography and orthography, down the long congested road to concrete poetry. Birney is a constant reviser of poems and a contributor to little magazines. 'I don't know exactly where the literary Dew Line is this moment,' he says, 'but I'm sure it lies somewhere in the complicated world of today's little-little magazines and small-press chapbooks.'

Birney's life is as colourful as his art—and as controversial. He was born in 1904 in Calgary, but spent most of his youth in Banff and in Creston, B.C. He graduated from the University of British Columbia in 1926. His graduate studies in California were interrupted by difficulties, mostly financial, which took him to Utah to teach, and to New York to work for the Trotskyites. With a grant from the Royal Society he completed his doctoral studies in London, Eng., and at the University of Toronto, where he lectured for several years and served as literary editor of the *Canadian Forum*. During the Second World War he was a Personnel Selection Officer overseas and then for a short time was Supervisor of Foreign Language Broadcasts to Europe for the CBC. Later he joined the English Department at UBC and was head of the Department of Creative Writing. Birney has been writer-in-residence at the University of Toronto and has travelled widely throughout Asia, Europe, South America, and the United States. He now resides in Toronto.

Birney's reputation as a poet was established with *David and Other Poems* (1942) and *Now Is Time* (1945), for both of which he won a Governor General's Award. Further books have followed, including *The Strait of Anian: Selected Poems* (1948),*Trial of a City and Other Verse* (1952), *Ice Cod Bell or Stone* (1962), *Near False Creek Mouth* (1964), *Selected Poems* (1966), *Rag and Bone Shop* (1970), *The Collected Poems of Earle Birney* (1975), and *Ghost in the Wheels: Selected Poems 1920 - 1976* (1977). Birney has also written two novels—*Turvey* (1949), which won the Stephen Leacock medal for humour, and *Down the Long Table* (1955)—and a series of lectures prepared for the CBC, *The Creative Writer* (1966).

GEORGE BOWERING

Critics have consistently linked George Bowering's poetry to that of Charles Olson and other poets of Black Mountain College in North Carolina. It is true that Bowering has learned from Olson to reject the closed form in poetry, with its clichés of thought and manner, in favour of the open form, or what Olson calls 'composition by field'. Olson insists that a poem is a *thing*, a unit of energy passed from writer to reader, and that it has its own laws, the most important being that form and content must unfold simultaneously, grow out of each other. The other side of 'objectism' is that the poet himself is a thing, an object, and must continually face the fact of his existence in the physical world. He must begin with the literal fact of being; thus his preoccupation with his breathing, the rhythms of his body, the objects he has contact with. It is not so much Bowering's subscription to this poetic, however, as his identification with certain anarchic elements in the American tradition that troubles his readers.

Bowering's primitivism involves certain gestures that one associates with Irving Layton: the urge to throw off the yoke of tradition, the use of barbarisms, the rejection of familiar poetic devices such as rhyme, metrics, alliteration, and the simile. Bowering is aware that his poetic is no more than a single pattern imposed on experience to make it tolerable. In 'Circus Maximus' he speaks of being 'lost in my own particularity', but subsequently admits: '(pattern I deny/and that/is part of a pattern)'. It is not surprising that Bowering, whose energies were once channelled into the publication of a magazine with the anagrammatical title of *Tish*, should be drawn to an aesthetic that serves as a healthy antidote for his academic existence and for the conforming, repressing elements at work in his society.

Many of Bowering's comments about technique relate to the question of *voice*. 'Not just Wordsworth's vague idea of using common speech,' he says, 'but *how to get your own voice on the page.*' In his recent book on the poetry of Al Purdy, Bowering explains the notion of finding your own voice as 'a writing-school aphorism that inadequately describes the process whereby the poet comes to avail himself of ways to get the individualities of his speech habits into his prosody.'

There is no one way to achieve this end. Bowering rejects all the familiar trappings in favour of a 'plain style' consisting of vacabulary and sentence structure that are casual and simple. He avoids the phrasally determined line and the line that is always a unit of sound and sense. His irregularly determined lines and use of syncopation free his verse from the tedium of easily anticipated line breaks, but occasionally the conversational style he aims for results in a certain flatness. The relation between 'voice' and prosody may be closer to Wordsworth than Bowering admits; after all, the question still rests in the poet's choice between his tired breakfast voice and his animated evening voice.

The poet's work is also affected by his notion of subject. If he begins always with the fact of his own being, he may perhaps get no further. Alden Nowlan states the dangers in this way:

The most vulnerable part of poetry born of immediate experience is its tendency to slide into banality, where the incident or subject itself does not seem to the reader to have warranted the importance attached to it by the poet.

Bowering was born in Penticton, B.C. in 1935. He completed a B.A. in History and an M.A. in English at the University of British Columbia. As well as being an editor of *Tish*, a controversial little magazine on the west coast, he did the usual odd jobs that poets do to support themselves between sessions at the desk, at college, and at the pub. He was in the RCAF for a while and travelled to Mexico, where, he says: 'I first saw strangers as individuals. I got close to people and that has always been a hard thing for me: to be close to people.' Bowering was the founding editor of *Imago*, a magazine devoted to the publication of the long poem. He has taught in Calgary and Montreal and is now a member of the English Department at Simon Fraser University in Burnaby, B.C.

Bowering's publications include *Sticks & Stones* (1963), *Points on the Grid* (1964), *The Man in Yellow Boots* (1965), *The Silver Wire* (1966), *Baseball* (1967), *Two Police*

Poems (1968), and his two Governor-General's-Award-winning books: *Rocky Mountain Foot* (1969) and *The Gangs of Kosmos* (1969). He has published two novels— *Mirror on the Floor* (1967) and *A Short Sad Book* (1977)—as well as a collection of short stories: *Flycatcher* (1974).

LEONARD COHEN

The movement of Cohen's poetry is toward greater simplicity, toward verse that is free of artifice and the colouring of the individual ego. Speaking of these changes, Cohen says: 'Well, you know, you get wiped out. And the deeper the wipe-out, the deeper the reluctance to use ornament or to use any other faculties that brought you to the wipe-out.' In 'Style', a poem that is central to his work aesthetically and pyschologically, Cohen hints at the potential for brotherhood and harmony existing (in an electric reality that could be either Buddha's or Marshall McLuhan's) beyond the trappings of ego, culture, and nationalism. The search for a 'plain' style in poetry does not mean simply the slap-it-all-down manner that characterizes so much recent writing. It suggests rather a desire to eliminate all clichés of thought and expression that could interfere with the poet's efforts to give imaginative expression to his vision of things. In Cohen's own words:

I think that a decent man who has discovered valuable secrets is under some obligation to share them. But I think that the technique of sharing them is a great study. . . .

Now, you can reveal secrets in many ways. One way is to say this is the secret I have discovered. I think that this way is often less successful because when that certain kind of conscious creative mind brings itself to bear on this information, it distorts it, it makes it very inaccessible. Sometimes it's just in the voice, sometimes just in the style, in the length of the paragraph; it's in the tone, rather than in the message.

Cohen has learned many ways to share his secrets. In *Let Us Compare Mythologies*, the first book in the McGill Poetry Series, and *Spice-Box of Earth* he wrote in a traditional manner but was able to surprise his readers with unexpectedly bizarre images and witty about-faces. He experiments with the surreal, the lyrical, and the anti-poetic. Here Cohen explores in a light, youthful manner the mysteries and paradoxes of the Jewish and Christian religions. He also reveals a romantic obsession with regeneration and transcendence through varieties of physical love, sacrifice, violence, and degradation that ultimately finds its fullest statement in *Beautiful Losers*. The tone of joyous celebration gives way in *Flowers for Hitler* to darker imaginings. This book is Cohen's dark night of the soul. He discovers his heart of darkness in the Nazi atrocities of the Second World War; he descends morally and imaginatively into the fiery furnaces of Belsen and Auschwitz where, like Conrad's Marlow, he comes face to face with his own emptiness, his own capacity for evil.

At times, when he is too close to his subject, when the materials seem to call for irony or some other distancing technique, Cohen tries unsuccessfully to speak in his own voice. However, he is at his best when he adopts the obliqueness of symbolism rather than direct statement (of the kind found in Bowering's verse, for example). As F. says in *Beautiful Losers*, 'We who cannot dwell in the Clear Light must dwell in Symbols.' Cohen has a unique capacity for creating weird psychological parables, such as 'Story', 'You Have the Lovers', and a number of the recorded songs. Among popular contemporary lyrics, Cohen's songs most resemble the symbolic narratives of Bob Dylan. The symbolic mode suits Cohen well; it is like the Buddhist notion of the beautiful answer that asks a more beautiful question.

Cohen was born in 1934 in Montreal's Westmount district. He graduated from McGill and went on to an abortive three-week venture in graduate studies at Columbia University. Cohen returned to Montreal to read in night clubs, to write *Ballet of Lepers* (a novel that was never published), and to try a stint in the family clothing business. Eventually he received a Canada Council grant to go to England, where he worked on his first published novel, *The Favourite Game*. From England he set out for Greece and the island of Hydra, where he wrote much of his poetry and fiction. Cohen then returned to Montreal and New York to take up a full-time career as a composer-singer. He has had several albums of songs produced, including *Songs of Leonard Cohen, Songs from a Room,* and *Death of a Ladies' Man.* Despite his considerable success as a performer, he lives a quiet, almost ascetic life in Montreal. When his *Selected Poems* was awarded the Governor General's Award, Cohen wrote to say:

May I respectfully request that my name be withdrawn from the list of recipients of the Governor-General's Award. . . . I do sincerely thank all those concerned for their generous intention. Much in me strives for this honor but the poems themselves forbid it absolutely.

His collections of poetry include *Let Us Compare Mythologies* (1956), *Spice-Box of Earth* (1961), *Flowers for Hitler* (1964), *Parasites of Heaven* (1966), *Selected Poems, 1956-1968,* and the forthcoming *Death of a Lady's Man* (1978). His two novels are *The Favourite Game* (1963) and *Beautiful Losers* (1966).

VICTOR COLEMAN

Victor Coleman was born in 1944 in Toronto and grew up there and in Montreal. He submitted his early poetry to a variety of little magazines and edited *Island* (which ran to eight issues), with encouragement from Raymond Souster. His work as a production assistant and a linotype operator and editor eventually took him to Coach House Press, Toronto, where he served for several years as production manager. He attended the Berkeley Poetry Conference with Jack Spicer, Charles Olson, Gary Snyder, Robert Duncan, Allen Ginsberg, Robert Creeley, and others, and was one of the poets who read in the New American Poetry Circuit for 1970-1. His publications include *From Erik Satie's Notes to the Music* (1965), *one/eye/love* (1967), *Light Verse* (1969), *America* (1971), *Parking Lots* (1972), *Stranger* (1974), *Speech Sucks* (1975), and *Terrific at Both Ends* (1978). He now lives on Ward's Island, Toronto, and is Director of the Nightingale Arts Council, operating as A Space.

Coleman has always insisted on going his own way. He does not subscribe to the poetics of Black Mountain College, or to the 'realist' and 'myth-making' fashions in Canada. Coleman's tastes as an editor are catholic: the early issues of *Island* contain poems by Newlove, MacEwen, Bowering, Souster, and Purdy. He reads and is willing to learn from such contemporaries as Jack Spicer and Charles Olson, but remains very much his own poet. His earliest poetry is often personal and idiosyncratic to the point of being inaccessible, but it is seldom without interest. The one characteristic that persists throughout his still short career as a poet is a disarming playfulness. He has always had a more than mild obsession with rhymes, internal and external, and with alliteration, as is evident in this early poem, 'a song', from *Island* #3:

> sung as the shrill
> bird. the word
> offers the ear
> cheer, as it be
> to be the chor-
> us for us, &
> by our sense of
> hear, as ear, here

This kind of playfulness, this delight in language, is a great asset to a young poet, because it enables him to learn about the essentials of the craft instead of striving unduly for meaning or statement that is beyond his experience.

Robert Duncan expressed considerable delight in Coleman's *Light Verse*, and in the fact that the book is dedicated to Jack Spicer: 'Always such an intense, intent, thereness to the line that all the emotion is true to the poem. It's that, something more than authenticity, that Jack insisted upon. . . . it is a rare poet who comes thru for me bringing such a delite, winning me to whole-hearted reading.' The *thereness* Duncan speaks of refers not only to the consistent intelligence that informs the poetry, but also to the linguistic and typographical precision with which the poems are made. Coleman concerns himself not merely with the fantastic image or the profound thought (though these may come naturally to a poem), but rather with a maximum use of every word. In Coleman's poems there are no second-class words; if placed in the right context, or position, the most common word may be made to give out new energies or meanings. Articles, prepositions, suffixes may jump off the page by virtue of being given prominence in a line. It is a poetry directed more to the ear than to the eye or to the mind, so there is no need in a single poem for verbs and nouns and adjectives to crowd out other parts of speech. In this way Coleman not only increases the linguistic resources at his disposal, but also pulls the reader more intimately into the actual texture of sounds in the poem, rather than sending him off on analytical cul-de-sacs.

Although he does not eschew the most useful of the age-old poetic techniques, Coleman has been reluctant to accept the closed form. Readers are fascinated by his break-away from the notion of the poem as a set-piece, and the notion of a feeling or experience as a 'subject' to be worked up. In *one/eye/love* and *Light Verse* he is somehow able to hold together within a single imaginative context an unusually wide range of diction and feeling. The poem does not have to have a consistent mood, or stick to a single theme.

Allen Ginsberg speaks of Coleman's poems as 'improvizations'. In a letter to

Coleman he says: 'Read *Parking Lots*—was thumbing thru *radiofreerainforest* I saw the line "I have taken the liberty ... afterlife" which was so odd and intelligent I went back to the beginning. The whole poem or spout was funny & of lovely nature. There aren't many improvizations I can read with detail & humour any more & this poesy was *interesting. . . .* ' Improvisation is a good term, especially for its associations with jazz. Coleman's ear and imagination explore a word or a phrase in much the same way that a jazz musician searches out the contours of a note or musical phrase—pushing the phrase in a number of directions, building on it, using it as a springboard. In one of his recent poems, 'America', Coleman has invented his own equivalent of the closed form. In each section he accepts the limitations of a tarot card randomly drawn (e.g., the NINE OF SWORDS), the first word in each line beginning with the corresponding letter from the card. This formal limitation frees him, as the sonnet freed the Elizabethan poet, to discover new combinations of sound and sense.

'We make up a different language for poetry/And for the heart—ungrammatical', Coleman says in 'Transformations II'. In his search for a new language he does not sit still; his discoveries influence him, make him rethink his poetic directions. But he is self-taught, so his discoveries and subsequent developments come with surprise and delight and, of course, a certain roughness, which is a small price to pay for poetry that escapes the tiring slickness of professional imitation.

D. G. JONES

Doug Jones was born in Bancroft, Ont., in 1929 and educated at McGill and Queen's Universities. He began writing as an undergraduate at McGill, where he won a number of prizes in creative writing. His early work was encouraged and ultimately published by Louis Dudek and Raymond Souster in magazines and in book form by Contact Press. Jones has taught at several universities in Canada and is a member of the English department at the University of Sherbrooke, where he is an editor of *Ellipse*, a quarterly review designed to present the work of French and English writers in translation. He has published four books of poetry—*Frost on the Sun* (1957), *The Sun is Axeman* (1961), *Phrases from Orpheus* (1967), and *Under the Thunder the Flowers Light Up the Earth* (1977), for which he received the Governor General's Award—and a major analysis of image and theme in Canadian literature, *Butterfly on Rock* (1970). He lives in North Hatley, Que.

There is a passage in *Butterfly on Rock* that is both an acute comment on the state of poetry in Canada and a useful summary of Jones's own poetic development: 'Having reached the Pacific, Canadians have begun to turn back on themselves, to create that added dimension Teilhard de Chardin calls the noosphere. . . . more than ever before, we have arrived at a point where we recognize, not only that the land is ours, but that we are the land's.' His first three volumes of poetry represent the stages in his own journey towards a 'true' landscape. In *Frost on the Sun* Jones was preoccupied with violence and disintegration, but only as poetic *subjects*, not as pressing realities that must find poetic resolution. In *The Sun is Axeman*, however, a

hostile nature is presented, one that is stunted and barren, mute and unsympath-
etic, unlike anything in the pastoral world of his early poems. Many of the poems
present the unpredictable landscapes of dreams, landscapes that may splinter into
betrayal and degeneration. 'Little Night Journey' is a Whitmanesque symbolic
narrative that suggests rather than describes the violence lurking beneath the still
surface of consciousness. In *Phrases From Orpheus* Jones experiences some sort of
dark night of the soul, arrives at his own underworld. This is Jones's *Flowers for
Hitler*, his descent into the heart of darkness, in which he asks: 'how shall I love/
this earth,/which is my certain death?' 'All earth is now an underground', he says
in 'En Guise d'Orphée'. Jones feels in all things a potential for violence, for
disintegration, but he understands this at a psychological level to be a fundamen-
tal aspect of reality. In the later poems, myth functions not as ornament but as a
controlling structural element; these poems are successful, not because they re-
write old myths, but because they reveal something of the poet's own world. In a
letter to the editors, Jones wrote: 'It is always a case of seeing through a conven-
tional pattern or faded myth to something more immediate, vital or violent, and
the renewal of the old or the creation of a new myth more adequate to that
immediate experience.' *Orpheus* also includes a number of poems that grow out of
very personal emotional experience, but experience that is controlled and manipu-
lated. These poems are extremely well turned and yet they retain a psychological
depth that is quite remarkable.

As important as Jones's discovery of his own noosphere is his discovery of the
means with which to give it imaginative expression. In 'Clotheslines' he argues
that 'the most common things/clothes hung out to dry/serve as well as kings/for
your imagery.' The truth is that common things serve *better* than kings, as Jones
discovers in *The Sun is Axeman*. His early poetry had been too general, too abstract.
The sense of logic, or intellect, was oppressive; too often sound and image were
under severe strain from having to flesh-out the skeleton of thought that held a
poem together. However, in poems such as 'Portrait of Anne Hébert' and 'For
Françoise Adnet', the images grow with the poem; they are not grafted on. The
metaphors are organic, drawing the reader toward, rather than away from, the
subject. Jones begins to use common objects quite naturally and his poetry makes
its appeal through the senses, not merely through the intellect. He forsakes his
idealized landscapes for the colour and texture of the actual world around him.

Jones's concern for a more personal, affective style is not limited to imagery. In
'A Problem of Space' he suggests the directions he would like his poetry to take. 'I
would eliminate this bombast, this/Detail of type,' he says, 'and leave an image/
And a space'. The search for a more precise and more immediate form of expres-
sion took him briefly to Pound and the Imagists and then to moderns such as
Auden. In 'Portrait of Anne Hébert' the language is natural, the syntax simple and
insistent, suggesting that the poet is too caught up in the *making* to be fanciful or
verbose. Here, and in the more complicated poems of *Phrases from Orpheus*, Jones is
concerned with 'articulating a highly intense and obscure complex of feelings with
extreme economy ... with a certain simplicity and yet dramatic power.' One poem
that seems to realize this difficult goal is 'These Trees Are No Forest of Mourners';
it has a sureness and a simplicity that are quite striking. The best of Jones's later
poems have this sculptural quality, this sharpness of outline. Their success lies not

in an exhaustiveness of detail, but rather in their precision and economy of phrasing. We are left, as in the Chinese paintings that Jones admires, with only an image—and a space in which that image can grow. In his latest book, *Under the Thunder the Flowers Light Up the Earth* (1977), Jones explores metaphors of growth and decay, love and violence, in poems that attain a lyrical intensity not present in his earlier work. He also writes a remarkable poem-sequence from the persona of Archibald Lampman to 'Kate' that touches upon the violence and prudery of the Canadian psyche.

PATRICK LANE

In an essay entitled 'To the Outlaw', first published in John Gill's *New: American & Canadian Poetry* (1971), Patrick Lane writes passionately of the poet as an outlaw, a half-mad fugitive who inhabits the margins of society, the darkest corners: 'A poet is neither trained nor taught. He is the outlaw surging beyond the only freedom he knows, beauty in bondage.... The poem is a place of beauty that goes beyond knowledge and understanding.' For Lane, then, the poem would appear to be a sort of prison or cage in which experience is captured, its terrors rendered beautiful in words. Appropriately, images of confinement—jails, cages, rooms, attitudes, roles, social classes, political systems—abound in his poems. Animals—creatures that ought to exist outside the mental and physical prisons man makes, but are constantly being trapped, victimized, or rendered extinct—stalk through the pages of Lane's books—especially birds, those exotic and romantic reminders of our earthbound nature and our deepest yearnings for escape.

Another facet of Lane's romantic stance is his conviction that he writes about lower-class working experience from the INSIDE IN, rather than from the OUTSIDE IN. He insists that 'the personal is the only universal truth, the "everyman"', and argues that his 'search for enlightenment... is always balanced with my social commitment to the lower class, of which I am a member, with all its rage and pathos.' Thus he identifies strongly with Chilean poet Pablo Neruda and with the plight of peoples in the Third World countries he has visited; so, too, he advocates a poetry along lines suggested in Neruda's essay 'Towards an Impure Art': 'A poetry impure as the clothing we wear, soup-stained, soiled with our shameful behaviour, our wrinkles and vigils and dreams....'

The form and content of most of Lane's early work falls within such 'impure' bounds. His messages are not pretty; they are full of guilt and suffering, separation and loss. Gradually, however, the image of the tight-lipped loser who inhabits these poems gives way to a wiser, more reflective persona, capable of greater understanding and a broader historical reference. Where the early work had been excessively anecdotal, Lane began to discover in the basic materials of his poetry *significant* form, which has more to do with the resources of language than with events themselves. Similarly, his considerable metaphorical gifts, which previously seemed unsuited to an age committed to understatement and economy, became more and more capable of profound and startling effects: the metaphor in 'Stigmata', for example, 'the scrimshawed teeth of endless whales,/the oceans it took to carve them', derives its power not from mere cleverness, but rather from the poet thinking his way into the image. For the reader, this results in the shock of recognition, and delight at being confronted with a proposition (the creature shaped by the element it inhabits) that is so profoundly simple it has escaped our attention.

Whether he is writing about love, nature, the destruction of the Incas, or the castration of a ram, Lane is capable of a delicate but biting lyricism. In 'Mountain Oysters', for example, the speaker describes the quick and efficient slitting of the ram's scrotum and subsequent eating of the fried testicles with an excruciating matter-of-factness and verbal understatement ('brushed the tail aside/slit the bag/ tucked the knackers in his mouth/and clipped the cords off clean'); these techniques, and the colloquial indifference of the farmer's off-hand remarks, serve to heighten the sense of pain and horror Lane wishes to communicate. The idea of 'cutting delicately' and then eating the testicles invokes a sense of incongruity, as well as calling up old-wives' tales about strength and sexual prowess being derived from eating the organs of certain animals; then Lane beautifully juxtaposes the dining scene with an image of rams in the field, 'holding their pain/legs fluttering like blue hands/of tired old men.'

Ultimately there is a degree of poetic learning and a real commitment to literature in Lane's work that is of greater significance than his 'outlaw' stance. As he works with the longer line and explores certain metrical and syllabic possibilities that he had eschewed in his earlier work, Lane becomes more and more capable of appropriating other voices, other times.

He was born in 1939 in Nelson, B.C. and has lived intermittently in the interior of British Columbia, mostly in Vernon, until recently, when he settled on the coast at Half Moon Bay. His travels have taken him to various parts of North, Central, and South America. As his poems indicate, he has tried his hand at a wide variety of jobs, mostly manual. He was co-founder of Very Stone House, a small publishing venture Lane often operated in transit out of a series of doomed Volkswagen vans, and has been appointed writer-in-residence at the University of Manitoba for the 1978-9 year. His books include *Letters from a Savage Mind* (1966), *Separations* (1969), *Mountain Oysters* (1971), *The Sun Has Begun To Eat the Mountains* (1972), *Passing Into Storm* (1973), *Beware the Months of Fire* (1973), *Unborn Things* (1975), and *Albino Pheasants* (1977).

IRVING LAYTON

Layton is the best-known and most controversial figure in Canadian poetry, because he is so outspoken and graphic in his denunciations. Like Auden, he believes that the writing of poetry is a political act; as he explains in the Preface to *The Laughing Rooster:*

In this country the poet has always had to fight for his survival. He lives in a middle-class milieu whose values of money-getting, respectability, and success are hostile to the kind of integrity and authenticity that is at the core of his endeavour. His need to probe himself makes

him an easy victim for those who have more practical things to do—to hold down a job, amass
a fortune, or to get married and raise children. His concern is to change the world; at any
rate, to bear witness that another besides the heartless, stupid, and soul-destroying one men
have created is possible.

Layton's barbs are not limited to the middle-class. He is equally critical of educational institutions. He rejects Culture as 'that underarm perspiration odour of impotent old men'; and he describes good taste as 'something to wipe our unstodgy behinds with'.

Layton is a man of contradictions. He would have us believe that he is a 'brawling, irreverent', wild-eyed poet with no use for conservative values. Despite his swagger and cultivated disdain, however, Layton is neither a primitive nor a sensualist. His satire, bombast, and erotica are the masks for his fine, beleaguered sensibility. His need to project an image of controversy has often made him espouse issues and causes that seem inconsistent with his expressed poetic vision, with the vision of poetry as freedom. Perhaps it is a comment on our country, rather than on Layton, that his second-rate poems of social gesture should attract more attention than his most delicate, refined verse.

If Layton himself remains an enigma, his literary significance is more certain. Like Whitman in the United States, he has done much to stimulate interest in poetry and to loosen its choking collar. He has reminded us that there are no inherently unpoetic subjects—there are only unpoetic minds. Poetry, he says, is 'a self-authenticated speaking, a reaching down into the roots of one's being'. The poet is someone who knows 'the terror and ecstasy of living daily beyond one's psychic means'. Layton is a conscious craftsman, but he insists that 'without the material given the poet when his Unconscious (soul) is stirred into activity by a powerful emotion, his intelligence and craftsmanship are of no use to him whatever'. His own best poems are a perfect blend of passion and restraint, of a conscious and an unconscious ordering of materials.

Layton's poetry is concerned with three main subjects: sexual love, power, and imagination. Like most men he is attracted to the subject of large-scale expenditures of energy, especially violence. He believes that men are basically aggressive and that battles and wars are a means of psychic cleansing. Sexual love is, for Layton, another form of encounter that has its creative and destructive aspects. His poetic treatment of sex would hardly meet with the approval of the Women's Liberation Movement. Man can dominate reality, Layton tells us in 'The Fertile Muck', not only by love, but also by imagination. Art is the supreme synthesizer; it can contain paradox and contradiction because it deals with the truth that lies between opposites, as we have learned from poets like Blake and Yeats. As Layton explains in 'The Birth of Tragedy': 'Love, power the huzza of battle/are something, are much;/yet a poem includes them like a pool/water and reflection.'

Layton was born in Romania in 1912. While a child he went with his parents to Montreal, where he has spent most of his life. He studied agricultural science at Macdonald College and economics at McGill University. He taught in a boys' private school before taking up his teaching position at Sir George Williams University. In the forties Layton was associated with Louis Dudek and John Sutherland in the editing of *First Statement*, a controversial magazine that later merged with *Preview* to become *Northern Review*. In the fifties he joined with Dudek and Raymond Souster in the founding of the influential Contact Press. Since then Layton has taught, travelled, edited books, read his poetry on campuses across the country, and been an active commentator on current affairs. He was a professor of English at York University, but is now retired.

Since the publication of *Here and Now* (1945), Layton has published many books of poetry, including *The Improved Binoculars* (1956), *A Red Carpet for the Sun* (1959), for which he received the Governor General's Award, *Balls for a One-Armed Juggler* (1963), *The Laughing Rooster* (1964), *Collected Poems* (1965), *Periods of the Moon* (1967), *The Shattered Plinths* (1968), *The Whole Bloody Bird* (1969), *The Collected Poems of Irving Layton* (1971), *Lovers and Lesser Men* (1973), *The Darkening Fire: Selected Poems 1945-1968* (1975), *The Unwavering Eye: Selected Poems 1969-1975* (1975), *For My Brother Jesus* (1976), *The Covenant* (1977), and *The Poems of Irving Layton* (1977).

DOROTHY LIVESAY

In an essay entitled 'Song and Dance' (*Canadian Literature*, No. 41, Summer 1969), Dorothy Livesay says: 'I suppose that all my life I have fought against obscurantism! For me the true intellectual is a simple person who knows how to be close to nature and to ordinary people. I therefore tend to shy away from academic poets and academic critics. They miss the essence.' Livesay's search for the 'essence' has led her through a series of transformations, from her earliest imagist and symbolist lyrics about love and isolation; through her activist 'agit-prop' writings of the forties and fifties; and, finally, to her confessional and feminist writings of the sixties and seventies.

The constant fact in her art, as in her life, has been the struggle to reconcile her need for privacy and her need for community. At times Livesay has likened this struggle to the search for the 'perfect dancing partner' or the perfect muse. As she says in 'Song and Dance', writing was a form of dance which 'could extend to an identification with a community, a nation, a world.' Poetry is for Livesay a manifestation of that ideal union between two people, poet and reader: 'Not a dance of touch, but one where the rhythm itself created an unseen wire holding two people together in the leap of movement.'

At various points in her life, Livesay has espoused a 'realist' credo, such as that expressed in 'Without Benefit of Tape', where she insists that poetry must originate in everyday experience and 'living speech'. Her documentary poems clearly grow out of this 'realist' impulse. She describes 'Call My People Home' as her 'most thoroughly documented "public" poem', one that is able to 'combine a sense of personal poignancy and alienation with a sense of social purpose.' What interests her about this form, as she says in 'The Documentary Poem: A Canadian Genre' (*Contexts of Canadian Criticism*, edited by Eli Mandel), is its capacity to create a 'dialectic between the objective facts and the subjective feelings of the poet.' Livesay's best work certainly lies at the extremes of private and public statement—in the lyric and the narrative; and the documentary is the form in which, for her, both of these elements come together. The passion of the poet finds its engagement and release, not in didacticism or righteous indignation, but rather in a total absorption in character and event. And yet, regardless of the documentary impulse that gives rise to it, 'Call My People Home' derives its illusion of reality less from accurate reference to historical fact than from the linguistic inventiveness and imaginative sympathy of the poet. The subjective needs of the poet drive her to penetrate the surfaces of history in order to create myth, to plumb the depths of what we call archetypal experience.

Although her recent work has been more stridently feminist in its utterances, Livesay has always been concerned about the role of women in society. There is no shortage of women in her poetry, from ruined maids and overburdened house-wives to political activists. The world of these women is often circumscribed by roles, attitudes, domestic conditions. They move awkwardly and uncomfortably within rooms, framed windows, magic circles of children, drowning in, but mirac-ulously saved by, the incredible detail of their lives; and rejoicing in the evidence of growing things—a bird, a grandchild, a geranium.

Livesay rejects the elegaic preoccupations of much modern writing. 'We are optimists', she says, 'Blakean believers in the New Jerusalem. We cannot see man's role as tragic but rather as divine comedy. We are alone—so what? We are not always lonely. Laughter heals, the dance captures, the song echoes forth from the tree-top. I won't stop believing this until every tree in Canada's chopped down; I thumb my nose at those who say that nature and with it, human nature, is becoming "obsolete".'

No doubt she inherited both her interest in poetry and her concern for social issues from her parents, who were literary people and active in the field of journalism. Livesay was born in Winnipeg in 1909 and lived there for ten years before her family moved to Ontario. She graduated from the University of To-ronto in 1931 and then studied at the Sorbonne, exploring the influence of the French Symbolists on modern English poetry. During the Depression she was a social worker in Toronto, Montreal, and New Jersey. After 1936 she lived in Vancouver, where she worked at the YWCA, taught, and contributed to political and literary magazines, including Alan Crawley's *Contemporary Verse*. When her husband died, Livesay returned to Paris, where she worked for UNESCO before being posted to Zambia for three years. She has taught widely and been a writer-in-residence at various Canadian universities. She now lives in Winnipeg, where she founded and edits *CV/II*, a periodical of poetry and reviews.

Livesay's works include *Green Pitcher* (1928), *Signpost* (1932), *Day and Night* (1944), *Selected Poems* (1957), *The Unquiet Bed* (1967), *Collected Poems: The Two Seasons* (1972), *Ice Age* (1975), and a new Selected Poems, *The Woman I Am* (1978). Her two prose books are *A Winnipeg Childhood* (1975) and *Right Hand Left Hand* (1977). Livesay has edited *The Collected Poems of Raymond Knister* (1949) and two anthologies of poetry by women: *Forty Women Poets of Canada* (1972) and *Woman's Eye* (1974). She was twice the recipient of the Governor General's Award for poetry and received the Lorne Pierce Medal for Literature in 1947.

PAT LOWTHER

Pat Lowther was born in 1935 and grew up in North Vancouver, at that time a rugged, sparsely populated landscape such as the one she describes in 'Coast Range': 'Just north of town / the mountains start to talk / back-of-the-head buzz / of high-stubbled meadows / minute flowers / moss gravel and clouds.' This close proximity to, and awareness of, nature in its raw and primitive state was to be a constant in her life and poetry. She reveals an almost visceral awareness of the terrain she inhabited, participating in its energy and transformational character whether her subject is mountains, craneflies, or the waters of Furry Creek.

Images of earth, and stone in particular, are everywhere present in her poetry. She identifies strongly with Chilean poet Pablo Neruda and his involvement with his people at the baserock level of their work upon the earth. Neruda, she says, is 'the man who moves / under the hills, / the man who kisses stone'; he is someone who, transported suddenly to the west coast of Canada, 'would know where / the clamshell middens are'. Like Neruda, Lowther knows that it 'isn't easy / to keep moving thru / the perpetual motion / of surfaces' in a world were the bodies are 'laid / stone upon stone'; but the process is necessary: 'You are changing, Pablo, / becoming an element / a close throat of quartz / a calyx / imperishable in earth'.

At the psychological level, Lowther's preoccupation with stone, the most resistant of the things in the physical world, represents a desire to eliminate the surfaces, edges, boundaries that separate man from man and man from objects in nature. The sense of *relation* fascinates her, the position objects bear in relation to one another: thus she concerns herself with the silence between words, or the spaces between notes of music; she regards love as a kind of intersection; she sees certain gadgets and phenomena, such as phone booths and hot-line shows, as symbols of our struggle to reach beyond the limits of our own skin into other spheres of knowing. 'The world falls through my forehead', she says, 'resistlessly as rain.'

Lowther is intensely conscious of the major intellectual issues of her time: the role of women in society and the nature of political involvement. Yet her feminist concerns are only a part of her larger concern with extending consciousness, as she suggests in a note to her poems in *Mountain Moving Day* (1973, edited by Elaine Gill for The Crossing Press):

> I see the woman's revolution as part of a new outreach of consciousness. The liberation of women from imposed self-images is happening. Even the most hostile and fearful women are absorbing it subliminally right along with the cream depilatory commercials. New assumptions are being accepted below the level of consciousness. . . .
>
> At one time I believed we humans were coming to the end of our evolutionary cycle— devolving like dandelions. Now I see the half-breeds of the future passing like migrating birds, and I begin to have a kind of tentative hope.

For Lowther, poetry is a means of effecting change in individuals *and* in society. In 'Regard to Neruda', she states: 'Often now I forget / how to make love / but I think I am ready / to learn politics.' Learning politics, for the poet, involves exercising full control over the language and its precious resources. The poem itself becomes a magical tool or vehicle for transporting the reader from one level of consciousness to another, and from a position of estrangement from the things, events, and people of this world to one of full participation and involvement.

Although many of her poems are political at this deeper, more profound level, Lowther has also written about specific political events in recent history. 'Chacabuco, The Pit', which deals with the aftermath of the U.S.-assisted overthrow of the government of Salvador Allende in Chile, is a powerful hymn to survival, to the earth and its people. What interests Lowther is not so much the betrayal of human values evident in the overthrow, but rather the miraculous persistence of the human spirit which, like the sexual energy that keeps the species from extinction, is a 'holy mystery / beyond refusal.'

Lowther's poetry is remarkable less for its 'fashionable' content than for its maturity and control. Whether she is writing brief imagistic pieces, confessional lyrics, or passionate meditations, she is extremely conscious of prosody—not with rhythm as an aspect of poetry, but with what Pound called the 'articulation of the total sound of the poem'.

Before her untimely death in 1975, Pat Lowther had published three books of poetry: *This Difficult Flowering* (1968), *The Age of the Bird* (1972), and *Milk Stone* (1974). Her reputation was growing rapidly. She had been elected national chairman of The League of Canadian Poets and was teaching Creative Writing at the University of British Columbia. *A Stone Diary*, which had been accepted before her death, was published posthumously in 1976.

GWENDOLYN MacEWEN

Gwendolyn MacEwen rejects self-indulgent, therapeutic poetry and the 'terribly cynical and "cool" poetry written today'. She believes that the poet can and must say things; and she writes with the conviction that she has discovered things sayable, and worth saying. 'I write basically to communicate joy, mystery, passion,' she says, ' . . . not the joy that naively exists without knowledge of pain, but that joy which arises out of and conquers pain. I want to construct a myth.'

MacEwen's poetry might well be discussed in terms of the peculiar ground it inhabits between the 'realists' and the 'myth-makers' in Canadian poetry. From the beginning she has repudiated the actual world for one that is ancient and mythic, believing that imagination can reconcile the antinomies in life. 'I believe there is more room inside than outside,' she says in the introduction to *A Breakfast for Barbarians*. 'And all the diversities which get absorbed can later work their way out into fantastic things, like hawk-training, IBM programming, mountain-climbing, or poetry.' Like Blake and Yeats, she draws her inspiration from things occult, mystical, rather than from traditional mythology. She is most alive to the myth and ritual contained in ordinary experience; her motorcycle Icarus bears little resemblance to the original. Her landscapes and figures are mostly dream-like, not bound by normal conventions of space and time; her characters are symbolic, their movements ritualistic.

'I am involved with writing as a total profession, not as an aesthetic pursuit,' she says. 'My prime concern has always been with the raw materials from which literature is derived, not with literature as an end in itself.' Of course one of the primary sources of raw material for the writer is literature itself. MacEwen has long been preoccupied with the figure of the artist, whether the Egyptian scribes 'who drew/eyes right into their hieroglyphs' or the solitary figure of the dancer. As she says in 'Finally Left in the Landscape',

> Yet still I journey to this naked country
> to seek a form which dances in the sand.
> This is my chosen landscape.

She chooses this landscape but not without certain misgivings, as she suggests in 'Poems in Braille'. Here she expresses the conflict she feels between art and life, between the world of names and the world of things, between dance and action. For her, as for the Platonist, things are but the shadows of a real world. Words, the names we give to things, are more real because they are our attempt to describe the other-worldliness of things; they are the windows through which we view reality. However attractive this landscape, the poet cannot help but doubt its sufficiency at times. MacEwen is aware that the whole of the message may not be contained in the medium, that it may be found in the very *things* she eschews. 'I do not read the long cabbala of my bones/truthfully', she admits. She asks to follow Wenceslas, who could behold a peasant gathering fuel and be moved and involved in that experience—that is, see it in terms of itself. 'I should read all things like braille in this season', she concludes:

> with my fingers I should read them
> lest I go blind in both eyes reading with
> that other eye the final hieroglyph

Although her usual method has been to begin with names, to decode language for what it may reveal about the human condition, MacEwen appears, in the *The Shadow-Maker*, to be moving more in the direction of realism. There is one poem, 'The Compass', which is a comic exaggeration of an encounter with a fool who abuses language profoundly on a train between Fredericton and Halifax. Two others, 'Inside the Great Pyramid' and 'One Arab Flute', are reflective accounts of actual experiences and impressions during travel. In terms of poetic technique, MacEwen resembles the incantatory and prophetic Yeats. Yeats claimed to have 'tried to make the language of poetry coincide with that of passionate, normal speech', to have searched for 'a powerful and passionate syntax'. Although she emphasizes the passionate more than the normal aspect of speech, she often combines, like Yeats, the oracular and the vernacular in a single poem. 'O baby, get out of Egypt', she writes in 'Cartaphilus'. 'An ancient slang speaks through me like that.' She employs the dramatic gesture and direct speech ('listen—there was this boy, Manzini') of the actor or storyteller who is intent upon delivering his message. It is a spoken poetry, a poetry of chant or incantation. MacEwen has the habit of reciting her own poetry from memory; and the ritual is quite spellbinding. Hers is a passionate plea for life, for beauty. 'To live consciously is holy', she says. The conscious man will not be one-sided; he will find a balance between his passion and his reason, between 'the complex dance of fire and blood' and 'the accurate self'.

Gwendolyn MacEwen was born in Toronto in 1941. She first published poetry when she was fifteen, in the *Canadian Forum*. At eighteen she left school to take up a full-time career as a writer. Her activities and achievements are impressive. Since her Canada Council grant in 1965 to research a historical novel in Egypt, she has received the CBC New Canadian Writing Contest Award (1965), the Borestone Mountain Poetry Award, and the Governor General's Award for *The Shadow-Maker* (1969). She has translated, prepared plays and talks for radio, and reads poetry in universities and schools.

Her poetry publications include *Selah* (1961) and *The Drunken Clock* (1961) (both privately printed), *The Rising Fire* (1963), *A Breakfast for Barbarians* (1966), *The Shadow-Maker* (1969), *The Armies of the Moon* (1972), *Magic Animals: Selected Poems Old and New* (1974), and *The Fire-eaters* (1976). She has published two novels—*Julian the Magician* (1963) and *King of Egypt, King of Dreams* (1971)—and a collection of short stories, *Noman* (1972).

ELI MANDEL

Eli Mandel was born in 1922 in Estevan, Sask., and lived in that province until he joined the Army Medical Corps in 1943 and went overseas. When he returned from the war, he completed an M.A. from the University of Saskatchewan and taught at the Collège Militaire Royale de St Jean. He has since completed a PH.D. in English at the University of Toronto, taught at the University of Alberta, and become a Professor in the Fine Arts and Humanities departments at York University. His first poems were published in *Trio* (1954) with those of Gael Turnbull and Phyllis Webb. He has published numerous books of poetry: *Fuseli Poems* (1960); *Black and Secret Man* (1964); *An Idiot Joy* (1967), for which he received the Governor General's Award; *Crusoe: Poems Selected and New* (1973); *Stony Plain* (1973); and *Out of Place* (1977). Mandel is also an important critic and anthologist; he has an unusual talent for critical synthesis. Apart from his numerous essays, he has published *Criticism: The Silent-Speaking Word*, a series of broadcasts for the CBC, and *Another Time* (1977), a collection of essays on Canadian poetry. He edited *Poetry '62* (with Jean-Guy Pilon), *Five Modern Canadian Poets* (1970), *Contexts of Canadian Criticism* (1971), and *Poets of Contemporary Canada: 1960 - 1970* (1972).

Mandel's early poetry was admired for its use of classical mythology as a means of exploring experience obliquely. His 'Minotaur Poems' and many of the Fuseli poems were written under the critical inspiration of Northrop Frye and the poetic example of James Reaney and Jay Macpherson. The early poems, though they are well-turned, polished pieces, often lack conviction, as if the weight of the traditional masks weakens, or stifles, the poet's own voice. In all of these poems there is a lyrical poet caged and threatening to break out. In *Black and Secret Man* Mandel becomes more personal, more inward. He is, to use his own definition of the modern poet, a man in search of himself; and his voyage of discovery takes him into difficult, troubled waters. He wanders through the ranks of his own ghosts, rifles his personal files of guilt and suffering, discovering in the process new and exciting materials.

The form of Mandel's verse has changed radically. It has moved from a rational ordering of materials in the direction of fragmentation and logical discontinuity, from language that is heavily rhetorical to a more colloquial idiom. Gradually he leaves behind 'the poise and thrust of speech' that 'gleams like polished steel' for a rougher, more halting, though possibly incoherent, form of expression. Some of his latest poems echo the last speeches of Beckett's characters in combining grunts, non-sequitars, and erratic description with philosophical profundities and lyrical outpourings. Mandel has read and absorbed the critical theories of George Steiner in *Language and Silence*. As a Jew, a writer, and an academic, he is in a natural position to understand the limitations of rational discourse and also the dangers inherent in the indiscriminate use of language. Although his poetic explorations of these themes are sometimes too self-conscious and academic, his new directions are undeniably promising. The Auschwitz poem, for example, is a beautiful rendering of the intellectual and verbal disintegration that accompanies extreme psychic shock, as well as being a profound comment on the labyrinthine nature of moral perception.

Like Atwood, Mandel is fond of perceptual tricks, of unexpected shifts in tone or diction or point of view that startle the reader into consciousness. However, his verse always seems more personal and affective. Atwood, like Flaubert's ideal artist, is everywhere felt but nowhere seen in much of her verse; Mandel, on the other hand, is a poet who is both seen *and* felt. He does not use alienating devices to refine himself out of existence but to give another dimension to his poetry. It would be foolish to argue that Mandel's materials are more genuinely personal than Atwood's. In a poem such as 'Pictures in an Institution' he claims to reject his Greek and anthropology, his second-hand textbook knowledge, for the raw materials of memory. 'I take,/brutal to my thoughts, these lives, defy/your taste in metaphor', he says. The three self-consciously comic and anti-poetic 'notices' in the poem seem at first designed to cover up the poet's embarrassment at the deeply personal nature of the materials. But that is only one view. It is well to remember that poets are good liars, creatures with a 'forked tongue', to use Mandel's phrase, in which case the 'notices' in the poem could be regarded as devices calculated to *heighten* the personal emphasis by trying to call attention away from it to the banal or the merely comic. That such questions should be raised at all is a fair indication that Mandel is successful in his efforts to create the illusion of fact. Mandel would no doubt agree with Frederick Philip Grove's view that the artist's concern is not with fact but with truth.

For Mandel, the poet is a paradoxical creature, one who partakes of the divine but who also needs to be carefully watched like the wizards, thieves, hunchbacks, and idiots that inhabit his poetic world. The poet, like Houdini, is an escape artist, continually seeking newer and more difficult emotional and verbal nets or mazes to escape from, because he is most alive during those moments of struggle, of challenge. 'I am crazed by poetry,' Mandel admits; but he means the kind of madness that is truly sane, that demands the experience of bondage in order to understand the meaning of liberty. He describes himself as a man 'reeling with messages' and there is in his verse a kind of apocalyptic frenzy, or passionate intensity, that reminds one at times of Layton, at times of Yeats.

JOHN NEWLOVE

There are many dimensions in John Newlove's poetry. To readers familiar with his recent verse the tone of 'wearied intellectuality' that he refers to in 'In This Reed' seems predominant. He writes from a mood of despair and disenchantment that reminds one of post-war English poets such as Philip Larkin. Newlove's is a poetry of alienation, peopled with derelicts, hitch-hikers, whores, outsiders of all sorts. The poet himself appears as an outsider wandering in some no-man's-land between a vanishing past and a never-to-be-realized future. Memory is another country he inhabits frequently, as he explains in 'The Double-Headed Snake':

> The greatest
> beauty is to be alive, forgetting nothing,
> although remembrance hurts
> like a foolish act, is a foolish act.

But memory, like everything else in Newlove's cosmos, breaks down. The vision of *Black Night Window* is dark indeed; but in *The Cave* Newlove's landscape is even more desolate. He moves from the bleakness of the Prairies and the unending highway to a more primal landscape of swamps and sea. It is a book of terse confessions, tortured examinations of failed relationships and breakdowns in communication, cynical meditations upon history and 'progress'. The poet experiences not only the disintegration of personality, of identity, but also the collapse of the objective world; he is a man caught between the engine and the sea; in 'the cave/ of time/with trees/and war/falling/down . . . —and/Jesus,/goodbye,/goodbye.'

In these poems Newlove often writes in a halting, disjunctive, matter-of-fact manner, as in 'Crazy Riel', where he gives the impression of resistance to the poetic process itself. As his vision darkens there is a corresponding paring down of language. The poems become like etchings, painstakingly made, or distillations of complex thoughts and feelings. In *The Cave* Newlove's spareness reaches such a point that he says in 'The Flower': 'I am too tense/decline to dance/verbally.'

There is little reason to expect that Newlove will refine himself out of existence poetically. He has too much talent and has discovered too many new imaginative possibilities. Alongside the poetry of exhaustion and despair are poems of historical interest and poems of great lyrical intensity. He has an exceptional concern for rhythm and cadence and has written short lyrics that rival the best of Cohen and Layton. 'Ride Off Any Horizon' best illustrates Newlove's lyricism and his range of poetic materials. It is interesting first of all because it demonstrates one of the primary ways in which Newlove's imagination works. To ride off any horizon is to let the mind follow any idea or feeling for which there is an appropriate sound pattern, to let the mind be carried along by the verbal associations. A similar process is obviously at work in 'Crazy Riel', where the repetition of idea and sound draws attention to the incremental or associational structure of the poem.

The various sections of 'Ride Off Any Horizon' contain almost all of the areas of experience that concern Newlove in his poetry: the vast, untamed Prairies barely touched by the forces of industrialization; the Prairies of the Depression; the destruction of the Indians that finds its most powerful expression in 'The Pride', an imaginative recreation of part of our aboriginal heritage; the place of boyhood and family memories and emotional relationships; and, finally, the lonely crowds and concrete wilderness of the city. These images are held together by the refrain both aurally and grammatically, so that the poem has the kind of unity that is usually associated with the narrative or ballad.

Newlove writes with disarming directness and candidness about personal relationships. His is not simply a poetry of self-exposure; he seldom stops short of a precise, rhythmical expression of feeling. Where he cannot find the measure to control a feeling, he will occasionally turn on a gentle but perfectly pitched irony.

Newlove was born in Regina in 1938 and lived for a number of years in Russian farming communities on the eastern edges of Saskatchewan, where his mother was a school teacher. He has lived and worked in various parts of Canada, in Vancouver, in Terrace, and now in Toronto; but the major geographical influence on his life and verse is the Prairies, with its oppressed Indians, ethnic minorities, and the vastness and austerity of its terrain. As he says in *Black Night Window*: 'Everyone is so/lonely in this/country that/it's necessary/to be fantastic.' Newlove's poetry has been widely published in magazines in Canada and abroad and has appeared in numerous anthologies. He has worked as a publisher's editor and been writer-in-residence at several Canadian universities. His publications include *Grave Sirs* (1962), *Elephants, Mothers & Others* (1963), *Moving in Alone* (1965), *Notebook Pages* (1966), *What They Say* (1967), *Black Night Window* (1968), and *The Cave* (1970).

ALDEN NOWLAN

Alden Nowlan has chronicled movingly and convincingly the harshness and hypocrisy of life in the Maritimes. His poems tell of the repressions that are a part of that heritage. 'I am a product', he says 'of a culture that fears any display of emotion and attempts to repress any true communication.' Like Souster, he is moved by his immediate environment, especially by economic conditions that grind down the human spirit. He is a poet of the underprivileged. 'In my childhood and early youth I experienced the kind of poverty that scarifies and warps the soul.' His is a dark world indeed, a world brutalized by poverty, ignorance, fear, greed, and lust. Anyone familiar with the fictional world of Hugh MacLennan's *Each Man's Son* will recognize Nowlan's landscapes at once.

Poetry for Nowlan is a means of establishing communication; like the atheist's prayer, it is a 'reaching out in fear and gentleness'. He is a man who can write of violence, loneliness, and despair with great compassion. In 'Britain Street' he tells of the unhappy conditions between parents and children in the depressed areas, 'where the very names/of their young were curses'. In this climate of brutality and hatred, the poet reclaims the abused, debased·names and restores to them some dignity; he gives them a newer, more humane context, invests them with beauty and feeling. He is not a moralist but he is a man capable of fine moral discriminations, as in 'In Those Old Wars', where he reflects upon the debasing effects of power and the (sometimes) ennobling effects of defeat. His attitude towards his own serious illness is typical:

When I was in hospital, every time that I was operated on I thought I was going to die. The thing I was worried about after worrying about what would become of my wife and son was how much I wanted to write—how much time I'd wasted when I could have been writing.

Every time I went down in the elevator to get operated on, I thought . . . how many more things I wanted to say. For that reason, my illness was good for my writing. As Nietzsche says, 'What does not kill me, strengthens me.'

Nowlan claims that his work as a journalist gave him a sense of writing for an audience. 'You learn a great respect for the audience when you do newspaper work,' he says. 'And, another thing, it made me very aware of people.' Not content to be a mere recorder of experience (from the outside), he tries to fathom the psychology that underlies experience, the relation between the feeling and the act. He brings to poetry the novelist's gift of characterization, the capacity to embody a feeling or idea in an image of action. 'I don't like hypocrisy and I don't like fakes,' he says in typical fashion. 'I think the most important division in the world is between the people who are real and the people who are fakes.' Journalism has also left its mark on his style. He writes with a disarming directness and simplicity, as if he had time for neither fakes nor literary games. The pressure to 'get things said' seems to preclude rhetoric, ornament. As he explains in 'And He Wept Aloud':

> oh, admit this, man, there is no point in poetry
> if you withhold the truth
> once you've come by it

The naturalness of Nowlan's diction, his ear for the nuances of the speaking voice, the rightness of his enjambment—these things speak for the sincerity of his desire to offer his truth in the simplest, most unadorned manner possible. As Robert Bly suggests in the prefatory note to *Playing the Jesus Game*, Nowlan is a poet entangled not in words, but in the universe.

Nowlan seems to be a man with few pretensions, personal or literary. Of his own life he says:

Rationally I know that my life is no more important to the cosmos than the life of a housefly or a blade of grass. . . . Emotionally, I can't help but feel that my death will be the end of a world that was created the day I was born.

And of literature? 'Human feeling is all that counts,' he says. 'To hell with *literature* . . . it's a kind of reassurance that there *are* people out there, listening. Makes me sort of visualize my poems wandering all over the place tapping people on the shoulder and saying: 'Hi there, I'm Alden Nowlan, who are you?' To the charge that he is a regionalist, Nowlan replies: 'I don't write about Maritime people in capital letters, as if they were some special species. I have certain feelings and responses—I could well have these same feelings and responses if I lived in Montreal, but I'd write about them in a different way, simply because I'd have a different experience and see different things if I lived in Montreal.' Nowlan's portrayal of human emotions has moved from the objective early poetry, which was often saved from lapsing into sentimentality by his sense of irony and wry humour, to a more personal, confessional poetry. Whatever his subject or manner, however, his unusual moral sympathy gives the poetry a warmth and an appeal that are unique.

Nowlan was born in the Nova Scotia backwoods in 1933. He left school at twelve and worked as a farm labourer, a sawmill helper, the manager of a hillbilly orchestra, and the editor of the Hartland *Observer*, finally joining the *Telegraph-*

Journal of Saint John, N.B. Nowlan has received a number of awards, including Canada Council grants, a Guggenheim fellowship, and a Governor General's Award (for *Bread, Wine and Salt*). He engages in freelance writing projects and is writer-in-residence at the University of New Brunswick.

Nowlan has recently worked closely with theatre people in the Maritimes, writing a play called *Frankenstein* (1976) with Walter Learning, one called *One Dollar Woman*, and another about Sherlock Holmes. His published collections of poetry are *The Rose and the Puritan* (1958), *A Darkness in the Earth* (1959), *Wind in a Rocky Country* (1960), *Under the Ice* (1961), *The Things Which Are* (1962), *Bread, Wine and Salt* (1967), *the mysterious naked man* (1969), *Playing the Jesus Game* (1970), *Between Tears and Laughter* (1971), and *I'm a Stranger Here Myself* (1974). Some of his short stories are collected in *Miracle at Indian River* (1968).

MICHAEL ONDAATJE

Michael Ondaatje was born in Ceylon in 1943, where he lived for eleven years. He was educated at Dulwich College in England before coming to Canada in 1962. He studied at Bishop's University, the University of Toronto, and Queen's University, where he completed an M.A. on Edwin Muir. He has published four books of poetry: *The Dainty Monsters* (1967), an exceptionally strong first book; *The Man With Seven Toes* (1969), a macabre narrative set in the primitive wilds of Australia; *The Collected Works of Billy the Kid* (1970, winner of a Governor General's Award), a novelistic sequence of poems and prose that explores, often in a stream-of-consciousness manner, the physical and psychic life of the famous American folk-hero; and *Rat Jelly* (1973). *Coming Through Slaughter* (1976) is a poetic novel that deals with the madness and death of American jazz musician Buddy Bolden. Ondaatje has published one critical study, *Leonard Cohen* (1970); made several short films, including one on concrete poet bp nichol called *Sons of Captain Poetry*, and *The Clinton Special*, a film about Théâtre Passe Muraille's 'The Farm Show'; and edited *Personal Fictions* (1977), an anthology of four Canadian short-story writers. He lives in Toronto and teaches at Glendon College.

Ondaatje has an acute eye for the bizarre, the 'abnormal', the out-of-the-way. His landscapes are peopled with strange beasts, cripples, lost, violent souls, animals—all moving in and out of focus, emerging from and receding into some uncharted region of racial memory. He is fascinated with energy, especially as it is manifested in the form of violence. His poetry is a catalogue of scars, whether the psychic scar that defines an emotional relationship or the disastrous historical event that shapes the destiny of a nation or civilization. Even in the domestic world, which he calls 'a cell of civilized magic', the poet perceives division, the struggle for space and survival.

Thomas Mann remarked that the 'abnormal', the bizarre, is the best, if not the only, route to the 'normal'. Ondaatje's figures, like the parade of freaks and grotesques in a Fellini film, are important for what they reveal of the obsessions, perversions, and fears of so-called normal men. This is not to suggest that his poetry is unrelentingly black or morbid. It is not. He does not revel in the depiction of violence, but brings to bear on his materials considerable integrity and restraint. This is especially obvious in 'Elizabeth' and 'Peter', where the use of understatement heightens the dramatic impact of events. Ondaatje also has a sense of humour, a capacity for the comic and the ironic that is quite engaging. If his characters often have blood on their hands and violence on their minds, they are just as likely to have shaving-cream on their chins and dragons in their tennis nets. His poems never seem to be reworkings of a single feeling or mood, because his ability to assume a variety of points of view enables him to describe events and sensations from the inside, as it were. Furthermore, the strong narrative element keeps him from overloading or overworking a single image and gives the poetry a sense of movement and space.

If Ondaatje has anything that might be called a poetic, it is expressed in his poem '"The gate in his head": for Victor Coleman'. 'My mind is pouring chaos/ in nets onto the page', he writes. Words are the unique threads that, properly woven, can snare strange, unexpected things. Ondaatje recognizes the importance of form in poetry; even his most casual, personal poetry is held together by some linguistic device. But he rejects an undue emphasis on formal structure. In a letter to the editors he states his 'distrust of *all* critics and nearly all dogmatic aesthetics and all rules and all clubs/cliques/schools of poetry'; instead, he expresses a 'wish to come to each poem and let it breed in its own vacuum and have its own laws and order.' He prefers the 'caught vision' of a blurred photograph to the standard reproduction of a recognizable reality:

> The beautiful formed things caught at the wrong moment
> so they are shapeless, awkward
> moving to the clear.

The wrong moment is the right moment: that is the secret of his peculiar form of myth-making. He catches his subject when it is moving *towards* clarity, when it is neither completely vague and unrecognizable nor completely clear and obvious. He can only use the traditional nets of classical mythology by altering our perception of them, by coming at them from unexpected angles. Otherwise they are too static and destroy the subject they are called upon to illuminate.

Ondaatje says that he has always loved movies and lists his favourites as *The Hustler, Sands of the Kalahari, Once Upon a Time in the West*, and *Point Blank*. Ondaatje's poems have a number of things in common with films: they are intensely *visual*; also they are frequently *dramatic*. Like the dramatist and film-maker, he is drawn to people and situations and landscapes that are extreme or, at least, uncommon—princesses or escaped convicts, rapes or turning-points in a war, deserts or lush tropical gardens. He is a kind of dramatist of disaster, with a cinematic concern for detail, for the appropriate image, for angles of vision. Like Bergman and Fellini, he has a special talent for finding the striking image, the image that remains hooked in the mind long after other details or events have faded.

P.K. PAGE

'I am a traveller', P. K. Page has written. 'I have a destination but no maps. Others will have reached that destination already, still others are on their way. But none has had to go from here before—nor will again. One's route is one's own. One's journey unique. What I will find at the end I can barely guess. What lies on the way is unknown. How to go? Land, sea or air? What techniques to use? What vehicle?' ('Traveller, Conjuror, Joureyman', *Canadian Literature*, No. 46, Autumn 1970.)

Patricia Kathleen Page has been a traveller in both her life and art. She was born in England in 1917 but raised in Calgary and Winnipeg, where her father was stationed in the Strathcona Horse. From her family, which she describes as closely knit and not at all typical, she seems to have gained an appreciation for the arts, as her parents engaged in writing and drawing and were excellent carvers. She says she 'first came to writing by being an adolescent, which is enough to make anyone write.' After living briefly in the Maritimes, she moved to Montreal, where she worked as a scriptwriter for the National Film Board and became associated with Patrick Anderson and F. R. Scott in the editing of *Preview* magazine. Her first major publication was in *Unit of Five* (1944), an anthology of five poets edited by Ronald Hambleton. Page lived abroad for many years, in Mexico, Australia, and Brazil, where she began to draw under her married name, P. K. Irwin. She now lives in Victoria, B.C.

Page's search for the techniques with which to make her spiritual and aesthetic journey is a fascinating study. Her early poetry, which she now describes as 'clotted with images', explores the contradictions that underlie everyday experience: the terrible and explosive beauty of childhood; the haunting presence of boredom and madness associated with the deadly routine of jobs; the vanity and self-delusion that infects the most charitable and earnest of actions and statements. Such subjects lent themselves readily to a richly textured and highly allusive style, in which the interplay of elements of prosody and figurative language served to heighten the sense of irony and paradox. A poem such as 'The Stenographers', for example, strikes one as a kind of tapestry of metaphor, on which the routines and nitty-gritty of office life are described in terms that draw attention to their tedium, mechanization, and mind-deadening qualities: 'the brief bivouac of Sunday', 'the inch of noon', 'the winter of paper'. Such detail and stylization give imaginative expression to the problem of workers alienated from the product of their labours as no Marxist treatise could do. Page does not glorify or romanticize the secretaries; but her metaphors leave no doubt in the reader's mind that such conditions are, ultimately, dehumanizing: 'In their eyes I have seen/the pin men of madness in marathon trim/race round the track of the stadium pupil.'

Time and travel have altered Page's conception of life and art, shifting her attention from social and political surfaces to internal psychological states. Actually, her account of her development as an artist serves as a useful analogy for her poetic progress as well. The shock of learning another language, as she says in 'Questions and Images' (*Canadian Literature*, No. 41, Summer 1969), was like being born a second time, growing from silence through a linguistic childhood and adolescence towards a radically altered adulthood, in which all one's perceptions underwent a sea-change. Since she could not write poetry, she began to draw, going first through a realist phase in which she had to 'see with the eye of an ant' in order to appropriate the new and exotic environment; then, she says, 'the pen began dreaming. It began a life of its own', to the point where the painter could look into the Macaw's eye and be 'drawn through its vortex into a minute cosmos which contained all the staggering dimensions of outer space.'

Here the poet and painter speak the same language, both being concerned, as she says in 'Stories of Snow', with that 'area behind the eyes/where silent, unrefractive whiteness lies.' No other poet in Canada, with the possible exception of Atwood, has been so intensely concerned to explore the nature of visual perception. Eyes abound in her poems, as do lenses, cameras, field glasses. Perspectives are almost always unusual; compositional elements play an important part; images may be blurred, superimposed, surprisingly juxtaposed, viewed through strangely distorting lenses. These perceptual elements, including a concern for colour and light and shade, combine with an imagistic precision that recalls her experience in film. As Munro Beattie has observed, 'Several of her poems might serve as scripts for little experimental films for "art" theatres. Action flows into action, image melts, "by a slow dissolve", into image.'

After Canada, which she has described as a 'whim-oriented culture', Page found the order and interconnectedness of the cultural symbols in Mexico liberating. She came to realize that, for her, art was not an end in itself so much as a means to an end, a path to wisdom. 'Poetry', she says 'was more than ever in the perceiving.' Art, whether poetry or painting, becomes a technique of transformation or metamorphosis, a vehicle for conducting us on that route that leads through the looking-glass, beyond the senses to 'some unseen centre'. 'Without magic the world is not to be borne', she insists. 'A good writer or painter understands these laws and practices conjuration.'

Page's skills as a conjuror are everywhere present in her poetry, from the metaphysical wit that draws strange and wonderful analogies to the deftness and precision with which she uses words: she is a master of her craft. However, the formal or manipulative aspect of her work seldom submerges the realistic, or referential, side; her best poems remain immediately accessible and thoroughly mysterious.

Page's publications include a novel, *The Sun and the Moon*, which was published in 1944 under the pseudonym Judith Cape and reprinted with eight short stories in 1973 under the title *The Sun and the Moon and Other Fictions*. Her books of poetry are *As Ten As Twenty* (1946); *The Metal and the Flower* (1954), which won the Governor General's Award; *Cry Ararat!* (1967); *Poems Selected and New* (1974); and *Leviathan in a Pool* (1974).

AL PURDY

Purdy was born in Wooler, Ont., in 1918 and educated at Albert College in Belleville. At sixteen he dropped out of school and began his wanderings, working at odd jobs, putting in time with the RCAF in British Columbia, and trying his hand at writing. Although his first book of poems was published in 1944, he did not seriously consider supporting himself by writing until he sold a script to the CBC in 1955. He moved to Montreal and then to Roblin Lake at Ameliasburg, where he has lived on and off for the last fifteen years. From Ameliasburg he has travelled to the Cariboo, Newfoundland, Baffin Island, Cuba, Greece, and England, and has been writer-in-residence at various universities. Of this incessant wandering he says: 'I write poems like spiders spin webs, and perhaps for much the same reason, to support my existence . . . unless one is a stone one doesn't sit still. And perhaps new areas of landscape awaken old areas of one's self. One has seen the familiar landscape (perhaps) so often that one ceases to really see it.'

Purdy's development has been haphazard and independent, a product of his continued experiment and chance discovery of interesting talents rather than of absorbing any major influences. He objects as much to the 'sweetness and iambic smoothness' of academic poets like Richard Wilbur as to the 'togetherness . . . of the Duncan-Creeley-Olson bunch.' 'I have no one style,' he said in a letter to Charles Bukowski, 'I have a dozen: have got to be virtuoso enough so I can shift gears like a hot-rod kid—I doubt that my exact combo ever came along before. Unlike some, I have no ideas about being a specific kind of poet. I mean, I don't make rules and say THIS is what a poet HAS to be. I don't know what the hell a poet is or care much. I do know what he isn't sometimes.'

Despite his objections to the contrary, Purdy has developed a speaking voice that is unmistakable. His poetry is most recognizable in terms of its language and structure. One of its main characteristics is a peculiar mixing of chattiness and profundity, of homely observation and mythical or historical allusion. Purdy is an extremely well-read poet. He has a firm grasp of what he calls 'the gear and tackle of living'; the imagery in a single poem can be drawn from a number of different sources, sometimes with considerable success. He peoples his rural Ontario with ghosts from the near and distant past, with echoes of ancient Greece and United Empire Loyalist salons; in his particular Baffin Island may be seen the shades of Diefenbaker, Odysseus, Laurence Oliver, King John, and Gary Cooper.

Structurally, Purdy's verse is equally recognizable. He has a tendency to leave his poems open-ended, to leave a subject deliberately unresolved. In poems of this sort there is no subject outside the poem other than the perceiving consciousness of the poet; in other words, the subject of the poem is *the process itself*, the process of trying to come to terms with a feeling or experience. Philosophically, a preoccupation with process is understandable; it implies an awareness that at best 'truth' is difficult to discover, at worst it is completely relative. From an aesthetic point of view, however, a desire for honesty and verisimilitude in this area does not always work to the poem's advantage. Carried too far it can become a cliché, a short-cut. If this happens the reader is likely to feel that at times a poet should lie, that he should be prepared to offer up small truths directly rather than try successfully for the larger truth.

Whatever objections one may have to Purdy's open-endedness and his habit of undercutting something that is obviously important to both himself and the reader, there can be no doubt about his very considerable talent. His 'exact combo' is unlike anything else in Canadian poetry. He has an inexhaustible capacity to surprise and delight, to upset whatever critical expectations his own poems might encourage. His answer to his critics, and perhaps the reason for his popularity, is suggested in the following comment he makes on the nature of the poetic process:

There ought to be a quality in a good poet beyond any analysis, the part of his mind that leaps from one point to another, sideways, backwards, ass-over-electric-kettle. This quality is not logic, and the result may not be consistent with the rest of the poem when it happens, though it may be. I believe it is said by medicos that much of the human mind has no known function. Perhaps the leap sideways and backwards comes from there. At any rate, it seems to me the demands made on it cause the mind to stretch, to do more than it is capable of under ordinary and different circumstances. And when this happens, or when you think it does, that time is joyous, and you experience something beyond experience. Like discovering you can fly, or that relative truth may blossom into an absolute. And the absolute must be attacked again and again, until you find something that will stand up, may not be denied, which becomes a compass point by which to move somewhere else.... And sometimes—if you're lucky—a coloured fragment may slip through into the light when you're writing a poem.

There are many coloured fragments in Purdy's poetry. The way his mind stretches to assimilate new areas of experience, the way it leaps in unexpected directions, often at considerable psychic cost to the poet, is truly remarkable.

Purdy's best verse is predominantly elegaic. Like Roberts and Carman, he is sensitive to manifestations of change, to the passing of time. He loves to reflect upon things historical. There is something about events and people out of the past that releases his imagination in new and exciting ways. Thus his identification with the decaying world of Prince Edward County, his attraction to the outbacks of British Columbia, and his passionate response to the Inuit's encounter with the white man's technology on Baffin Island. Perhaps the values, the certainty, that the shifting present never affords him are found in abundance in the past. In poems such as 'The Runners' and 'Lament for the Dorsets' there is little uncertainty or self-consciousness; instead, the poet achieves a rare beauty and precision.

Since the publication of his first book in 1944, Purdy has published a number of major collections, including *Poems for All the Annettes* (1962, 1968, 1973); *The Cariboo Horses* (1965), for which he received the Governor General's Award; *North of Summer* (1967); *Wild Grape Wine* (1968); *Love in a Burning Building* (1970); *Selected Poems* (1972); *Sex and Death* (1973); *The Poems of Al Purdy* (1976); *Sundance at Dusk* (1976); and *No Other Country* (1977). He has also published a limited deluxe edition of poems from his trip to Greece called *The Quest for Ouzo* (1970). In addition, Purdy has edited two anthologies—*Storm Warning* (1971) and *Storm Warning II* (1976)—and a collection of Canadian views of the United States, *The New Romans* (1968).

RAYMOND SOUSTER

Souster's chief concern has been to keep singing in the face of despair. As he says in 'Good Fortune', 'life isn't a matter of luck/of good fortune, it's whether/the heart can keep singing/when there's really no reason/why it should.' His imagination is peopled with the victims of wars and industrial 'progress', whores, cripples, beggars, down-and-outs of every sort. He takes upon himself their guilt and shame and tries to communicate the terrible sense of human waste that weighs upon him. Souster is equally troubled by the impermanence of things. At times he displays a gentle nostalgia for the innocence and good times of the past, lamenting the passing of friends and shared interests and the disappearance of familiar landscapes under a jungle of concrete and cereal-box architecture. Although he is incapable of sustained irony or satire, Souster often strikes out at the instruments of change and destruction like an animal that has been hurt or cornered. His most convincing response is to celebrate signs of man's capacity for joy or, at least, survival; he searches out pockets of beauty and spontaneity in the rubbish-heap of the century, as in 'Top Hat' or 'Victory', where he celebrates the determination of a 'bum' who beats the street-cleaning machine to a castaway cigarette butt.

Souster is predominantly a poet of content. Robert Creeley applies this name to the poets of the thirties. 'There are also those men', he says, ' . . . who extend to their writing of verse concerns which haunt them, again reasonably enough, in other areas of living. They are in this way poets of "content", and their poems argue images of living to which the content of their poem points. They argue the poem as a means to recognition, a signboard as it were, not in itself a structure of "recognition" or—better—cognition itself.' Creeley is thinking here of Kenneth Fearing, but his description applies well to Souster, for whom the sociological impulse seems more pressing than the aesthetic. This view is not inconsistent with Souster's idea of the poet's function. In 'The Lilac Poem' he speaks of the impermanence of all things, even poetry. If art itself is subject to the eroding effects of time, the artist is best employed as a recorder or photographer of the human condition at a particular moment in history; or rather—and perhaps this is his main function—as an entertainer who can divert man's attention away from the sources of his despair. The short poem is itself a function of the poet's view of the impermanence of all things; and it is especially characteristic of modern poetry. As Frost suggests, the good poem provides 'a momentary stay against confusion.'

This does not mean that Souster has no interest in form, in prosody. He is sufficiently steeped in American poetry, especially in the work of Ezra Pound and William Carlos Williams, to have absorbed not only a distaste for the baggage of poetic tradition, but also a preoccupation with certain formal elements in verse. His own poetry is not metrical; he prefers the shifting rhythms of speech to the monotony of the metronome. Like Bowering, he avoids the use of mythical allusion and archaism, preferring instead poetry with a base in actual experience. Souster understands Pound's dictum that 'It is better to present one Image in a lifetime than to produce voluminous works.' He has written a number of excellent imagist poems, such as 'Study: The Bath' and 'The Six-Quart Basket', that have the clarity and economy of the *haiku*. Occasionally Souster is tempted to comment on the image, to tag on a moral that leaves attention outside the poem, as in 'The

Hunter'; but his best poems are either pure image or pure voice. The poems of lyrical reflection are less likely to misfire, because the poet begins with a mood that is strong enough to arrange the materials it gathers to express itself, rather than with an image that is often too weak to support itself without assistance from the voice of the poet. These reflective verses speak for Souster's integrity as a man and as a poet; they are beautifully turned and reveal a quiet concern, or empathy, that is always surprising, sometimes moving.

Souster was born in Toronto in 1921 and has spent all of his life there except for the war years, 1941-5, when he was in the RCAF in the Maritimes and in England. Of his beloved Toronto, he says:

> I suppose I am truly an unrepentant regionalist. As Emile Zola put it to Paul Bourget: 'Why should we be everlastingly wanting to escape to lands of romance? Our streets are full of tragedy and full of beauty; they should be enough for any poet.' All the experiences one is likely to encounter in Paris can be found in this city. Toronto has a flavour all its own. . . . My roots are here; this is the place that tugs at my heart when I leave it and fills me with quiet relief when I return to it.

Like Wallace Stevens, Souster is wedded simultaneously to the muses of poetry and commerce: as well as being a serious poet, he has been employed for many years by the Canadian Imperial Bank of Commerce in downtown Toronto. His involvements in the poetic community are many. He edited a mimeographed magazine called *Combustion* (1957-60) and was a founder-editor of Contact Press. He edited *New Wave Canada: The New Explosion in Canadian Poetry* (1966), and *Generation Now* (1970), an anthology of poetry for schools.

Souster has published more than a dozen books of poetry, including *When We Are Young* (1946); *Go to Sleep, World* (1947); *Shake Hands With the Hangman* (1953); *Selected Poems* (1956), edited by Louis Dudek; *A Local Pride* (1962); *Place of Meeting* (1962); *The Colour of the Times* (1964), his collected poems, which received the Governor General's Award; *Ten Elephants on Yonge Street* (1965); *As Is* (1967); *Lost & Found* (1968); *So Far So Good* (1969); *Selected Poems* (1972); *On Target* (1973); *Double-header* (containing *As Is* and *Lost & Found*, 1975); *Rain-check* (1975); and *Extra Innings* (1977).

PHYLLIS WEBB

Phyllis Webb's poetry, because it presents a world that often seems devoid of meaning and consolation—a world of suffering, betrayal, gratuitous violence, and death—raises questions about the aim of art. What, we find ourselves asking, can be the point of writing about such things? Is the aim of art—if indeed it can be said to have an aim—to confirm our suspicions that life has no meaning, or that its purpose is by no means certain or benign? Can so unrelentingly bleak a picture be anything but depressing?

However bleak it may appear to be at the level of content, Webb's poetry is an affirmation of the human spirit, of the power of the imagination to confront and reshape reality. As Albert Camus argues in his famous treatise, *The Rebel*, there is no such thing as a nihilistic work of art; even if literature 'describes nostalgia, despair, frustration, it still creates a form of salvation. To talk of despair is to conquer it. Despairing literature is a contradiction in terms.' What is important in Webb's poetry is the style, the way in which she imposes *form* on whatever elements from reality she uses.

One has only to look closely at 'Love Story' to understand the terrifyingly delicate balance Webb can achieve between the realist and formalist elements, by virtue of an unremitting attention to the visual, auditory, and intellectual nuances of words. Rather than describe the death of the infant in graphic detail, Webb chooses rather to stylize the killing, speaking of the ape's biting of the neck in metaphorical terms as 'tasting time' and of the attack as something general rather than specific: 'and his nails rooted sudden fire in the ribs of Adam.' Reference to the infant's belly as 'plush' on which the ape 'bobbed nervously' serves, finally, to heighten rather than diminish the horror of the imaged scene by drawing attention to elements of texture and cushioning effect that the reader would otherwise gladly forgo.

On the rare occasions when she has spoken about her art, Webb's concern has been, primarily, with craft. In an article called 'Polishing Up the View', which appeared in *CV/II*, Vol. 2, No. 4, December 1976 (transcribed from a tape in the Aural History Department of the Provincial Archives, Victoria), Webb speaks briefly of the influence of American poets Charles Olson, Robert Creeley, and Robert Duncan, all of whom she met in the summer of 1963 at the University of British Columbia. She singled out Duncan on the grounds that he had 'the most to offer me because he is a great explorer in the realm of form.' Of her own explorations in form she is very specific, talking about the difficulty of ordinary sentence structure, which is 'based on an opposition of ideas, so that you get "buts" and "thoughs" and "althoughs" and "ifs" and so on.... it seemed to me that this had some philosophical significance and that I had to break through the oppositions that are presented to us in everyday thought and get a more refined synthesis.'

In the same article she ranges widely in her consideration of form to include a discussion of punctuation—the comma, which 'looks so big in a little poem'—the significance of line-lengths, and her aims in writing the *Naked Poems*:

The Naked Poems *... are attempts to get away from a dramatic rhythm, from a kind of dramatic structure in the poem itself, and away from metaphor very often, so that they are very bare, very simple. In a suite like this where the image is not realized in terms of metaphor, but is simply named, the* thing *is named—like the room, the plum colour, the curtains and the gold colour. These are not in effect metaphors but they have a kind of image-like impact as they build up through the two suites. And like the various kinds of rhyme I use in the poem, they too seem to me to have a linking effect and are part of what I'd call the total music of the poem.*

Webb is an extremely conscious craftswoman who seldom rests in her artistic explorations, no matter how successful she may be with a particular form. No sooner has she written *Naked Poems*, with its short lines and minimalist criteria, than she anticipates experimenting with long poems. She deals rather humorously with these formal preoccupations in 'Poetics Against the Angel of Death', in which she apologizes for her compulsion to speak of death yet again and goes on to assert that she wants to die

writing haiku
or, better,
long lines, clean and syllabic as knotted bamboo. Yes!

And yet she seems equally unwilling to rest in her explorations of life and its meaning, personally and collectively. Her work touches not only upon the philosophical anguish of modern life, but also upon some of the issues, events and personalities that have shaped our age.

Phyllis Webb was born in Victoria in 1927 and raised there and in Vancouver. She studied English and Philosophy at UBC from 1945 to 1949, ran unsuccessfully as a CCF candidate in the provincial elections, and worked as a secretary in Montreal, where she also attended Macdonald College and McGill and came into contact with F. R. Scott and Ronald Sutherland. Her poems were first published in *Trio*, along with those of Eli Mandel and Gael Turnbull. For the next fourteen years she lived intermittently in England, Montreal, Paris, Vancouver (where she taught English at UBC) and Toronto, where she produced the CBC 'Ideas' program. She now lives on the Gulf Islands. Her publications include *Even Your Right Eye* (1956), *The Sea Is Also a Garden* (1962), *Naked Poems* (1965), and *Selected Poems* (1971).

SUPPLEMENTARY MATERIALS

1. Criticism: General

Atwood, Margaret. *Survival: A Thematic Guide to Canadian Literature* (Toronto, 1972).

Davey, Frank. *From There to Here: A Guide to English-Canadian Literature Since 1960* (Erin, Ont., 1974).

Dudek, Louis, and Michael Gnarowski, eds. *The Making of Modern Poetry in Canada* (Toronto, 1967).

Frye, Northrop. *The Bush Garden: Essays on the Canadian Imagination* (Toronto, 1971).

Jones, D. G. *Butterfly on Rock* (Toronto, 1970).

————— . 'The Sleeping Giant; Or the Uncreated Conscience of the Race', *Canadian Literature*, 26 (Autumn 1965); Repnted in *A Choice of Critics*, ed. George Woodcock (Toronto, 1966).

Klinck, Carl F., ed. *Literary History of Canada: Canadian Literature in English* (Toronto, 1965).

Mandel, Eli. 'A Lack of Ghosts: Canadian Poets and Poetry', *The Humanities Association Bulletin*, XVI, 1 (Spring 1965).

————— . 'Modern Canadian Poetry', *Twentieth Century Literature*, XVI, 3 (July 1970).

————— , ed. *Contexts of Canadian Criticism* (Chicago, 1971).

Reaney, James. 'The Canadian Poet's Predicament', *University of Toronto Quarterly*, XXVI, 3 (April 1957).

Smith A. J. M. 'The Canadian Poet: Part I. To Confederation; Part II. After Confederation', *Canadian Literature*, 37 & 38 (Summer & Autumn 1968).

————— . 'Eclectic Detachment: Aspects of Identity in Canadian Poetry', *Canadian Literature*, 9 (Summer 1961). Reprinted in *A Choice of Critics*, ed. George Woodcock (Toronto, 1966).

————— . 'Introduction', *The Oxford Book of Canadian Verse*, ed. A. J. M. Smith (Toronto, 1960).

————— , ed. *Masks of Poetry* (Toronto, 1962).

Staines, David. *The Canadian Imagination: Dimensions of Literary Culture* (Cambridge, Mass., 1977).

Waddington, Miriam. 'Canadian Tradition and Canadian Literature', *Journal of Commonwealth Literature*, 8 (December 1969).

Wilson, Milton. 'Other Canadians *and After*', *The Tamarack Review*, 9 (Autumn 1958). Reprinted in *The First Five Years*, ed. Robert Weaver (Toronto, 1962).

Woodcock, George, ed. *A Choice of Critics: Selections from 'Canadian Literature'* (Toronto, 1966).

————— . *Poets and Critics: Essays from 'Canadian Literature' 1966-1974* (Toronto, 1974).

2. Criticism: Individual

MARGARET ATWOOD

Foster, J. W. 'Poetry of Margaret Atwood', *Canadian Literature*, 74 (Autumn 1977).

Malahat Review, 41, Margaret Atwood symposium.

Marshall, Tom. 'Les animaux de son pays: Notes sur la poésie de Margaret Atwood', *Ellipse*, 3 (Spring 1970).

Onley, Gloria. *'Power Politics* in Bluebeard's Castle', *Canadian Literature*, 60 (Spring 1974).

Rogers, Linda. 'Margaret the Magician', *Canadian Literature*, 60 (Spring 1974).

Ross, Gary. 'Circle Game', *Canadian Literature*, 60 (Spring 1974).

———— . 'Divided Self', *Canadian Literature*, 71 (Winter 1976).

MARGARET AVISON

Bowering, George. 'Avison's Imitation of Christ the Artist', *Canadian Literature*, 54 (Autumn 1972).

Doerksen, D. W. 'Search and Discovery': Margaret Avison's Poetry', *Canadian Literature*, 60 (Spring 1974).

Ghiselin, Brewster. 'The Architecture of Vision', *Poetry*, LXX, 6 (September 1947).

Jones, Lawrence M. 'A Core of Brilliance: Margaret Avison's Achievement', *Canadian Literature*, 38 (Autumn 1968).

Moisan, C. 'Rina Lasnier et Margaret Avison', *Liberté*, 18 (November-December 1976).

Redekop, Ernest. *Margaret Avison* (Toronto, 1970).

Wilson, Milton. 'The Poetry of Margaret Avison', *Canadian Literature*, 2 (Autumn 1959). Reprinted in *A Choice of Critics*, ed. George Woodcock (Toronto, 1966).

EARLE BIRNEY

David, J. 'Alphabeings & other seasyours', *Fiddlehead*, 114 (Summer 1977).

New, W. H. 'Prisoner of Dreams: the Poetry of Earle Birney', *Canadian Forum*, 52 (September 1972).

Smith A. J. M. 'A Unified Personality: Birney's Poems', *Canadian Literature*, 30 (Autumn 1966).

West, Paul. 'Earle Birney and the Compound Ghost', *Canadian Literature*, 13 (Summer 1962). Reprinted in *A Choice of Critics*, ed. George Woodcock (Toronto, 1966).

Wilson, Milton. 'Poet Without a Muse', *Canadian Literature*, 30 (Autumn 1966).

LEONARD COHEN

Davey, Frank. 'Leonard Cohen and Bob Dylan: Poetry and the Popular Song', *Alphabet*, 17 (December 1969).

Djwa, Sandra. 'Leonard Cohen: Black Romantic', *Canadian Literature*, 34 (Autumn 1967).

Ondaatje, Michael. *Leonard Cohen* (Toronto, 1970).

Pacey, Desmond. 'The Phenomenon of Leonard Cohen', *Canadian Literature*, 34 (Autumn 1967).

Purdy, A. W. 'Leonard Cohen: A Personal Look', *Canadian Literature*, 23 (Winter 1965).

Scobie, Stephen. *Leonard Cohen* (Vancouver, 1978).

D. G. JONES

Blodgett, E. D. 'Masks of D. G. Jones', *Canadian Literature*, 60 (Spring 1974).

Bowering, George. 'Coming Home to the World', *Canadian Literature*, 65 (Summer 1975).

PATRICK LANE

Bowering, Marilyn. 'Pine Boughs and Apple Trees: The Poetry of Pat Lane', *Malahat Review*, 45 (January 1978).

IRVING LAYTON

Doyle, Mike. 'Occasions of Irving Layton', *Canadian Literature*, 54 (Autumn 1972).

Geddes, Gary. 'Our Most Erotic Puritan', *Books in Canada* (December 1977).

Mandel, Eli. *Irving Layton* (Toronto, 1969).

Smith, P. K. 'Irving Layton and the Theme of Death', *Canadian Literature*, 48 (Spring 1971).

Waterston, Elizabeth. 'Irving Layton: Apocalypse in Montreal', *Canadian Literature*, 48 (Spring 1971).

Woodcock, George. 'A Grab at Proteus: Notes on Irving Layton', *Canadian Literature*, 28 (Spring 1966).

DOROTHY LIVESAY

Leland, D. 'Dorothy Livesay: Poet of Nature', *Dalhousie Review*, 51 (Autumn 1971).

Lever, Bernice. 'Interview with Dorothy Livesay', *Canadian Forum*, 55 (Spring 1975).

Mitchell, B. '"How Silence Sings" in the Poetry of Dorothy Livesay 1926-1973', *Dalhousie Review*, 54 (Autumn 1974).

Stevens, Peter. 'Out of the Silence and Across the Distance: the Poetry of Dorothy Livesay', *Queen's Quarterly*, 78 (Winter 1971).

Zimmerman, Susan. 'Livesay's Houses', *Canadian Literature*, 61 (Summer 1974).

PAT LOWTHER

Geddes, Gary. 'A Stone Diary', *Globe and Mail*, 9 April 1977.

Ryan, S. 'Florence McNeil and Pat Lowther', *Canadian Literature*, 74 (Autumn 1977).

GWENDOLYN MACEWEN

Atwood, Margaret. 'MacEwen's Muse', *Canadian Literature*, 45 (Summer 1970).

Geddes, Gary. 'Now You See It . . .', *Books in Canada* (July 1976).

Warwick, Ellen D. 'To Seek a Single Symmetry', *Canadian Literature*, 71 (Winter 1976).

ELI MANDEL

Geddes, Gary. 'Out of Place', *Globe and Mail*, 31 December 1977.

Ower, John. 'Black and Secret Poet: Notes on Eli Mandel', *Canadian Literature*, 42 (Autumn 1969).

ALDEN NOWLAN

Cook, Gregory. 'An *Amethyst* Extra: Interview with Alden Nowlan', *Amethyst*, II, 4 (Summer 1963).

The Fiddlehead, 81 (August, September, October 1969). Special issue devoted to Alden Nowlan.

Metcalf, John. 'Interview with Alden Nowlan', *Canadian Literature*, 63 (Winter 1975).

MICHAEL ONDAATJE

Kahn, Sy. 'Michael Ondaatje, *The Dainty Monsters*', *The Far Point*, 1 (Fall/Winter 1968).

Scobie, Stephen. 'Two Authors in Search of a Character', *Canadian Literature*, 54 (Autumn 1972).

P. K. PAGE

Keeler, Judy. 'Interview with P. K. Page', *Canadian Forum*, 55 (Spring 1975).

Namjoshi, S. 'Double Landscape', *Canadian Literature*, 67 (Winter 1976).

Rooke, Constance. 'P. K. Page: The Chameleon and the Centre', *Malahat Review*, 45 (January 1978).

Smith, A. J. M. 'Poetry of P. K. Page', *Canadian Literature*, 50 (Autumn 1975).

AL PURDY

Bowering, George. *Al Purdy* (Toronto, 1970).

Doyle, Mike. 'Proteus at Roblin Lake',

Canadian Literature, 61 (Summer 1974).

Duffy, Dennis. 'In Defence of North America: the Past in the Poetry of Alfred Purdy', *Canadian Studies*, 6 (May 1971).

Geddes, Gary. 'A. W. Purdy: An Interview', *Canadian Literature*, 41 (Summer 1969). Reprinted in *20th-Century Poetry & Poetics*, ed. Gary Geddes (Toronto, 1969).

Stevens, Peter. 'In the Raw: The Poetry of A. W. Purdy', *Canadian Literature*, 28 (Spring 1966).

RAYMOND SOUSTER

Carruth, Hayden. 'To Souster from Vermont', *Tamarack Review*, 34 (Winter 1965).

Dudek, Louis. 'Groundhog Among the Stars: The Poetry of Raymond Souster', *Canadian Literature*, 22 (Autumn 1964). Reprinted in *A Choice of Critics*, ed. George Woodcock (Toronto, 1966).

Geddes, Gary. 'Cursed and Singular Blessing', *Canadian Literature*, 54 (Autumn 1972).

PHYLLIS WEBB

Hulcoop, John. Introduction to Phyllis Webb, *Selected Poems* (Vancouver, 1971).

Sonthoff, Helen W. 'Structure of Loss: The Poetry of Phyllis Webb', *Canadian Literature*, 9 (Summer 1961).

Stainsby, Mari. 'Interview with Phyllis Webb', *B.C. Library Quarterly*, 36 (October 1972-January 1973).

3. Audio-Visual Aids

RECORDS

Alden Nowlan's Maritimes. CBC Learning Systems T-57193-4, 1972

Canadian Poets I, Eight poets, including Birney, Bowering, Cohen, Layton, MacEwen, Newlove, Purdy, and Webb, reading selections from their own works on two 12-inch LPs. CBC publications, $7.50

Canadian Poets II: The Journals of Susanna Moodie by Margaret Atwood. Read by Mia Anderson. CBC publications, $5.00

Death of a Ladies' Man by Leonard Cohen. Warner Brothers WAR 3125

Layton Reads His Own. Caedmon ML 7002

The Poetry and Voice of Margaret Atwood. Caedmon TC 1537

Six Montreal Poets. Includes Cohen and Layton. Folkways 9805

Six Toronto Poets. Includes Avison and Souster. Folkways 9806

Songs from a Room by Leonard Cohen. Columbia 9767

Songs of Leonard Cohen. Columbia 2733

33/3. A recording by Victor Coleman. Music Gallery Editions.

FILMS

Espolio. Earle Birney. National Film Board. 6 min.

Ladies and Gentlemen, Mr Leonard Cohen. National Film Board. 44 min.

A Moving Feast. Includes Birney, Layton, MacEwen. May be rented from Metropolitan Educational Television Association (META), 31 Wellesley St. E., Toronto 284. 18 min., 40 sec.

TAPES

Canadian Poets on Tape. Nine audio tapes available from Van Nostrand Reinhold Ltd, 1410 Birchmount Rd, Scarborough M1P 2E7. Included are Birney, Layton, Livesay, MacEwen, Mandel, Purdy, and Souster. 30 min., $5.00 each

High Barnet cassette tapes. Ten poetry tapes available, including Atwood, Birney, Layton, MacEwen, Mandel, Purdy, and Souster. High Barnet, 503 Merton St, Toronto 7. 1 hr, $12.95 each

Irving Layton. 2-inch video. May be rented from Metropolitan Educational Television Association (META), 31 Wellesley St E., Toronto 284. 28 min., 45 sec.

Irving Layton: Under Attack. Explains the role of the poet and defends Canadian poetry. Audio tape may be obtained from Traffic Department, Screen Gems, 72 Carlton St, Toronto 200. $10.00-$15.00

Portrait of a Canadian Poet—Earle Birney. Talks to students about poetry and recent social issues. 2-inch video. May be rented from META. 28 min., 32 sec.

The Twist of Feeling. Margaret Atwood. CBC Learning Systems 755, 30 min.

INDEX